"Christopher Katulka has written a masterful reader through the whole counsel of God and ...... pur- pose and role in redemptive history—past, present, and future. I readily recommend this book to anyone who wants to know why, when other nations come and go in history, Israel always will exist. This book is desperately needed in this day when the church is losing its understanding of Israel's relevance and importance."

Jim Showers, DMin
Executive Director/President
The Friends of Israel Gospel Ministry

"Christopher faithfully presents the purpose of the nation of Israel in God's plan from early history until today, helping the reader understand why the land and the people are called 'the center of the earth.'

"He helps readers to understand contemporary politics and how to treat God's cho- sen people in a way that will glorify His name. Had this knowledge been accepted in the hearts of those in the medieval institutional church, as well as those in Israel's neighboring countries, much of history could have been different."

Meno Kalisher, DMin
Pastor of Jerusalem Assembly House of Redemption

"Israel is miraculous. Its landscapes and biblical sites inevitably turn tourists into pil- grims! With the logical 'yesterday, today, and tomorrow' approach taken in *Israel Always*, as well as the touching personal stories, this an excellent resource for any traveler. And Christopher, with a precise and loving pen, adds an extra dimension beyond historical chronology: his faith in the divine purpose for the chosen people in the land. Unlike any other, this book prepares Christian readers for an unforget- table visit as well as a spiritual journey to their origins."

Tito Anidjar
Licensed Israeli tour guide with 40 years' experience

"Books on Israel abound, but each tends to focus on one aspect of Israel's history, politics, or prophetic role. Christopher Katulka has provided readers with a rare service—a comprehensive, up-to-date survey of Israel in almost every important aspect, yet as a succinct and compelling story. His background in Jewish ministry has given him a unique and necessary perspective for this work, and I enthusiastically commend *Israel Always* to a wide readership!"

J. Randall Price, PhD
Distinguished Research Professor, Biblical & Judaic Studies
The John Rawlings School of Divinity
Liberty University

ISRAEL
ALWAYS

CHRISTOPHER J. KATULKA

HARVEST HOUSE PUBLISHERS
EUGENE. OREGON

Cover design by Brock Book Design Co., Charles Brock

Cover photos © Kvitkanastroyu, ronib1979, Sanychs / Depositphotos

Interior design KUHN Design Group

For bulk, special sales, or ministry purchases, please call 1-800-547-8979.
Email: Customerservice@hhpbooks.com

This logo is a federally registered trademark of the Hawkins Children's LLC. Harvest House Publishers, Inc., is the exclusive licensee of this trademark.

Israel Always
Copyright © 2022 by Christopher J. Katulka
Published by Harvest House Publishers
Eugene, Oregon 97408
www.harvesthousepublishers.com

ISBN 978-0-7369-8312-9 (pbk)
ISBN 978-0-7369-8313-6 (eBook)

Library of Congress Control Number: 2022938667

Printed in Colombia

22 23 24 25 26 27 28 29 30 / NI / 10 9 8 7 6 5 4 3 2 1

To my wife, Karen.
One inch at a time.

And to my children,
Olive
Cohen
Preston
Levi

ACKNOWLEDGMENTS

As you read through *Israel Always*, I hope you sense my passion to communicate biblical truth about Israel and the Jewish people. I want to thank Dr. Jim Showers and the leadership of the Friends of Israel Gospel Ministry, who graciously provide me the platform to do ministry and live out my calling from the Lord. I'm honored to serve with such an amazing ministry.

My passion for Israel and the Jewish people started in high school at the dinner table of Steve and Alice Herzig, 25 years ago. Steve and Alice's hospitality, kindness, grace, generosity, encouragement, and meals with lots of food sparked my interest in Jewish ministry. One of my favorite aspects about serving at the Friends of Israel is ministering side by side with Steve, my mentor, my friend, and my Jewish sage!

I wouldn't have this passion for the Lord or ministry without the love and support of my mother—Michelle Katulka. During my childhood, my mom directed me and my sisters, Caleigh and Olivia, to the relentless love of Jesus. Thank you, Mom, for always placing God at the center of our family and endlessly investing in my relationship with the Lord. And to my dad—Bob Katulka, who is now with Jesus—thank you for always believing in me and always telling me how proud you were of me. I miss you, Dad. I wish you were here so I could hear you laugh at the idea of me authoring a book.

Years ago, I studied at Dallas Theological Seminary to learn more about the Bible; and there I met Karen, my best friend and the love of my life. Karen, no one believes in me like you do. You've championed me every day in my ministry. You encouraged me to keep pushing forward with *Israel Always*, despite the craziness surrounding the pandemic. The Lord has blessed us with a full and meaningful life of love, four beautiful kids, very little sleep, and lots of laughs. I love you!

I also want to thank Steve, Becky, and Nate Miller, along with the entire Harvest House team, for their long-suffering spirit as my young family lived through a once-in-a-century pandemic. The Miller family have become friends; they made my writing experience enjoyable from start to finish, even during a difficult time.

I am not ashamed of the gospel, because it is the power of God that brings salvation to everyone who believes: first to the Jew, then to the Gentile. For in the gospel the righteousness of God is revealed—a righteousness that is by faith from first to last, just as it is written: "The righteous will live by faith."

ROMANS 1:16-17

CONTENTS

PART 1:

YESTERDAY

CHAPTER 1

THE BIBLICAL
STORY OF THE JEWS

*"Listen to me, you who pursue righteousness and who seek the
LORD: Look to the rock from which you were cut and to the
quarry from which you were hewn; look to Abraham, your
father, and to Sarah, who gave you birth. When I called him he
was only one man, and I blessed him and made him many."*

ISAIAH 51:1-2

The Bible is the best-selling book of all time. According to researcher,
James Chapman, four billion Bibles were sold worldwide in the
past 50 years.[1] Year after year, the Bible's reach expands as it's translated
into more languages, giving more people around the world access to
God's Word.

The Bible that is read in numerous countries and various cultures;
among different people and also by you—even if it is in a digital for-
mat—hasn't changed through the ages. It's been telling the same story
for thousands of years to billions of readers.

It tells the biblical story of the Jewish people.

The Old and New Testaments progressively unfold Israel's history, revealing the people's origins, laws, practices, festival celebrations, worship of God, and how they interacted with the nations
around them.

The authors of the biblical books were Jewish and their original readers were Jewish as well. For the multitude of Christians who worship Jesus Christ it's vital to always remember Jesus Himself was Jewish, the apostles were Jewish, and so was the early church.

Within this book are heroic accounts we have tucked away in our hearts and minds from our youth: the parting of the Red Sea, David's victory over Goliath, Jesus walking on water, and Jesus rising from the dead. These are accounts of faith placed in the God of Abraham, Isaac, and Jacob. He is the God who watches over Israel, and over you and me (Psalm 121).

When you read the Bible, you are ushered into the unfolding narrative of God's chosen people. The fact they are chosen is the heartbeat of the story of the Jewish people. It's what defines them and separates them from everyone else in the world.

The Jewish prayer book, the *siddur*, is full of prayers thanking God for choosing them out of all the nations. For instance, when the Torah (the first five books of the Old Testament) is read in the synagogue, worship begins with a prayer acknowledging God's kindness in choosing the Jewish people to be the recipients of His law. "Blessed are you, Lord, our God, King of the Universe, who has chosen us from all the nations and given us His Torah. Blessed are You, Lord, who gives the Torah" (Birchot HaTorah).

Sabbath prayers remind the Jewish people weekly that God chose them and gifted them with a day of rest, which serves as a visible indication that they are set apart from all the other nations: "For you have chosen us and sanctified us out of all the nations, and have given us the Sabbath as an inheritance in love and favor. Praised are you, Lord, who hallows the Sabbath."

Even in the closing of the morning, afternoon, and evening services, the *Aleinu* prayer, which grapples with the great responsibility of being the chosen people, reconfirms their faith and dedication to God. "It is our duty to praise the Master of all, to exalt the Creator of the Universe, who has not made us like the nations of the world and has not placed us like the families of the earth; who has not designed our destiny to be like theirs, nor our lot like that of all their multitude."

To be chosen in the eyes of God means to be different from all the other peoples of the earth. According to the Bible, the Jewish people were set apart to accomplish a divine task. God defined their uniqueness to Moses at Mount Sinai:

> "Now if you obey me fully and keep my covenant, then out of all nations you will be my treasured possession. Although the whole earth is mine, you will be for me a kingdom of priests and a holy nation." These are the words you are to speak to the Israelites (Exodus 19:5-6).

As an outsider looking in, for a people to be chosen by God can sort of seem like those who are within are members of an exclusive club. However, God chose Israel to be a "kingdom of priests" who would reach out to connect a broken world to Himself. For some of God's chosen people, this position was considered more of a curse than a blessing.

In the musical *Fiddler on the Roof*, the main character, Tevye, struggles as a religious Jew to uphold his beliefs and traditions with his family, which includes five daughters. The pressures and influences from the outside world were quickly eroding the vision he had for his family and their way of life. Tevye, knowing that God has chosen his people and set them apart from the rest of the world, desperately cries out in a Job-like fashion, "I know. I know. We are the chosen people. But, once in a while, can't You choose someone else?"

To fully understand all the prayers, cultural references, and even comedic relief connected to God's choosing of the Jewish people, you must go back to where it all started, in the earliest parts of the Bible.

The biblical story of the Jewish people begins with a journey, an odyssey that is both physical and spiritual in nature. God called Abraham to step out in faith to follow Him into places unknown. The step of faith required a trust in God's voice that gave him the confidence to start walking in a new direction. The journey did more than change his physical surroundings; God chose Abraham to reintroduce the world to its Creator.

A PROMISE BUILT ON FAITH

There are 50 chapters in Genesis. Only 11 are dedicated to creation, the fall, the great flood, and the dispersion of mankind throughout the world. You might think an entire biblical book would be dedicated to the earliest movements of creation and human history, but that wasn't God's intention. The plotline in Genesis uses the creation account as a vehicle to introduce one specific man to the one true God who created the heavens and earth.

Let me introduce you to Abraham who, at the time, was called Abram. Genesis 12 opens with God's call to this man:

> The LORD had said to Abram, "Go from your country, your people and your father's household to the land I will show you. I will make you into a great nation, and I will bless you; I will make your name great, and you will be a blessing. I will bless those who bless you, and whoever curses you I will curse, and all peoples on earth will be blessed through you" (Genesis 12:1-3).

God's call to Abraham time-stamped the official beginning of the biblical story of the Jewish people. Abraham was asked to leave behind his family, people, culture, and religion to embark on a faith journey to start a new family, new people, new culture, and new faith.

DID YOU KNOW?

According to Jewish tradition, Abraham is the father of both the race and religion of the Jewish people. He is fondly remembered and honored as "our Father Abraham."

Abraham was raised in a polytheistic world, which means his people worshipped a multitude of gods. But the God who called Abraham didn't sit among a cohort of Mesopotamian idols. Abraham's God stood out. He was different from the gods who were often represented by carved images. According to the beginning of Genesis, He was the One true invisible God who created the heavens and the earth and shared His majesty with no one.

God's promise to Abraham in Genesis 12:1-3 is the foundation of the biblical story of the Jews and the thread that's woven throughout all the Scriptures. The voice who commanded Abraham "Go" promised that if Abraham would step out in faith, he would receive the three necessary ingredients to become a nation with God's divine imperative:

1. Land (Genesis 12:1)

2. Descendants (Genesis 12:2a)

3. Blessing (Genesis 12:2b-3)

First, God would give Abraham a land, a place he and his family could inhabit. Every nation needs territorial boundaries (chapter 2 will

A 4,000-year-old Canaanite gate is dubbed "Abraham's Gate." Tradition holds the patriarch passed through this gate to rescue his nephew Lot.

provide more details on the role the land plays in the biblical story). According to God's promise, this land stretched from "the Wadi of Egypt to the great river, the Euphrates" (Genesis 15:18).

Second, the citizens of Abraham's nation would consist of his descendants. God tested Abraham's faith with this promise. The patriarch's wife, Sarah, was 90 years old and barren since her youth. This facet of the promise would require a deep trust that God could perform a miracle.

Finally, God promised Abraham and his descendants a multifaceted blessing on this journey. First, Abraham's name would always be associated with blessing: "I will make your name great, and you will be a blessing." Second, God would protect Abraham's family wherever they went: "I will bless those who bless you, and whoever curses you I will curse." Last, Abraham's divine purpose is wrapped up in the blessing: "All peoples on earth will be blessed through you."

DID YOU KNOW?

"I will bless those who bless you, and whoever curses you I will curse" is the promise given to assure Abraham of God's protection. The phrase "whoever curses you I will curse" consists of two different Hebrew words translated "curse." The first use of "curse" (*qālal*) literally means "to take lightly," while the second "curse" (*'ārar*) was God's oath that anyone who took Abraham or this promise lightly would be excluded from the blessing of the covenant.

This three-part promise—the land, the descendants, and the blessing—is foundational to the story of the Jewish people in the Bible because it's the basis for their identity as a chosen nation. But it was all predicated upon Abraham's willingness to step out in faith and follow God. And according to the text, "Abram went, as the LORD had told him" (Genesis 12:4).

Abraham's step of faith shook the world and changed the course of human history forever. Through this unsuspecting individual, God would intervene—He would bring redemption to all families of the earth through a promised land, a chosen people, and an eternal blessing.

TURNING GOD'S PROMISE INTO A CONTRACT

On the journey there were moments of deep trust in the Lord and anxiety concerning the future. In these ways, Abraham's faith journey is no different than yours or mine.

> [The LORD] took [Abram] outside and said, "Look up at the sky and count the stars—if indeed you can count them." Then he said to him, "So shall your offspring be." Abram believed the LORD, and he credited it to him as righteousness. He also said to him, "I am the LORD, who brought you out of Ur of the Chaldeans to give you this land to take possession of it." But Abram said, "Sovereign LORD, how can I know that I will gain possession of it?" (Genesis 15:5-8).

In the span of just two verses, Abraham experienced great faith in God's ability to provide and real doubt when he didn't see the proof of God's promise.

PLACES TO VISIT: **TEL DAN**

A beautiful nature reserve in northern Israel that houses the ancient Canaanite gate that's been dubbed "Abraham's Gate." It is likely that the gate was standing in the days of Abraham when he went through the land in Genesis 14, and possibly even earlier during his original travels into the land of Canaan.

To prove His dedication to Abraham and cement His promise, God entered into a contractual agreement through an ancient ritual. The more literal term used to explain what happened is that God "cut" a covenant with Abraham.

God commanded Abraham to collect a heifer, a female goat, a ram, a turtledove, and a young pigeon. After hearing these instructions, Abraham instinctively acted. He cut the land animals in half while leaving the birds whole. To the modern reader, this probably sounds otherworldly, but for Abraham and the people of his time, this was a common procedure for making a binding contract.

In a normal covenant ceremony, two parties would walk side by side between the animal parts. A simple curse was placed on the two parties: If one party didn't live up to their end of the bargain, their fate would be that of the animals they passed through.[2] The prophet Jeremiah alluded to this ancient contract: "Those who have violated my covenant and have not fulfilled the terms of the covenant they made before me, I will treat like the calf they cut in two and then walked between its pieces" (Jeremiah 34:18).

However, there is a twist in this covenant God made with Abraham. Just as you expect God and Abraham to walk between the split animals, the text finds our nomadic patriarch asleep as God passed through the pieces alone. This covenant left the realm of the temporal and entered the realm of the eternal with Abraham's absence. The destiny of Israel and the Jewish people were tied solely to God's name.

DID YOU KNOW?

The everlasting covenant God cut with Abraham is symbolically remembered through the act of circumcision (Genesis 17:9-14). Circumcision is a customary religious practice called *Brit Milah* (Covenant of the Circumcision) and is performed on Jewish males eight days after birth.

If God doesn't fulfill the promise, then He is a liar. It's God's holy name and reputation at stake here. The biblical story of the Jewish people rests solely on God's faithfulness to see this covenant promise through to the end—to use His chosen people the way He pledged He would. The promise to Abraham is an unbreakable vow ensuring the divine task of bringing blessing to all the families of the earth would not be thwarted.

TRACING THE COVENANT
THROUGH THE BIBLE

The covenant that started with Abraham didn't rest with him. If it had, the biblical story of the Jewish people would be buried with Abraham in Hebron at the Machpelah—the burial cave of the patriarchs. The following chart shows that all throughout Scripture God remembers and honors His promise to Abraham.

GOD'S COVENANT TO ABRAHAM THROUGH THE BIBLE		
Isaac	God's covenant to Abraham passed on to Isaac	Genesis 26:2-4
Jacob	God's covenant to Abraham and Isaac passed on to Jacob	Genesis 28:13-15
Joseph	Joseph wishes to be buried in the Promised Land based on God's covenant to Abraham, Isaac, and Jacob	Genesis 50:24
Moses	Moses' famous words "Let my people go!" were rooted in God's covenant to Abraham, Isaac, and Jacob	Exodus 2:24-25
Israel Enters the Promised Land	God reminded the Israelites before they entered the Promised Land that their inheritance wasn't of their own righteousness, but grounded on an unconditional pledge to Abraham, Isaac, and Jacob	Deuteronomy 9:5
Israel During the Reign of Kings	Despite Israel's disobedience to the Lord, God remained compassionate toward them because of His covenant with Abraham, Isaac, and Jacob	2 Kings 13:22-23

GOD'S COVENANT TO ABRAHAM THROUGH THE BIBLE		
Israel's Prophets	Despite Israel's continual disobedience to the Lord and their impending judgment, the prophets remain confident that God will restore Israel's fortunes to her former glory because of His covenant with Abraham, Isaac, and Jacob	Micah 7:20
Jesus' Ministry	The coming of Jesus was seen as God's faithfulness to remember Israel through His covenant with Abraham, Isaac, and Jacob	Luke 1:72-73
The Church Age	In the book of Acts and the epistles, the promise made to Abraham, Isaac, and Jacob remains a vital part of reaching the world with the gospel of Jesus Christ	Acts 3:25; Galatians 3:7-9
Israel's Prophetic Future	God's covenant with the patriarchs remains intact and will guarantee Israel's protection and restoration because of His faithfulness to fulfill the oath He swore to Abraham	Romans 11:28-29

The covenant was passed to Abraham's descendants as an inheritance, pushing the biblical plotline forward. The divine purpose of a promised land, a chosen people, and an eternal blessing began at the roots—Abraham, Isaac, and Jacob—and continued upward to all the branches of Abraham's family tree.

PLACES TO VISIT: **HEBRON**

Abraham purchased a plot of land here to bury his wife Sarah (Genesis 23). Later, Abraham, Isaac, Rebekah, Jacob, and Leah would also be laid to rest here in what is now known as the Machpelah.

TENSION IN THE BIBLICAL
STORY OF THE JEWISH PEOPLE

Generation after generation, God protected the heirs of the covenant promise. The holy and perfect God—who freed His chosen people from slavery in Egypt, gave them the law, and guided them into the Promised Land—worked with fallible and imperfect humans. Frequently, God would discipline the people of Israel for their disobedience, but He would never forsake them because of the covenant promise. Remember, it was only God who walked between the pieces of the animals. It is His holy reputation that is on the line.

Do you see why God was the only one to walk through the pieces, making a covenant with Himself? Had Abraham entered the covenant with God, the Bible would have been a much shorter book; the promise would have been broken before the close of the book of Genesis. The writer of Hebrews wrote it perfectly: "When God made his promise to Abraham, since there was no one greater for him to swear by, he swore by himself" (Hebrews 6:13).

This book is called *Israel Always* because the biblical story of the Jewish people extends throughout all of Jewish history. It is built on the eternal promise that God gave a promised land, to a chosen people, to fulfill a divine mission to bless all the families of the earth. God will sustain the Jewish people during their darkest moments and even guide them to return to their ancient homeland all because of an oath He made to Abraham.

The divine mission mentioned above includes God's pursuit of you, and all others who answer to His call for salvation in Christ. Come with me and we will experience the Holy Land and the epic of the Jewish people together, and along the way, witness God's continuing work through His chosen people from the book of Genesis all the way into eternity.

CHAPTER 2

THE PROMISED LAND AND THE TEMPLE

"This is what the Sovereign LORD says:
This is Jerusalem, which I have set in the center of
the nations, with countries all around her."

EZEKIEL 5:5

L et me tell you about a *tel*.

That's not a misspelling, tels are man-made hills that have layers of civilizations buried beneath them. A tel forms over the ages when a group of people settle on top of a natural hill that has natural resources like rain, drinking water, good soil for crops, and pastures for animals. Over time the settlement would grow until, one day, enemies would appear at the gate and destroy the city, leaving behind nothing but smoke, rubble, and ash. The ruins would be leveled out and a new town would be built atop the old one. Then enemies would appear at the gate—wash, rinse, repeat—I think you get the picture.

More than 200 tels dot the map in Israel. Excavations of Tel Megiddo, in the Lower Galilee region of northern Israel, unearthed 26 layers of civilizations, the most of any tel in the land. Why would so many people throughout history fight to conquer this area of the world?

PLACES TO VISIT: **TEL MEGIDDO**

With 26 layers of civilizations stacked upon itself dating back to the Canaanite period, this strategic location on the International Coastal Highway made it the epicenter of several battles throughout history. The book of Revelation also mentions a prophetic battle from Har-Megiddo, more commonly known as Armageddon (Revelation 16:16). Tel Megiddo is a UNESCO World Heritage Site.

Megiddo was strategically located near the Aruna Pass, a narrow stretch of the International Coastal Highway, that connected much of the known world. For that reason, Megiddo has a checkered history of international conflict. Whoever controlled Megiddo controlled international trade; this is the reason Solomon increased the fortification of the city during his reign (1 Kings 9:15).

Tel Megiddo is a microcosm of the Promised Land. Israel was highly valued because it was the only land bridge that connected three major continents. Much of the world's trade traffic moved through here.

An aerial view of Tel Megiddo. The hill contains 26 layers of civilizations dating back thousands of years.

When you think of the world, picture a dartboard: the Temple is the bull's-eye, then outside of that Jerusalem, then Israel, and then the world, all in concentric circles. When God sent Abraham to the Promised Land, He didn't select it haphazardly; He providentially placed the Jewish people directly in the bull's-eye of the world.

THE PROMISED LAND—
THE CENTER OF THE WORLD

There is no better map to display God's intent for the Promised Land than the Bünting Clover Leaf Map. Created by the sixteenth-century German theologian and cartographer Heinrich Bünting, the map depicts the world in a colorful cloverleaf array. Each of the three cloverleaves features a major continent: Europe appears on the upper left side, Asia is on the upper right side, and Africa is located on the bottom in the middle. The continents are depicted as floating independently of each other on a large body of water but they are anchored where the leaves all converge in the center. This anchor is Jerusalem.

"Jerusalem is a port city on the shore of eternity."[1]

Israeli Poet Yehuda Amichai

Bünting's map geographically places Israel at the center of the world because it bridged the continents of Europe, Asia, and Africa. Caravans, armies, and messengers traversed that part of the world by using two international highways that ran north and south through the Promised Land. Israel is flanked by the Mediterranean Sea and the Syro-Arabian Desert; any shortcut to circumvent Israel could spell disaster for the traveler.

The International Coastal Highway, one of antiquity's most significant transportation arteries, connected Egypt in the south with Mesopotamia, Syria, and Phoenicia in the north. The highway followed the length of the Mediterranean coast until it reached the Carmel mountain range near Megiddo. Some 37 exits branch off the International Coastal Highway in the coastal plain of Israel alone, connecting travelers to various cities and seaports. That is why the International Coastal Highway is also dubbed the Great Trunk Road.[2]

The King's Highway was situated on the east side of the Jordan River, connecting Egypt with Damascus and reaching as far as the Euphrates River. This trade route was used to transport spices and perfumes from the Arabian Peninsula to the north.

So why have a history lesson on roads from the past? What do ancient highway systems have to do with the purpose of the Promised Land?

Caravans, armies, and messengers carried goods and currency between the continents, but they also intrinsically moved humans. People who disseminated culture, religion, and new ideas from one area of the world to another. These ancient roads transmitted "information travelers" all of the time from one place to another, like the wires that digitally transfer information online today. Travelers would learn about the God of Abraham, Isaac, and Jacob as they were passing through the Promised Land.

Throughout the course of their journey, they would converse with others about the uniqueness of Israel's God. The God of Israel was much different than the gods of the surrounding nations. The Israelites proclaimed that their God was the one and only Creator of the heavens and the earth, and that they were commanded to worship no other gods. This alone was a radical concept among ancient civilizations.

DID YOU KNOW?

The phrase "a land flowing with milk and honey" is a popular way of describing the Promised Land. The phrase comes from Exodus 3:8, which illustrates the fertility of the land. Goats' milk spoke of the land's good pastures for grazing. The flowing of goats' milk also illustrated an abundance of meat for food and wool for clothing. The mention of honey probably refers to a syrup from the date fruit and also signifies the endless horticultural resources available in the land.

The rituals and practices of the Israelites would have been noted and shared abroad—like how they maintained a kosher diet, refrained from work one day a week to honor their God on the Sabbath, and circumcised their sons to mark their covenant loyalty to God. The Israelites' adherence to the laws of God, as found in the Torah, was designed to mark them as separate and different from the rest of the world.

The land of Israel was God's switchboard to communicate His truth to a lost world. In Deuteronomy, Moses explained to the Israelites—before they entered the land—that their obedience to the Lord while they lived in the land would produce spiritual fruit among the nations:

> See, I have taught you decrees and laws as the Lord my God commanded me, so that you may follow them in the land you are entering to take possession of it. Observe them carefully, for this will show your wisdom and understanding to the nations, who will hear about all these decrees and say, "Surely this great nation is a wise and understanding people." What other nation is so great as to have their gods near them the way the Lord our God is near us whenever we pray to him? And what other nation is so great as to have such righteous decrees and laws as this body of laws I am setting before you today? (Deuteronomy 4:5-8).

As a nation, the Israelites were never commanded to venture outside of the Promised Land to make God known. Instead, they were commanded to remain obedient within the land, and through their obedience, nations would witness the closeness of God.

TEL ISRAEL

Just as Tel Megiddo has layers of civilization stacked upon one another, the same could be said for the whole of the Promised Land. As you tour the Holy Land, your guide is equipped to dispense copious amounts of historical insights wherever you're standing—and the information can be overwhelming at times. One minute your guide is discussing an Egyptian outpost from 3,500 years ago and before you know it your guide has moved on to the waves of Jewish immigration from the late nineteenth century AD that settled in that same place. Below are the strata of Tel Israel—the layers of the Promised Land that will give you a point of reference as you travel through time.

THE LAYERS OF CIVILIZATION OF TEL ISRAEL		
Era	Events	Name of the Region
Canaanite Period 2000 BC–1200 BC	Several ethnic groups, including the Canaanites, lived throughout the Promised Land	The Land of Canaan
Israelite Period 1200 BC–922 BC	The Israelite Period includes the conquest and settlement through to the unified kingdom established under David and Solomon	Israel
Divided Israelite Kingdom 922 BC–586 BC	The unified kingdom split after Solomon's death; both Israel and Judah were exiled from the land by 586 BC	Israel (northern ten tribes) Judah (southern two tribes)
Persian Period 537 BC–333 BC	Israelites were permitted to return to the Promised Land to rebuild Jerusalem and the Temple under the authority of the Persian Empire	Yehud
Hellenistic Period 330 BC–142 BC	Alexander the Great defeated the Persians; he imposed Greek culture (Hellenism) throughout his empire, heavily influencing the Jewish community	Judea
Hasmonean Monarchy 142 BC–63 BC	Mattathias, a zealous Jewish priest, and his children pushed back against Greek assimilation and gained Jewish independence; his family expanded the reaches of Judea	Judea

THE LAYERS OF CIVILIZATION OF TEL ISRAEL		
Era	Events	Name of the Region
Roman Period 63 BC–AD 330	Rome usurped Hasmonean rule and installed a client-king, Herod the Great; Judea was divided after Herod's death, but remained under Roman control	Judea (63 BC–AD 135) Palaestina (AD 135–AD 330)
Byzantine Period AD 330–AD 638	The Roman Empire coalesced into the Byzantine Empire; Roman emperor Constantine the Great converted to Christianity and established it as the state religion; he shifted the empire's capital from Rome to the ancient Greek city of Byzantium, located in what is now modern-day Turkey	Palestine
Arab (Umayyad) Period AD 638–AD 1098	The Byzantine Empire crumbled under the weight of Islam spreading north from Saudi Arabia; the Arab army conquered Christian lands after the powerful Umayyad Caliphate made Damascus its capital; Jerusalem was captured by the Arab army in AD 638	Palestine
Crusader Period AD 1098–AD 1187	In AD 1099, the Crusaders from Europe captured Jerusalem and massacred thousands of Muslims and Jews; Catholic Christians controlled Jerusalem for nearly a century, until Saladin recaptured Jerusalem and a large part of Palestine in AD 1187	Palestine
Arab (Mamluk) Period AD 1087–AD 1517	Mamluks were slave-warriors of medieval Islam; they deposed their masters and defeated the remaining Crusaders in Palestine to establish a dynasty that lasted 300 years; Cairo rose to prominence as the superior city of the Muslim world under Mamluk control	Palestine
Turkish Period AD 1517–AD 1917	Ottoman Turks seized control of Palestine from the Mamluks; Suleiman the Magnificent renovated much of the Jerusalem we see today as well as the Dome of the Rock and the walls of the Old City	Palestine

THE LAYERS OF CIVILIZATION OF TEL ISRAEL		
Era	Events	Name of the Region
British Period AD 1917–AD 1948	After World War I concluded, the vast Ottoman Empire was divided and the British controlled the Holy Land; the Balfour Declaration stated the British government would endeavor to establish a Jewish homeland in Palestine	Mandatory Palestine
Israeli Period AD 1948–Present	The sovereign Jewish State of Israel declared independence on May 14, 1948, after the United Nations approved the partition plan permitting a Jewish national homeland	Israel

THE TEMPLE

Walking toward the Western Wall in the Old City of Jerusalem, you'll see a sign that reads, "You are approaching the holy site of the Western Wall where the Divine Presence always rests." The Western Wall, or *Kotel* as it's called in Hebrew, is a small part of the retaining wall on which the Jewish Temple once stood—it is not part of the actual Temple itself. Nevertheless, Jewish sages teach that God's divine presence never departed. The Western Wall has been the centerpiece of Jewish worship for centuries because of its proximity to the Holy of Holies, where God once dwelled.

PLACES TO VISIT: **THE WESTERN WALL**

Since June 1967, this has been called the Western Wall. It is situated on the southwest side of the Temple Mount complex. It's a place of worship and prayer for those of the Jewish faith. The stones of the wall are part of the Herodian retaining apparatus the Temple was built upon. Jewish people are prohibited from worshipping on top of the Temple Mount where the Temple once stood. The Western Wall is the nearest locale they can access in relation to where the Holy of Holies was located.

The Temple is known as the place where the blood of bulls and goats was spilled on the altar, but the sacrificial system wasn't what set the Israelite Temple apart from pagan temples. Remember, the sign at the entrance to the Western Wall doesn't mention sacrifices. Rather, it speaks of God's divine presence. It was God's physical presence within the sanctuary that sanctified the Temple. And to fully understand God's presence in the Temple, we must first encounter the Tabernacle.

The Tabernacle

After the Israelites were freed from slavery in Egypt and they were making their way to the Promised Land, God commanded them to build a Tabernacle so that He might dwell with them: "Have them make a sanctuary for me, and I will dwell among them" (Exodus 25:8). The book of Exodus is all about God's deliverance and His dwelling with His chosen people. Exodus ends on a high note, with the physical presence of God settled in the Tabernacle: "Then the cloud covered the tent of meeting, and the glory of the LORD filled the tabernacle. Moses could not enter the tent of meeting because the cloud had settled on it, and the glory of the LORD filled the tabernacle" (Exodus 40:34-35).

God's presence in the Tabernacle shouldn't be overlooked; it marks the first time since the garden of Eden that God dwelled among His creation. Israel's God did not manifest Himself in the form of an idol, nor was He a distant, ethereal God disinterested in this world. Israel's God came down to be among His chosen people in the Tabernacle and the Temple. He's both holy and relational.

Solomon's Temple (957-586 BC)

The idea of a temple didn't arise until King David recognized that God's dwelling place was a tent and the king's dwelling place was a palace (1 Chronicles 17:1). In an effort to remedy this, David purchased the threshing floor of Araunah on top of Mount Moriah to build an altar. This is the same site where Abraham bound Isaac and placed him on an altar, then God intervened and provided a substitute sacrifice. David was denied the request to build the Lord a temple, an honor that would go to David's son Solomon.

Solomon's Temple was completed in the mid-tenth century BC. According to 1 Kings 8:10-11, the same glory that rushed into the Tabernacle flooded the First Temple at its inauguration. God's presence signified His approval of His new dwelling place in Jerusalem.

Solomon's Temple was patterned after the architectural layout of the Tabernacle, which was divided into sections by degrees of holiness. The center of the Temple was the most holy part—the Holy of Holies, where the physical presence of God dwelled. God's glory rested atop the Ark of the Covenant between the cherubim. Initially, the Ark held the tablets with the Ten Commandments, Aaron's rod, and a pot of manna (Hebrews 9:4). The Ark was much more than a box containing Israel's memorabilia of God's faithfulness, it was the throne of God, signifying His authority as the true King of Israel.

Entrance into the Holy of Holies was strictly prohibited. Once a year, on the Day of Atonement, the high priest was permitted to enter to make atonement for Israel's sins. A veil embroidered with cherubim separated the holy throne room of God from the rest of the Temple. The imagery on the veil hearkened back to the garden of Eden, where cherubim were stationed with a flaming sword to deny Adam and Eve reentrance into the garden after they fell into sin (Genesis 3:24).

On the other side of the veil within the sanctuary was the Holy Place, where the priests of Israel continually carried out their ministry and worshipped God. The Holy Place housed the menorah, the table of showbread, and the incense altar. Only the Levitical priests were permitted to enter the Holy Place.

The sanctuary opened to the Courtyard of the Priests, where sacrifices were offered on the brazen altar. The sacrifices were continually offered up as a "sweet aroma" to the Lord (Leviticus 1:9 NKJV).

Solomon's Temple served as a central place of worship for the Judahites until 586 BC, when the Babylonian king, Nebuchadnezzar, laid waste to Jerusalem and Solomon's Temple. The razing of the city and the Temple wasn't a consequence of ancient diplomacy gone wrong; its destruction was arranged by God Himself for His people's perpetual disobedience of Him. Before it was destroyed, the prophet Ezekiel vividly described God's physical presence departing the temple in Ezekiel chapters 9–11.

DID YOU KNOW?

Tisha B'Av (9th of Av) is an annual Jewish fast day to commemorate the destruction of Solomon's Temple in 586 BC and Herod's Temple in AD 70. This is considered the saddest day on the Jewish calendar. According to Jewish tradition, both Temples were destroyed on the same day of the calendar year and other tragedies took place on this day as well, such as the 12 spies returning from their journey through the Promised Land and reporting that the land was impossible to take. Their unfavorable report is what kickstarted Israel's 40 years of wandering in the desert.

The Second Temple (515-19 BC)

The Temple lay in ruins for 70 years, when a global power shift transitioned rule from the hands of the Neo-Babylonian Empire to the Persians. The new ruler of the largest and most influential empire of the day, Cyrus the Great, changed the policies of the Babylonians and permitted the Jewish people to return to the Promised Land and to rebuild the Temple in 538 BC (Ezra 1:1-4).

Certain vessels of worship that had been seized by Nebuchadnezzar were restored to the Israelites as well. This rebuilt Temple would go through stages of construction and renovations up through the time of Jesus. Yet God's glory that inhabited the Tabernacle and Solomon's Temple never returned; the Holy of Holies lacked God's physical presence.

By 515–516 BC, the new Temple was dedicated, and sacrificial worship to God was reinstituted. The dedication should have been a time of celebration and joy, but many of the Jewish people were depressed about the outcome of the new Temple. First, the structure paled in comparison to Solomon's Temple. Second, and most significantly, the Holy of Holies was an empty room, the Ark of Covenant was lost, and the physical presence of God had not returned.

Herod's Temple (19 BC–AD 70)

The most notable renovation and expansion work done on the Second Temple was spearheaded by Herod the Great starting around 19 BC. The structure received massive upgrades; it became the largest building project of its kind in the ancient world since the pyramids were erected in Egypt.[3]

Herod enlarged the Temple Mount complex by positioning a large platform over Mount Moriah. To accomplish this architectural feat, Herod erected retaining walls into the surrounding valleys and backfilled them with dirt. Archaeologists have exposed the original foundation stones of the retaining wall, and some of the largest stones are believed to weigh anywhere from 300 to 600 tons, supporting sections of the wall that rose more than 100 feet.

Herod's design doubled the size of the Temple complex, providing more room for the 100,000 Jewish pilgrims that worshipped each year in Jerusalem during the holy days of Passover, the Feast of Weeks, and the Feast of Tabernacles. Josephus stated that Herod's ambition was less about the betterment of Jewish worship and more about a structure that would serve as an everlasting memorial to his name.[4]

Even after all of Herod's splendid renovations were completed, the Holy of Holies remained void of God's presence. Interestingly, the apostle John opened his Gospel by employing the imagery of God's presence inhabiting the Tabernacle and the Temple when he described the incarnation of Jesus Christ. He wrote, "The Word became flesh and made his dwelling among us. We have seen his glory, the glory of the one and only Son, who came from the Father, full of grace and truth" (John 1:14). In the person of Jesus Christ, God dwelled with His people once again.

A Jewish rebellion against the Roman Empire that started in AD 66 was the impetus for the destruction of Herod's Temple in AD 70 by the Roman general Titus. Since then, the Jewish people have been praying and longing to rebuild a third temple on the Temple Mount.

PLACES TO VISIT: **THE TEMPLE INSTITUTE**

A Jewish organization committed to the rebuilding of the Third Temple on Mount Moriah. Located in the Old City of Jerusalem, the Temple Institute educates the public on the Torah's imperative for Temple worship and the need to rebuild. The Institute serves as a museum and houses "temple-ready" vessels and garments to be used in the next Temple.

THE KNOWLEDGE OF GOD

As you travel through Israel between the biblical sites, you may find yourself tempted to close your eyes and take a quick nap.

Don't do it!

You'll miss some of the best parts of the Promised Land. Some of the roads and highways in modern Israel sit above the routes traversed by the caravans, armies, messengers, and pilgrims of the ancient past. These roads were designed by men to connect the continents and carry out trade. But for God, these highways had a deeper spiritual purpose: to transmit to all peoples the knowledge of the one true God of Israel.

The Promised Land is alive. It cannot be explained in a map or chart alone; it must be treated as a special character, a character whose role in the Scriptures must be elevated to bring to light God's plan through the ages. God chose this place to make His name known and to dwell with His people, a theme that appears all throughout the Bible and will continue into eternity.

CHAPTER 3

THE EXILE
AND THE RETURN

*"If I forget you, Jerusalem, may my right hand
forget its skill. May my tongue cling to the roof
of my mouth if I do not remember you, if I do
not consider Jerusalem my highest joy."*

PSALM 137:5-6

M y freshman year of college was devoted to taking part in a year-long set of coursework called the Institute of Jewish Studies (IJS), developed by the Friends of Israel Gospel Ministry. The program was designed to prepare Christians to serve the Jewish community by engaging them with the Jewishness of the Bible. To this day, my time at IJS remains one of the most enlightening experiences I've had both academically and spiritually because it guided me to look at the Scriptures through a Jewish lens.

I absorbed a lot of information that year, but one lesson stood out. I vividly recall my professors highlighting four dates that radically enhance the way I read and interpret the Bible. The historical events associated with these dates not only influenced Israel's destiny in the Old Testament, but had a perpetual impact on the cultural, political, religious, and theological world of the Jewish people.

KEY EVENTS IN ISRAEL'S HISTORY

These life-changing events for the people of Israel resulted in paradigm shifts that are documented in the historical, prophetic, and wisdom books of the Old Testament. Knowing these dates and their corresponding events is helpful for giving context to the Bible. Understanding them has made me a better student and teacher of the Scriptures, and I believe that they will help you too.

Here are the dates you need to know:

- **722 BC:** The ten tribes in the northern kingdom of Israel were exiled by the Assyrian Empire.

- **586 BC:** Nebuchadnezzar, the king of the Neo-Babylonian Empire, destroyed Jerusalem and the Temple and exiled many of the inhabitants of the southern kingdom of Judah to Babylon.

- **538 BC:** Cyrus, the Persian king, permitted the Jewish community exiled by Babylon to return to Jerusalem to rebuild the city and the Temple.

- **AD 70:** Titus, a Roman general, destroyed Jerusalem and the Temple, which led to another Jewish expulsion from the land.

In this chapter we will cover three of the important dates, and we'll discuss the destruction of Herod's Temple in AD 70 in a later chapter.

Before we get into the events that took place on these dates, let's review some terms that will help enrich your journey through the Holy Land. These terms define three significant phases in Israel's history. The first one is *pre-exilic*. This descriptor summarizes events in Israel's history that occurred prior to the Jewish people's exile. For instance, the accounts of the patriarchs, the exodus and Passover, the giving of the law, the journey through the wilderness, the conquest of the Promised Land, and the eras of Israel's judges, kings, and some prophets all occurred during the pre-exilic period.

PLACES TO VISIT: THE CITY OF DAVID

Located south of the Temple Mount and the Old City of Jerusalem, the City of David brings many pieces of biblical history together in one location. The City of David is an interactive archaeological site where guests can experience remnants of the original Jerusalem. You can explore the likely foundation of King David's palace and step foot in Jerusalem's ancient water source, the Gihon Spring, as you wade through its water in Hezekiah's Tunnel to the Pool of Siloam.

The second term is *exilic*. This is the next phase in Israelite history, when the Jewish people were exiled from the Promised Land and lived among the Gentiles (non-Jewish people) in other nations. For instance, the prophets Daniel and Ezekiel wrote from Babylon. These men practiced godly living in a foreign world. God revealed through them that Israel's sin brought about their judgment, but they also offered a hope for when God would restore the Jewish people to the land of Israel.

The third term is *post-exilic*. This period includes events that took place after the Jewish people were permitted to return to the Promised Land. Ezra and Nehemiah were post-exilic leaders who detailed the trials and triumphs of the returnees as they set about rebuilding in the land of Israel. While post-exilic prophets like Zechariah, Haggai, and Malachi shared the deeper spiritual issues that plagued the Jewish community, they cast a prophetic hope for God's chosen people.

In Scripture, the exile and return of the Jewish people marks a seismic transition from an Israelite kingdom, when Israel and Judah had autonomy over the Promised Land, to the "times of the Gentiles" (Luke 21:24), when Gentile nations exercised authority over what God had promised to the Jewish people. Now let's discuss what happened.

JUDGMENT, DESTRUCTION, AND EXILE

Isaiah, a pre-exilic prophet, warned the divided kingdoms of Israel and Judah that God's patience with the people was waning. Because of their centuries of disobedience and sin, judgment was imminent. So, what exactly did judgment look like for these two wayward kingdoms? Let's go back to Deuteronomy 28, where we read Moses' reiteration of the law to a new generation of Israelites just before they settled in the Promised Land. There, God specifically stated that continual disobedience to His commands would result in the people's expulsion from the land. The judgment was harsh:

> The LORD will drive you and the king you set over you to a nation unknown to you or your ancestors. There you will worship other gods, gods of wood and stone. You will become a thing of horror, a byword and an object of ridicule among all the peoples where the LORD will drive you (Deuteronomy 28:36-37).

> Then the LORD will scatter you among all nations, from one end of the earth to the other. There you will worship other gods—gods of wood and stone, which neither you nor your ancestors have known. Among those nations you will find no repose, no resting place for the sole of your foot. There the LORD will give you an anxious mind, eyes weary with longing, and a despairing heart (Deuteronomy 28:64-65).

God's punishment for Israel's spiritual apathy was to temporarily exile His people from the land He promised to Abraham. Israel's God would orchestrate His judgment through shifts in political power in the Levant—the easternmost part of the Mediterranean region.

PLACES TO VISIT: **TEL LACHISH**

The strategic location of this second-most-important city in the ancient kingdom of Judah protected the road that stretched from

Egypt to Jerusalem. The remains of Tel Lachish visibly retell of Hezekiah's religious reforms and the Assyrian and Babylonian campaigns against Judah. Archaeological finds from Tel Lachish, such as the Lachish Letters, confirm the historical account of these biblical events.

Ancient Egypt's influence crumbled in 1200 BC, forming a power vacuum in Mesopotamia. Small kingdoms in the Levant, such as the Aramean states, Phoenician and Philistine cities, Transjordan kingdoms, and Israel all struggled to fill the void left in the region, but eventually, another power rose to the top—Assyria.

What started as a small trading community situated on the Tigris River in upper Mesopotamia (modern-day northern Iraq), became a major empire. Assyria developed a strategy that included the mining of raw resources for its own benefit and control over the vital trade routes of the ancient Near East.[1] These routes included the major highways we looked at in the previous chapter. Naturally, Assyria's strategy put Israel directly into the path of the ambitious empire.

The prophet Isaiah saw Assyrian expansion as a sign of God's judgment: "Woe to the Assyrian, the rod of my anger, in whose hand is the club of my wrath! I send him against a godless nation, I dispatch him against a people who anger me, to seize loot and snatch plunder, and to trample them down like mud in the streets" (Isaiah 10:5-6). According to Isaiah, it was Israel's God who was moving the pieces on the political chessboard to accomplish His goal of judgment. Assyrian pressure forced Israel and Judah to become vassal kingdoms that paid tribute to its foreign king.

King Hoshea, the northern kingdom's last ruler, halted tribute to Assyrian king Shalmaneser V and allied himself with Egypt to the south in order to gain independence from Assyrian rule. Unamused by Hoshea's decision, Shalmaneser began a siege on Samaria, the capital of Israel, that lasted for three years. This brings our first key date and event; in 722 BC, Samaria was captured, bringing an end to the northern kingdom (2 Kings 17). Israelites taken captive were removed from

Samaria and replaced by Assyrian captives from Babylon and Media (2 Kings 17:24). Mass deportation and resettlement of conquered peoples in the ancient Near East was a standard policy practiced by the Assyrians and later, the Babylonians, which forced the Jewish people to assimilate rapidly in pagan cultures.

The Assyrian resettlement policy in northern Israel encouraged the intermarriage of Israelites and Gentiles, which gave birth to the Samaritan people—a people that would appear during the post-exilic history of the land (Ezra 4:1-3; Nehemiah 4:7), the period between the Testaments, and the New Testament era (Luke 10:25-37; John 4).

PLACES TO VISIT: **MOUNT GERIZIM**

Situated in Samaria adjacent to Mount Ebal to its north and with the city of Nablus (Shechem) down in the valley between the two peaks, Mount Gerizim is home to a Samaritan temple that was most likely erected during Persian rule in the fifth century BC. Mount Gerizim is now both an archaeological park for visitors and an active site of Samaritan worship.

At the time of the Assyrian deportation, there was a contingency of Israelites who fled south, taking refuge in Jerusalem to escape Assyrian rule. Archaeologists believe Judah saw a massive spike in population and prosperity during the eighth century BC which was the impetus for King Hezekiah to expand the city walls of Jerusalem. He wanted to protect the Israelite refugees who were living outside the city's boundaries at the time (Isaiah 22:10).

The kingdom of Judah remained a vassal to the Assyrian Empire until the time of King Hezekiah. The king of Judah halted service to the king of Assyria. In 701 BC, Sennacherib responded to Hezekiah's rebellion and attacked the cities within Judah. Despite immense pressure from Sennacherib, Hezekiah pleaded with the Lord for deliverance and Jerusalem was spared by God (2 Kings 18–19).

However, this did not mean that Judah was off the chopping block. The godly leadership provided by Hezekiah and Josiah restrained judgment for a time. Assyrian power and influence ended in 612 BC with the rise of the Neo-Babylonian Empire, located on the Euphrates River, in what is now southern Iraq.

Judah's kings struggled to show allegiance to Babylon, which resulted in a series of deportations:

- 605 BC: Nebuchadnezzar campaigned in Jerusalem, deporting some of the young nobility of Judah to Babylon, possibly including at this time the prophet Daniel.

- 597 BC: Nebuchadnezzar returned and plundered Jerusalem, deporting King Jehoiachin and his family along with other Jewish leaders and the prophet Ezekiel.

- 586 BC: The final deportation came with the destruction of Jerusalem and Solomon's Temple (Jeremiah 52:12-16).

Our second key date, 586 BC and its events were devastating for Israel, and to this day, remains one of the most consequential moments in Jewish history. The Davidic dynasty that was to bring the promised Messiah seemingly vanished and Israel's independence faded. But, even in the darkness of all that was taking place, God did not leave His people without hope.

DID YOU KNOW?

In 1935, excavations on the site of Tel Lachish unearthed broken pottery shards with writing on them that documented the time period just prior to Babylon's conquest of Judah and Jerusalem. The Lachish Letters, as they are dubbed, preserve correspondence between a commander and his officer who was stationed not far from Lachish. The letters from the sixth century BC reveal the tensions felt leading up to Babylon's attack on the southern kingdom.

JEWISH LIFE AND FAITH IN EXILE

The forced deportation and resettlement policies of Assyria and Babylon were used to assimilate the Jewish people into pagan cultures, stripping them of their unique identity and independence.

The Jewish people who were forced to move to Babylon experienced a better quality of life than those who were left behind in Judah. The captives were encouraged to make a new life for themselves while in exile, and they were resettled in abandoned villages along the Chebar River (Jeremiah 29:4-7; Ezra 2:59; Ezekiel 1:1 [KJV]).

When it seemed like there was no hope for the Davidic dynasty, 2 Kings 25:27-30 (KJV) shows that Jehoiachin, Judah's king, deported in 597 BC, was relocated to the royal court of the Babylonian king Evilmerodach; a sign of hope that the Davidic dynasty would survive through the exile.

The book of Daniel opens with King Nebuchadnezzar inviting well-educated Jews into Babylonian royal service; they received all the trappings of royalty. However, Daniel, as a Jewish man, refused to defile himself with the royal food and wine (Daniel 1:8). Daniel's commitment to God—which meant he rejected the worship of false gods—would eventually land him in a lions' den (Daniel 6).

The prophet Daniel's spiritual posture toward God while in exile was representative of the entire Jewish community. The exile raised many questions: How do we maintain our Jewish identity outside of the Promised Land? How do we worship God apart from the Temple in Jerusalem? Did our sin nullify God's promise to Abraham, Isaac, and Jacob?

The Babylonian Jewish community was forced to alter the way they worshipped God, with changes that still affect Judaism to this day. While in exile, the Jewish people continued to practice the Sabbath, circumcision, and dietary restrictions, all of which were markers of the law that maintained their unique identity in Gentile territory.

DID YOU KNOW?

The Babylonian campaign against Judah and Jerusalem led to the exile of many Jewish people, but not all of them were taken to Babylon. Some of the poorest remained in Jerusalem and a contingency of Jewish refugees fled for Egypt (Jeremiah 43:1-7; 44:1).

The exiled Jewish communities were managed by elders. Synagogues became a fixture as a place of gathering and worship apart from the Temple, and scholars argue this transition could have its roots in Babylon. Prayers, fasting, charity, and suffering replaced the sacrificial system.

God's judgment over Israel's sin was palpable, but He did not abandon them. His presence remained with His chosen people during their suffering (Ezekiel 11:16). The displaced Jewish heart longed for Zion; the people pledged never to forget Jerusalem. In Psalm 137, which was written during the exile, we read the vow, "If I forget you, Jerusalem, may my right hand forget its skill. May my tongue cling to the roof of my mouth if I do not remember you, if I do not consider Jerusalem my highest joy" (verses 5-6). Prophets like Ezekiel gave hope that one day the people would return to the Promised Land (Ezekiel 36–37).

The exile shaped the Jewish people's view of God amid their suffering. After Jerusalem and the Temple were destroyed, the cultures of the ancient Near East would have considered Israel's God to be on life support. In the battle of the gods, Israel's God certainly looked weak or, at best, nonresponsive, after the Assyrians and Babylonians trampled Israel.

Yet the Jewish community refused to believe their God was dead. In Scripture, we never see the people blaming God for their plight. Instead, the exiles pointed the blame back on themselves. They recognized their disobedience was the impetus for their judgment. For the exiles, God became more alive than ever because His Word had come true—it was their sin that sent them into exile, just as God promised in His law (Leviticus 26; Deuteronomy 28).

A NEW ERA—THE RETURN

In time, Babylonian influence diminished in the Near East due to both internal and external pressures. Within a few short decades, the Persian Empire consolidated its power under the leadership of Cyrus and expanded its rule through the Levant into Egypt, northern Mesopotamia, and Anatolia.

This brings us to our third key date and event in the history of the Jewish people. Cyrus was chosen by God for a special purpose—the Persian king was called God's "shepherd" (Isaiah 44:28) and "anointed" (Isaiah 45:1). After 70 years of exile outside of the Promised Land, in 538 BC, Cyrus permitted the Jewish people to return to their homeland to rebuild their Temple and worship their God (Ezra 1:1-4). In fact, the Jewish people weren't the only ones to benefit from the king's benevolence—all captives in the empire were permitted to return to their lands and rebuild to honor their gods. Cyrus was tolerant to the claims of other peoples' gods and had no desire to supersede them with gods of his own.[2] His policy is well documented, seen in the Scriptures and in an edict found engraved on a barrel-shaped clay cylinder that was discovered in Iraq in 1879, called the Cyrus Cylinder.

DID YOU KNOW?

In the late 1960s, the Shah of Iran declared the Cyrus Cylinder the world's first charter on human rights, thus identifying Iran with the birthplace of tolerance. The Cylinder became a slogan of the Shah's new national identity in celebration of the 2,500th anniversary of the Persian monarchy.[3]

The Jewish people returning were assisted in every way possible by Cyrus. He even gave back the temple vessels that were seized by the Babylonians when they looted the Temple and destroyed it in 586 BC. The first wave that returned worked diligently to rebuild the Temple; a new altar was constructed above the old and a foundation marked the dimensions of the new Temple. Joy filled the air as the Feast of Tabernacles was observed at the new altar, but setbacks eventually halted the reconstruction.

The Samaritans obstructed the rebuilding efforts; this marked the beginning of ongoing tensions between the two peoples that would continue for hundreds of years and into the time of Jesus. And spiritual apathy paralyzed the newly settled Jews from carrying out the construction work, so the prophets Haggai and Zechariah had to urge them to continue to build.

The prophets envisioned a day when Israel and Judah would be united as one sovereign nation again and restored to her former glory under the rule of a new king from the line of David, a Messiah who would usher in a messianic age for Israel and put an end to the Gentile rule over the Promised Land:

> In that day I will restore David's fallen shelter—I will repair
> its broken walls and restore its ruins—and will rebuild it
> as it used to be...New wine will drip from the mountains
> and flow from all the hills, and I will bring my people Israel
> back from exile. They will rebuild the ruined cities and live
> in them. They will plant vineyards and drink their wine;
> they will make gardens and eat their fruit. I will plant Israel
> in their own land, never again to be uprooted from the land
> I have given them (Amos 9:11, 13-15).

God was faithful to restore His chosen people to the land He promised them; however, Gentiles still had authority over them. Jewish rulers like Zerubbabel and Nehemiah were given the title, governor of Judah, which means they were client rulers of the Gentile authorities. Yes, God's chosen people returned to the Promised Land, but a new era of Gentile control would continue reigning over them.

The Jewish community realized that this wasn't the way it should be, their prophets' visions of restoration never included the yoke of Gentile subjection. Daniel revealed that the Gentile kingdoms of the world would one day crumble under the weight of God's eternal kingdom

(Daniel 2:31-45). The Son of Man, a messianic ruler, would be given authority and power by God to rule over all the nations: "He was given authority, glory and sovereign power; all nations and peoples of every language worshiped him" (Daniel 7:13-14).

The Old Testament closes with the assurance that God's kingdom is coming. His presence will return to His people and Israel will dwell safely in the land. God's covenant to Abraham and to Israel would be fulfilled because God is a keeper of His promises. God will fully restore His people to the Promised Land, and all nations will be blessed.

CHAPTER 4

BETWEEN THE OLD TESTAMENT AND THE NEW TESTAMENT

"There will be a fourth kingdom, strong as iron—for iron breaks and smashes everything—and as iron breaks things to pieces, so it will crush and break all the others."

DANIEL 2:40

C an you find the page in your Bible that has no verses, yet encompasses nearly 400 years of Jewish history? I promise this isn't a riddle. I am referring to the single piece of paper that divides the Old Testament from the New Testament. The immense historical span of that one page has been labeled "the 400 years of silence." The "silence" is not referring to a lack of historical events, but instead to God's revelation through writing. The time between the last Old Testament prophet Malachi (445 BC) and the earliest New Testament writing from James (AD 45) is roughly 400 years. These years are better known as Intertestamental History or Second Temple Judaism.

There was a great deal of pressure placed on the Jewish community between the testaments. They had a choice to assimilate with the Gentiles who controlled the land or to resist. Assimilation into the Gentile culture was certainly comfortable, but it threatened Israel's unique identity and divine purpose. The intertestamental period tested Israel's resilience to stay true to God's election. As you'll soon find out, some Jewish leaders basked in the glory, power, wealth, prestige, and benefits of the Gentile culture, while others chose to stand firm in their biblical convictions to maintain their unique identity, even to the point of death.

When you travel to the land of Israel today you will be shocked about how much history you'll absorb that originated from this era; knowing the cast of characters, the politics, and the culture of the intertestamental period will enrich your journey through the Holy Land. The astounding thing about that single page in your Bible is, even though no words were added to the canon of Scripture for 400 years, there is no doubt that God shaped international events that paved the way for the coming of Jesus—the Messiah.

GREEK RULE (333–167 BC)

Alexander the Great and his armies swiftly conquered the entire Persian Empire and introduced Greek culture to the Middle East. The 20-year-old Macedonian king, who took the throne after the death of his father Philip II, forcibly freed the Greeks from the yoke of Persian power and reigned over what was then the world's largest empire. Within two years' time the entire geographical landscape of the Bible fell under his control.

This young ruler's quest for power lead him to the east, into the far reaches of the Indus Valley, an area that lies in modern-day Pakistan and India. By this point, the endless military campaigns depleted the morale of Alexander's men, forcing him to turn around and return. On his journey home, Alexander died in Babylon in 323 BC at the age of 33.

Alexander received the honorific title "the Great" for two reasons. First, for his brilliant military strategy—he warred against a giant empire and remained undefeated in battle. Second, for his ideological conquest. Greek culture permeated throughout his vast empire; the assimilation of conquered peoples to Greek culture became known as Hellenization.

The Jewish modus vivendi, or "way of life," was not immune to Hellenization; in fact, there were Jews who embraced it, both within the land of Israel and outside of it. Greek cities were established in Israel. Some of these cities became known as the Decapolis by New Testament times. Those who lived in Judea, the conservative center of Judaism, balked at the mingling of Jewish and Greek cultures, but even they would succumb to Hellenistic allure.

Almost overnight the Greek language became the lingua franca of the entire Near East. This paved the way for the creation of the Septuagint (LXX)—a translation of the Torah (Law) from Hebrew into Greek in the mid-second century BC. Greek would remain a common language into the Roman era, when the Greek New Testament books were written, and even longer still into the Byzantine era.

DID YOU KNOW?

The Septuagint (LXX) is a Greek translation of the Old Testament and was the first translation of the Hebrew Bible into another language. The Latin title *Septuaginta*, which means "70," refers to the 72 Jewish men commissioned by Ptolemy II Philadelphus (285–247 BC) to translate the Hebrew Scriptures held in the library of Alexandria. According to the *Letter of Aristeas*, the high priest sent six men from each of the twelve tribes of Israel to translate the Torah. Scholars believe the Septuagint was translated out of need, since Hebrew was not spoken by Greek-speaking Jewish people living outside of the land of Israel.

At the time of his death, Alexander had no viable heir to his throne, which created a power vacuum in his kingdom. Four power-hungry generals wrestled over the largest and most strategic portions of the empire. Daniel, the prophet, envisioned the rise and fall of Alexander and the division of his land (Daniel 8:5-8, 21-22).

As the dust settled, Israel was uncomfortably situated between two of the Greek kingdoms.

Two generals, who fought side by side with Alexander, Ptolemy I Soter and Seleucus I Nicator, took control of large swaths of Alexander's spoils. Ptolemy ruled Egypt, North Africa, Israel, Phoenicia, and a handful of the Greek Islands. While Syria, Asia Minor, Persia, and everything east to the Indus Valley, was under the dominion of Seleucus and his Seleucid Empire.

DID YOU KNOW?

Antioch was founded in 300 BC as the capital of the Seleucid Empire and would later become a pivotal location for the growth of the early church. After the martyrdom of Stephen, many Christians fled Jerusalem for Antioch, resulting in the conversion of many Gentiles to Christianity. It is there that followers of Jesus were first called Christians (Acts 11:19-26).

The Ptolemaic dynasty to the south controlled Israel from 323–200 BC. This ended when Antiochus III, the Seleucid king to the north, moved in to expand his empire. He was successful in defeating the Ptolemaic forces at Paneas (Caesarea Philippi) and ripping Israel from Ptolemaic rule.

The Jewish community in Judea responded positively to Antiochus III; they were tired of paying the burdensome taxes of their previous landlord. But all that optimism faded quickly when Antiochus IV Epiphanes claimed the throne of his father. Antiochus IV sought to unify and expand his kingdom under the banner of Hellenization, and the Jewish people became the target of much of his fury.

After an unpleasant run-in with Rome, in 167 BC Antiochus prohibited the Jewish people from practicing circumcision, offering sacrifices, reading the Torah, honoring the Sabbath, and celebrating Jewish festivals (1 Maccabees 1). To make matters worse, Antiochus desecrated the Jewish Temple when he dedicated it to Zeus, committing an "abomination of desolation" (Daniel 11:31 NKJV).

PLACES TO VISIT: CAESAREA PHILIPPI

Caesarea Philippi rests at the base of Mount Hermon in the Golan Heights 25 miles north of the Sea of Galilee. Formerly known as Paneas, its springs supply water to the Jordan River. The fertile site was dedicated to the Greek god Pan. It is where Antiochus III defeated Ptolemaic forces and seized control of Israel in 198 BC. Later, when Peter recognizes Jesus is the Messiah, it is here that Jesus tells Peter, "I tell you that you are Peter, and on this rock I will build my church, and the gates of Hades will not overcome it" (Matthew 16:18).

Jewish people were required to offer up pagan sacrifices to demonstrate loyalty to Antiochus. This included slaughtering pigs, an unkosher animal according to the Torah. Many Jewish people capitulated to preserve their lives. That is, until one man resisted the Greek pressure to assimilate.

THE MACCABEAN REVOLT (167–142 BC)

Antiochus' men arrived in Modi'in, a small town 20 miles northwest of Jerusalem, demanding Jewish loyalty. Mattathias, an elderly Jewish priest, unwilling to forsake God's law, protested, "'Let every one who is zealous for the law and supports the covenant come out with me!' Then he and his sons fled to the hills and left all that they had in the town" (1 Maccabees 2:27-28).

Mattathias was compelled to live as a Jew or die as a Jew. His zeal sparked the flame of Jewish independence. Mattathias and his five sons were associated with a group called the Hasidim (Pious Ones); they spearheaded a Jewish revolt against the Seleucid Empire. Their bravery pushed back the tide of assimilation that was meant to have erased Judaism.

In the Hebrew month of Kislev, 164 BC, the Jewish people received a boost of confidence when the elderly priest's son, Judas Maccabeus, recaptured the Temple in Jerusalem, cleansing it and reinstituting sacrificial worship to God (1 Maccabees 4:36-53).

Religious freedom returned to the Jewish people, but the revolt continued for more than 20 years. By 142 BC, Simon, the last surviving son of Mattathias, made a deal with the Seleucid ruler Demetrius II that exempted Judea from taxes, which moved the Jewish people into an era of independence, a freedom they hadn't tasted since before the Babylonian exile in 586 BC.

HASMONEAN RULE (142-63 BC)

The Hasmonean name originates from a family member of Mattathias according to Josephus. For liberating the Jewish people, Simon's reputation among his people was legendary; they endowed upon him the roles of high priest and ruler in perpetuity, "until a trustworthy prophet should arise" (1 Maccabees 14:41). His descendants ruled over the people and the land for nearly 80 years.

The Hasmonean kingdom expanded under Simon's son, John Hyrcanus. He forced the Idumeans (Edomites) in the south to convert to Judaism and he destroyed the Samaritan temple on Mount Gerizim to show priority of worship in Jerusalem, exacerbating the ongoing conflicts between the Jewish and Samaritan people.

PLACES TO VISIT: QUMRAN

Qumran, a community in the wilderness on the northwest side of the Dead Sea, is home to the famous Dead Sea Scrolls, which were first discovered in 1947. Developed during the Hasmonean period around 134 BC, the Qumran community is believed to be the home of the Essenes. The Dead Sea Scrolls give a glimpse into the strict monastic lifestyle of the Qumran community.

Over a short period of time the religious zeal of Mattathias, which started the revolution, was exchanged for the accumulation of wealth and power, corrupting the Hasmonean dynasty. As a result, anticipation among the people for the Messiah intensified; their longing for the promised Son of David to correct the woes of the Jews increased. Meanwhile, Rome was swallowing up the Hellenistic world piece by piece.

The Hasmonean dynasty, full of family drama and tension, fought to give the Jewish people autonomy and independence, yet they eventually sold themselves back into Gentile control. Later, Roman general Pompey conquered Jerusalem in 63 BC.

ROMAN AUTHORITY AND HEROD THE GREAT (63–4 BC)

Rome installed Herod as King of Judea in 37 BC, but the Jewish people were not comfortable with his presence on the throne. Promoting Roman ideals, he constructed a theater, hippodrome, and stadium in Jerusalem. To win Jewish affection, he gave the Second Temple a major renovation that he will always be remembered for. To this day, the retaining wall of the Temple Mount stands as a sign of his architectural legacy.

Herod also memorialized himself through other magnificent building projects all throughout Israel, many of which still stand today. He built the largest artificial port in the first century BC and dedicated it to Caesar Augustus—he called it Caesarea. The port city was Herod's way to connect Rome with Israel through trade, which brought along with it: wealth, jobs, and prosperity. Pagan temples, theaters, and bath houses lined the streets; you would be hard-pressed to find a religious Jew perusing Caesarea in this period. Other building projects by Herod spotted around Israel include Masada, Herodium, Sebaste, and Jericho.

PLACES TO VISIT: **CAESAREA MARITIMA**

Caesarea Maritima, also known as Caesarea by the Sea, sits on the coast of the Mediterranean Sea 20 miles north of Tel Aviv.

Originally Strato's Tower, master architect Herod the Great, turned Caesarea into a Romanized port city with theaters, baths, and a hippodrome. In AD 6, Caesarea became the capital of the Roman province of Judea where governors like Pontus Pilate ruled.

Herod trusted no one toward the end of his life. He feared those who had ties to his throne, so he murdered members of his own family. He also ordered that all boys under the age of two in Bethlehem be murdered after he heard about the birth of Jesus (Matthew 2:16). Herod feared this newborn king of the Jews could usurp his authority (Matthew 2:2).

The era between the Testaments set the stage for the coming of Jesus Christ. God continued to guide the course of history to accomplish His purposes. Despite living under Gentile control, the promises and prophecies of God in the Old Testament drove sects of Jewish people to trust that God still had a future for Israel. Instead of assimilating into Greco-Roman culture, many Jewish people maintained their unique identity as God's chosen.

CHAPTER 5

ISRAEL IN THE TIME OF JESUS

*"Your father Abraham rejoiced at the thought
of seeing my day; he saw it and was glad."*

JOHN 8:56

t's hard to wrap your mind around what Jerusalem looked like during
the days of Jesus from simply walking around the Old City. Archaeologists can only go so far. They can't ask everyone to move out of town
for a few decades while they dig down to the strata of the first century
AD, perform their studies, then place everything back and invite everyone back in. You'll understand what I'm talking about when you walk
through the Old City yourself. Outside of the Temple Mount, you can
feel helpless attempting to identify the bits and pieces of Jerusalem that
are exposed from the first century Roman era.

The best way to cure that helpless feeling is to get a bird's-eye view
of Herod's Jerusalem at its zenith, just prior to its destruction in AD
70. There is a way to do it that doesn't require a time machine; you
only need to ask your tour guide to take you to the model of Jerusalem
housed at the Israel Museum.

The Jerusalem Model was constructed in 1964 under the guidance of Professor Michael Avi-Yonah, professor of archaeology at
Hebrew University, historian, and the secretary of the Department

of Antiquities during the British Mandate. The benefactor of the 10,000-square-foot replica was Hans Kroch—owner of the Holyland Hotel at the time. Kroch commissioned the building of the Jerusalem Model in memory of his son, who died fighting in Israel's War of Independence. The model was moved from the Holyland Hotel to the Israel Museum in 2006.

Professor Avi-Yonah used the writings of Josephus, the Mishnah, and other historical and archaeological resources to reconstruct the Jerusalem of the first century AD. The replica is a 1:50 scale model of the city from around the time of Jesus. Craftsmen used authentic materials such as Jerusalem stone, marble, ceramics, and gold leaf for the Temple. The model is updated when new research gives clearer insights into the Jerusalem from that time. It's a must-see on any visit to Israel.

"One who did not see Jerusalem in its glory, never saw a beautiful city."

Babylonian Sukkah 51b, The Talmud

THE POLITICS

The taste of independence still occupied the minds of Jewish people living in the time of Christ. The memory of Mattathias, the aged priest who stood up against the Greeks, was still strong. His shout still resonated with the average Jewish citizen living in Judea or Galilee.

> Even if all the nations that live under the rule of the king obey him and have chosen to obey his commandments, every one of them abandoning the religion of their ancestors, I and my sons and my brothers will continue to live by the covenant of our ancestors. Far be it from us to desert the law and the ordinances. We will not obey the king's words by turning aside from our religion to the right hand or to the left (1 Maccabees 2:19-22).

The quest for Jewish sovereignty, the longing for the Messiah, and the aspirations to rid the land of Gentile oppression were not quenched during Rome's rule over the Holy Land. Every year on the 25th day of Kislev (November/December) the Jewish community celebrated Hanukkah (John 10:22); the zealous spirit of Mattathias and his sons was not forgotten. If the Maccabees could take back the land and the Temple, then surely the Jews of the first century thought they could as well.

DID YOU KNOW?

Archaeologists from the Israel Antiquities Authority uncovered a road connecting the Temple to the Pool of Siloam. The section of road, 100 meters long, likely traversed by Jesus, was constructed after Herod the Great's rule. Arrowheads and ballistic stone balls have been found on the road, projectiles used during the First Jewish Revolt.

Jesus was but a toddler when Herod the Great passed on; the kingdom Herod ruled over was divided between his three sons who survived his psychosis. When you read the birth story of Jesus in Matthew chapter 2, you get an inside look into Herod's insecurity and lunacy. He issued an edict to have all children under the age of two killed in Bethlehem after hearing of Messiah's birth. Herod wanted no one near his throne, not even his own children.

Archelaus, Herod's oldest son, received the coveted regions of Judea, Samaria, and Idumea. Herod Antipas, his youngest, received Galilee and Perea, and Philip received areas of lower Syria and the northeast section of the Sea of Galilee.

Archelaus' reign ended as soon as it began. His policies and personal life turned his Jewish subjects against him. Caesar Augustus dethroned Archelaus, banished him, and installed a Roman prefect (governor) in AD 6. Roman prefects of Judea were headquartered out of Caesarea

Maritima; they were tasked to police the jurisdiction, act as judges, and ensure taxes were paid.

Rome permitted Judea some degree of religious and political independence; this can best be seen in Luke's passion of Christ. After Jesus was arrested, the Jewish leaders interrogated Him and found Him guilty according to their laws. He was brought to Pontius Pilate, the prefect of Judea at the time, who just so happened to be in Jerusalem managing security during the Passover festival.

The Jewish leaders wanted Jesus put to death, but they had limited authority under Roman rule to enact their own form of capital punishment. Upon hearing Jesus was a Galilean, Pilate unloaded Jesus' fate onto Herod Antipas, who had jurisdiction over the region of Galilee. Antipas was in Jerusalem for Passover as well. After seeing Jesus, he found no wrong in Him—so Antipas sent Jesus back to Pilate.

Jerusalem was a potential powder keg during Passover. Messianic fervor was high during the holiday and the city's population swelled with Jewish pilgrims from all over. Pilate was convinced Jesus was innocent, but eventually, he caved to the wishes of the Jewish leaders in order to prevent a riot. Rome honored the justice system, but there were times when keeping the peace was more valuable to Rome's rulers than preserving the justice of one individual.

THE JEWISH SECTS

There's an old Jewish saying that goes, "Put three rabbis in a room and they leave with four opinions." Israel, in the time of Jesus, was full of opinions on the issues surrounding Roman occupation, Israel's spiritual condition, and the corrupt nature of the Jewish leaders. These opinions led to what Josephus calls the four "philosophies" of the Jewish people.[1] We will look at four significant sects of Judaism that existed at this time.

Pharisees

It's during the Hasmonean reign of John Hyrcanus that the title, Pharisee, first made its appearance. However, it is widely held that

Pharisees originated from the Hasidim who fought during the Maccabean revolt.

The Pharisees were less than enthusiastic about the direction the Hasmoneans were leading the Jewish people. Their strict adherence to the law turned them off to the Greek influence present in the upper ranks of the Hasmonean leadership, which put them at odds with the leaders of their day.

It's possible the name *Pharisee* comes from the Hebrew word for "separate." The Pharisees were demarcated from the rest of the Jewish people in the way they upheld the entire law, kept Shabbat, and maintained ritual purity. Those who were unable to live up to the Pharisaic standards were deemed "sinners."

In addition to the biblical law, the Pharisees equally valued the oral law—a set of standards that was developed to apply biblical law to everyday life. The oral law became a point of contention between Jesus and the Pharisees; He challenged the undue burdens that were placed on Israel: "Jesus replied, 'And you experts in the law, woe to you, because you load people down with burdens they can hardly carry, and you yourselves will not lift one finger to help them'" (Luke 11:46).

It should be noted that not all the Pharisees rejected Jesus. Nicodemus was a Pharisee and Joseph of Arimathea likely was a Pharisee, and they became believers in the Lord Jesus (John 3:1; 7:50; 19:38-39).

Pharisaic oral tradition was the soil that would later produce Rabbinic Judaism after the destruction of the Temple in AD 70.

Sadducees

The Sadducees first appear during the Hasmonean period like their counterparts the Pharisees. There is limited knowledge about this specific Jewish sect; there is speculation the name is associated with the Zadok priestly line who ministered during David and Solomon's reign.

They were the ruling elite, the party of the wealthy aristocrats connected to the high priestly families. The Temple and all its revenue were under their care.

PLACES TO VISIT: **THE JERUSALEM ARCHAEOLOGICAL PARK—DAVIDSON CENTER**

The Jerusalem Archaeological Park takes you down to the original road where worshippers walked on the western side of the Temple Mount. Herodian stones pushed over by Roman soldiers during the First Jewish Revolt lay in piles untouched. On the southern end of the Temple Mount, the original steps that led worshippers through the Huldah Gates that lead to the Temple Mount can still be used, just as Jesus used them.

The Sadducees opposed the oral traditions of the Pharisees, yet still would have been considered very conservative in their faith. The Pentateuch (the five books of Moses) was their primary authority.

Unlike most of Judaism in that day, the Sadducees were extremely worldly in that they did not believe in resurrection, life after death, angels, demons, or even that God was a personal being. They were more politically inclined to ally themselves with the ruling powers that be, like the Romans. Because of their social status, the common Jewish person of Jesus' day resented the Sadducees. And the Sadducees resented Jesus because He threatened their position of power, wealth, and influence.

Essenes

The discovery of the Dead Sea Scrolls raised a new awareness for one of the four Jewish sects—the Essenes. The Essenes abandoned the religious and political environment in Jerusalem to send a message that they were less than pleased with how the Temple was being managed. They created a community in the wilderness to wait for the end times, when God would rebuild a new Temple and establish a righteous priesthood.

Most scholars agree the Essenes were the sect who copied the scrolls in the Qumran community, which dates the group to around the time of the Hasmonean dynasty. According to the Dead Sea Scrolls, they believed in the coming of two messiahs: one from the line of King David and one from the lineage of the high priest Aaron. Ritual and ethical purity were of the utmost importance to the Dead Sea community, to a level even higher than the Pharisees' standards.

Zealots

Zealots were the radical nationalists of Jesus' day. They believed in obtaining liberty at any expense. While the Essenes retreated to the wilderness to wait for God, and the Pharisees demanded devotion to the law, the Zealots were fully engaged in toppling the Roman occupation—violence was not off the table. The Sicarii, known for carrying small, curved daggers, *sica*, were the most extreme group among the Zealots; they were very hostile to Rome, assassinating their political opponents. The Zealots are most known for their stand against the Roman siege at Masada, where, in the end, the Jews there took their own lives rather than being taken alive by the Romans. We will look at this event in more detail later in this chapter.

PLACES TO VISIT: MASADA NATIONAL PARK

Declared a World Heritage Site by UNESCO, the beauty and grandeur of Herod the Great's fortress palace built atop an isolated plateau in the Judean desert can still be appreciated today. The absurdity of undertaking such a building project brings to life the fear he felt that, at any moment, the kingdom he ruled could turn on him. The fortress Herod constructed eventually protected the Zealots, who were retreating from the Romans a little more than 100 years later.

Josephus blamed the Jewish revolt and destruction of the Temple in AD 70 on the Zealots. After the First Jewish Revolt, he used his pen to paint his heritage in a positive light for the Romans. He tried to show the problem wasn't the whole of the Jewish people, but rather, a part who created the most trouble—namely, the Zealots.

JESUS' PURPOSE

The sects mentioned above each had political and religious viewpoints on Israel's nationalism, Rome, the messiah, and God's intervention. But at that time, these all boiled down to whether you were a Roman sympathizer or in rebellion against their rule. The Pharisees wanted to trap Jesus by pulling out His thoughts on Rome's occupation. The religious leaders questioned Jesus in the presence of pro-Roman Herodians: "Tell us then, what is your opinion? Is it right to pay the imperial tax to Caesar or not?" (Matthew 22:17).

The question is a loaded one. If Jesus agrees to the tax, He is seen as a Roman sympathizer. If He denies the tax, He could potentially instigate a revolt against Rome. Jesus asked to see a coin used to pay the tax, and they brought Him a denarius.

> [Jesus] asked them, "Whose image is this? And whose inscription?" "Caesar's," they replied. Then he said to them, "So give back to Caesar what is Caesar's, and to God what is God's" (Matthew 22:20-21).

Jesus revealed His sovereign view on the political and religious structures of His day in this one statement. "Give back to Caesar what is Caesar's, and to God what is God's," is Jesus' way of saying that Israel wasn't a victim of Rome's oppression. They suffered because Israel's religious leaders had neglected to shepherd the Jewish people on paths of righteousness. Sin was Israel's greatest enemy, not Rome.

Read through the Gospels, and you will find that Jesus never indicted Rome. Instead, He severely judged the Pharisees and religious teachers: "Woe to you, teachers of the law and Pharisees, you hypocrites! You shut the door of the kingdom of heaven in people's faces" (Matthew 23:13).

Jesus knew the Roman Empire was just another Gentile kingdom God was using to move His plan of redemption forward. Rome too would one day crumble under the pressure of the "rock" cut out, "but not by human hands" of Daniel chapter 2. That same "rock" would grow to become a mountain that would fill the whole earth (verse 35). The apostle Paul comments on Jesus' ministry:

> Being found in appearance as a man, he humbled himself by becoming obedient to death—even death on a cross! Therefore God exalted him to the highest place and gave him the name that is above every name, that at the name of Jesus every knee should bow, in heaven and on earth and under the earth, and every tongue acknowledge that Jesus Christ is Lord, to the glory of God the Father (Philippians 2:8-11).

The "rock" that will crush Gentile oppression, provide forgiveness, and bring reconciliation with God is Jesus Himself. One day, the eternal kingdom that Jesus will establish will overshadow any previous kingdoms, will reign over the whole earth, and will defeat sin.

THE FALL OF JERUSALEM

After the death, resurrection, and ascension of Jesus Christ, the Jewish people still found themselves mired under the heavy hand of Roman occupation. Several events that happened back-to-back instigated Jewish riots in Jerusalem and Caesarea. The rebellion spread throughout the land and the Jews prevented sacrifices offered on behalf of Caesar and of the Roman people.

The confidence of the Jewish rebels grew after they staved off Roman advancement on Jerusalem. Roman general Vespasian was sent by Emperor Nero to stamp out the fires of revolt. Vespasian, along with his son, Titus, and nearly one-quarter of the Roman legions, besieged the Holy Land in three phases. First, in AD 67, Vespasian successfully campaigned in the north around Galilee, then he moved down the coast. The general set his sights on Jerusalem by AD 68, but Nero's death put a halt to the military campaign. Vespasian was proclaimed emperor of Rome, placing Titus in charge of stamping out the revolt.

"Jerusalem, Jerusalem, you who kill the prophets and
stone those sent to you, how often I have longed to
gather your children together, as a hen gathers her
chicks under her wings, and you were not willing."

Matthew 23:37

This brings us to our fourth key life-changing date and event for the Jewish people from chapter 3. Titus completely surrounded Jerusalem and in August AD 70, on the 9th of Av on the Hebrew calendar, the Temple fell in accordance with Jesus' prophecy, "Truly I tell you, not one stone here will be left on another; every one will be thrown down" (Matthew 24:2).

After the fall of Jerusalem, the Zealots fled to Herod's fortresses in the south. Masada was the last stronghold of the Jewish rebellion; 8,000 Roman soldiers surrounded the plateau, but its steep sides made it impossible to breach the walls. Jews who were already captured by the Romans were forced to build a massive siege ramp that took several months to complete. When the legion finally breached the fortress's wall in AD 73 they found 960 Jewish men, women, and children dead; they chose suicide over succumbing to Roman slavery.

DID YOU KNOW?

Excavations at Masada in the 1960s unearthed a 2,000-year-old Judean date palm seed. In 2005, Israeli scientists germinated that millennia-old seed and a new sprout came alive. The Judean date palm tree from Masada was appropriately named Methuselah.

The fall of Masada concluded the First Jewish Revolt, but it would not be the last time the Jewish people stood up against Rome's oppression.

When Jesus approached Jerusalem at the beginning of His Passion Week, He wept over the city knowing the judgment that would soon befall it, and said, "If you, even you, had only known on this day what would bring you peace—but now it is hidden from your eyes" (Luke 19:42). Though a short time earlier the crowds were proclaiming, "Blessed is the king…" (verse 38), Jesus knew the people would abandon Him. He would go to the cross to give His life to bless all nations, and, for the time being, destructive conflict would continue in the land of Israel.

PLACES TO VISIT: **THE GARDEN TOMB**

Jerusalem is a busy, congested city full of spectacular sights and sounds, but when you enter through the gates of The Garden Tomb, a calm comes over your soul. The Garden Tomb is a possible location where the death, burial, and resurrection of Jesus occurred. This Jewish tomb is said to date to the First Temple Period and was discovered in the latter half of the nineteenth century, adjacent to a rockface that resembled a skull. British Christians purchased the property and established The Garden Tomb Association. I always enjoy making The Garden Tomb my very last stop on tours I am leading. It is a refreshing place and an opportune time for visitors to reflect on God's grace through sending His one and only Son for mankind.

CHAPTER 6

THE DIASPORA JEWS: SCATTERED TO ALL THE NATIONS

"Then the LORD will scatter you among all nations, from one end of the earth to the other. There you will worship other gods—gods of wood and stone, which neither you nor your ancestors have known. Among those nations you will find no repose, no resting place for the sole of your foot. There the LORD will give you an anxious mind, eyes weary with longing, and a despairing heart."

DEUTERONOMY 28:64-65

South Korea isn't the typical place you would expect to find a large menorah standing outside of a modest home. The symbol of Judaism shines brightly among nearly ten million Koreans in Seoul, inviting displaced Jews to enter. The Tudor-style home serves as the Chabad center of South Korea. Chabad is not a Jewish-South Korean barbeque fusion restaurant; it serves a different purpose—to reach God's chosen people who live in predominantly Gentile cultures.[1]

The Chabad rabbi honors weekly Sabbath services, celebrates annual Jewish festivals (like Passover and Hanukkah), and hosts lectures and events that have plenty of Kosher food on hand. There are nearly 3,500 Chabad houses located in 100 countries around the world.

Chabad emissaries are stationed in some of the most unlikely places, like Uganda, Morocco, Thailand, Azerbaijan, Brazil, Argentina, and even Iceland. It's hard to imagine Jewish people living in Thailand or Azerbaijan. But this just goes to show, Jewish people are scattered all over the world, and it's been like this since the days of the prophets Ezekiel and Daniel.

Jewish people who live outside of Israel have a title: they are called, Diaspora Jews. *Diaspora* is a Greek word that means "dispersion." When the modern state of Israel was founded in 1948, 99 percent of the Jewish people lived in the diaspora. Only seven decades later, roughly 49 percent of the world's 14.7 million Jews are citizens of Israel. Those statistics reveal that a little more than half of the global Jewish population still remain living in towns, cities, and countries spread out across the continents.

So how exactly did God's chosen people, who were given land as a nation, find themselves in places like Seoul?

"In Jewish history there are no coincidences."[2]

Elie Wiesel

DIASPORA

The diaspora did not come about through one historical event; rather, it was a series of events that date all the way back to the Assyrian (722 BC) and Babylonian (586 BC) captivities.[3]

Assyria and Babylon forcibly resettled Israelites and Judahites east of the land, planting them in Middle Eastern culture for nearly 2,500 years.

The destruction of the Temple in AD 70 and the failure of the Second Jewish Revolt (AD 132–135) scattered more Jews into areas across the Roman Empire.

DID YOU KNOW?

The Arch of Titus, located in Rome, was constructed in AD 81 in honor of Emperor Titus and his victory over the Jewish rebellion. The honorific arch became a symbol of the Jewish diaspora. It was decorated with panels illustrating Temple artifacts like the Menorah and the Table of Showbread being carried through the streets of Rome to celebrate Titus' victory. The Menorah depicted on the Arch of Titus would become the future emblem of the State of Israel.

When Roman emperor Hadrian came to power, Jews were denied access to their ancient capital. Jerusalem was renamed Aelia Capitolina and a temple to Jupiter was erected on the sacred ground of the Temple Mount. To make matters worse, Hadrian renamed Israel after their biblical enemies the Philistines; he called it Palaestina (Palestine), a title that still exists in twenty-first-century Middle Eastern religion and politics. After the end of the Second Jewish Revolt, Hadrian erased all traces of Jewish identity from the land.

Hadrian's aggression pushed Jews westward toward Europe; cities like Rome, Antioch, Ephesus, and Sardis saw an influx of new Jewish residents. Even the most distant lands, northern and eastern Europe, northern Africa, Persia, and far to the east along the trade routes that went into India and China became homes to the displaced Jewish people.[4]

Diaspora Jews would spend the next 2,000 years running from persecution and chasing religious freedom. The population of Jewish people in the Promised Land dwindled down to next to nothing. During the next centuries, after Christianity was established as the official religion of the Roman Empire in AD 380, sadly, some of the greatest antisemitic atrocities were committed.

As Jewish people settled in various areas of the world, they maintained their identity, but they also created a unique Jewish culture in the diaspora. Below is a brief history of Jewish migration as it relates to three major ethnic groups.

ASHKENAZI

What image comes to mind when you think of a Jewish person? Probably a man wearing a black suit with a long black coat or robe, under which white fringes, *tzitzit*, are hanging from their waist. An ornate black hat covering his head and a long beard with curls of hair, *payot*, that are flowing down each side of his face. That mental image is that of a Jewish man from the Ashkenazic heritage.

The Ashkenazic Jewish culture, cuisine, and music are probably the most recognizable in Western society. Challah bread, lox, bagels, gefilte fish, strudels, kugel, and matzo ball soup are just some of the classic Jewish dishes that originate from the Ashkenazic tradition. Klezmer is the choice sound of the Ashkenazi people, music that is played traditionally during weddings. The klezmer fiddle plays with your feelings, while the clarinet squeaks in time.

"Ashkenazi" was a title given to those who settled along the Rhine River in what is now Germany and northern France. Today, nearly 80 percent of modern Jewry have Ashkenazic ancestry.[5]

Israeli scientists have discovered that 40 percent of Ashkenazic Jews are descendants of just four women.[6] Another study revealed that all Ashkenazim are thirtieth cousins that originate from the same population from almost 800 years ago; their DNA can be traced back to the Middle East from Jews who migrated from Israel to Italy in the first and second centuries, which fits perfectly with the time frame of Jewish expulsion from Israel in the First and Second Jewish Revolts.[7]

The Ashkenazic culture is a melting pot of Judaism from Israel and Babylon, infused with influences of the western Mediterranean and European cultures, with a dash, or better yet, a cup of *chutzpah*. They settled in what is now Germany as early as AD 321, but it's not until the Middle Ages that they were identified as Ashkenazi.[8]

Speaking of chutzpah, the Ashkenazi have their own language, you've probably uttered a few words a time or two. Maybe you *schmoozed* with a friend at the party or grew tired of *schlepping* around the luggage on your vacation. Now you may be saying to yourself, "*Oy vey!* This isn't a Yiddish lesson so let's move on already."

Yiddish is a perfect example of diaspora life; it reveals the practice of cherry-picking aspects of the surrounding culture, while still remaining separate. Yiddish combines High German with Hebrew, Aramaic, and Slavic languages. In its heyday, millions of Jewish people from various backgrounds spoke this unique Jewish language. Later, it unified the immigrant Jewish community in America. Sadly, after the Holocaust and Stalin's persecution, the use of this European Jewish language drastically declined. Recently, there's been a resurgence of Yiddish, namely among the ultra-Orthodox Jewish communities living in Israel and New York.[9]

Antisemitism was rampant during the Middle Ages. Jews were falsely accused of blood libels—when they were blamed for murdering Christian children to use their blood during Passover and other rituals. They were also accused of spreading the Black Plague which led to riots and massacres.

Economic and religious persecution tormented the Ashkenazic communities. They were targeted with discriminatory taxes, prohibitions on land ownership, and restrictions on certain kinds of employment. Under certain European rulers, Jews could face expulsion if they did not convert to Christianity. Persecution forced the Ashkenazic population to migrate eastward, where they found religious freedom in what is now Poland, Lithuania, and Russia.

Eastern European Jewry, especially in Poland, grew to become the largest Jewish community in the diaspora. Small Jewish villages, called *shtetels*, canvassed the eastern European countryside and they embodied the Ashkenazic lifestyle. Poland remained the religious and cultural center of the Ashkenazim until the Holocaust in the mid-twentieth century. The Nazis completely decimated shtetels and Jewish life in Europe was nearly eradicated at the cost of two-thirds of the Ashkenazic Jews' lives. Afterward, Ashkenazi Jews played a prominent role in the establishment of the State of Israel, and continue to influence the country today.

DID YOU KNOW?

The poetic lines "Give me your tired, your poor, your huddled masses yearning to breathe free," etched on a plaque at the base of the Statue of Liberty, were authored by Emma Lazarus. She was a Jewish woman who protested the rise of antisemitism and advocated for the rights of Russian-Jewish immigrants. As a Zionist, Lazarus saw the need for a Jewish homeland in Palestine as she witnessed antisemitism in the diaspora.

SEPHARDI

In 2015, the government of Spain passed a law that grants citizenship to any Jewish person with Spanish heritage who can prove that their ancestors were forcibly expelled from the country more than 500 years earlier. You know the saying, "In 1492 Christopher Columbus sailed the ocean blue." Well, as Columbus embarked on his transatlantic voyage, King Ferdinand and Queen Isabella of Spain imposed upon their Jewish population a choice with three options: convert to Catholicism, leave the country, or be killed. Jewish people now living in Mexico, Venezuela, and Columbia took advantage of the 2015 law and applied for citizenship in order to right a 500-year-old wrong.[10]

Sephardic Jews are those who settled in the Iberian Peninsula, namely Spain and Portugal. In Hebrew, *Sepharad* is translated "Spain," probably referring to an unknown, far-off place. Obadiah, the Old Testament prophet, mentions exiled Israelites in Sepharad (Obadiah 20).

Iberia has a unique history in Europe; for a time, it was controlled by Christians, then by Muslims, and then by Christians again, which meant the religious freedom of Sephardic Jews rested in the control of those in power. Early on, in the Roman era, the Sephardic community had the freedom to worship and engage in commerce with Jews and non-Jews alike. However, Sephardic persecution appeared in the fourth century AD after the establishment of the Roman Catholic Church.

The Church isolated the Sephardic community through laws prohibiting Christians from marrying or even eating with their Jewish neighbors. The Church became enemy number one—so much so, the Jewish community assisted the Muslim armies when they invaded Spain in AD 711, for they were seen as liberators from Catholic oppression.

The Golden Age of Judaism emerged under Islamic rule, a concept that's hard to imagine in today's religious and political climate. Together, Muslims and the Sephardic community built one of Europe's most advanced civilizations.

Under Islamic law, Jews were called *dhimmis*; they were "People of the Book" and were protected. They were permitted to study and practice their faith as long as they paid a discriminatory tax called the *jizya*.

Sephardic Jewry became entwined with their Muslim neighbors; they prayed in Arabic and dressed in a similar Moorish style. Sephardim were active in the Muslim government and military despite living in separate communities. Jews received fame in non-Jewish circles as poets, scholars, and physicians. Talmudic and halachic (Jewish law) study saw major strides during the Golden Age.[11]

Moses Maimonides (Rambam) is one of Judaism's most famous rabbis and philosophers. He was a Sephardic Jew brought up in Cordoba toward the end of the Golden Age. Maimonides is famously known in Judaism for his "13 principles of faith," a summary of Judaism's required beliefs. No rabbi before him took the endless corpus of rabbinical law and biblical law and summarized it in easy-to-read principles.

For nearly 400 years, Jews lived in peace with their Muslim neighbors, but the Golden Age of Judaism melted away when less-tolerant Muslim rulers came to power.

Christians began recapturing land in Spain in the eleventh century AD and the incoming Catholic governments demanded religious uniformity. Jews were again forced to choose: to convert or to face death. The Catholics' fear of forced converts secretly practicing Judaism and impacting the behavior of other Jewish people who had converted was one of the factors that drove religious and political leaders to initiate the Spanish Inquisition. In 1492, all practicing Jews were expelled from Spain in order to prevent those converts from returning to Judaism.

Sephardim migrated into northern Africa to what is now Morocco, Algeria, Tunisia, and Libya to integrate with the Arabic-speaking Jewish communities that were already established in those places. The Sephardic Jews could not settle north of Spain, in France, or in Germany because the Ashkenazi community had already previously been forced out of those areas by the ruling governments there. Other Sephardim migrated across the Mediterranean into the Ottoman Empire.

Sephardim were the first Jews to settle in the Americas; however, over time, the Ashkenazi would come to outnumber their Spanish counterparts living in the Western Hemisphere.

MIZRAHI

For nearly ten years, I organized a young adult volunteer trip to Israel. As the years passed, the relationships I made with the Israelis who worked at Kaplan Medical Center, where we served, deepened. I became part of the family at that hospital. During one of my trips, an Israeli friend of mine invited me to his daughter's pre-wedding party—a traditional Yemeni henna party.

Now let me tell you, I have studied Jewish culture and customs for years; I've honored Sabbath in synagogues and celebrated Passover in homes, but nothing prepared me for a Yemeni pre-wedding henna celebration. The bride, the groom, and their parents dress in colorful, ornate costumes that represent the regions of Yemen the families are from. Henna dye is painted on the skin of the bride and her guests. It's believed the henna dye symbolizes fertility—the darker the dye, the better. If you're wondering, yes, I was marked with henna.

Yemeni food was also a new experience for me. It was full of aromatic Middle Eastern spices and flavors. It was not the matzo ball soup I was used to eating. I had grown so accustomed to ministering in the Ashkenazi communities that this Yemeni party was a Jewish culture shock. The bride and groom, along with their family and friends, danced to exciting Middle Eastern music till late into the night.

The traditions of the Yemeni Jews make up only one part of the diverse culture within the vast Mizrahi community that is spread across the Middle East. In Hebrew, *Mizrahi* refers to "eastern" or "oriental." Jews migrated and established communities in what is now Iraq (Babylonia), Iran (Persia), Yemen, Egypt, northern Africa, and even as far as India and China. They belong to the group called Mizrahi.

DID YOU KNOW?

Beta Israel (House of Israel) was an isolated Jewish community in Ethiopia who claimed their Jewish heritage through Menilek I, the son of the Queen of Sheba and King Solomon. Waves of Ethiopians mass-migrated to the Holy Land with the help of the Israeli government. As a result, Israel is home to the largest Beta Israel community in the world, with more than 160,000 Ethiopian-Jewish citizens.

After the destruction of the Second Temple and Hadrian's expulsion, the center of Mizrahi Judaism transitioned to Mesopotamia and remained there for centuries. When the Muslim conquests began in the seventh century AD, Islam became the dominant religion in the region. Over time, the Jews' social position changed and, like the Sephardic Jews, Mizrahi were required to pay a tax for being non-Muslim and were treated as second-class citizens. Ancient synagogues scattered throughout countries like Iraq, Libya, Afghanistan, and Egypt still stand as testimonies to the Mizrahi Jews who were once embedded in Middle Eastern culture.

Today, the Jewish presence in the Middle East is scant after nearly 850,000 Jews were forced to migrate out of Arab countries between 1948 and the late 1970s. These predominantly Muslim countries made the Mizrahi communities abandon the homes that their families had lived in for centuries and the governments confiscated their land and any wealth that they had.[12]

Why did Muslim nations do this to the Jewish communities within their borders?

The United Nations had granted the Jewish people a homeland. Silence shrouds this twentieth-century human rights atrocity; very few talk about the 850,000 displaced Jewish refugees because Israel absorbed those refugees—making them citizens.

PLACES TO VISIT:
ANU—MUSEUM OF THE JEWISH PEOPLE

ANU, on the campus of Tel Aviv University is dedicated to describing what Jewish life was like in the diaspora outside of the land of Israel. Originally called Beit Hatfutsot, *anu*, Hebrew for "we," is one of the largest museums of its kind, immersing the visitor in Jewish history from all around the world.

JEWISH COMMUNITIES
IN THE LAND OF ISRAEL

As Jewish people were scattered among the nations, the presence of a small remnant remained in Israel to preserve that divine connection to the Promised Land. Tiberias, Safed, and Jerusalem became hubs of Jewish life, and for that reason, today they have been considered some of Israel's most holy cities.

Tiberias is the largest city on the Sea of Galilee. After the Second Jewish Revolt, the Jewish religious and political leaders who remained moved north to Tiberias. The Masoretes were a group of scribal scholars who created a system of pronunciation for the Hebrew Bible by adding vowel markers. Prior to the discovery of the Dead Sea Scrolls in 1947, the oldest complete Hebrew Bible was the Masoretic Aleppo Codex, which was copied in Tiberias around the tenth century AD and approved by Maimonides.

Almost directly north of Tiberias, in Upper Galilee, is the elevated city of Safed. Jewish history describes Safed as one of Israel's five designated cities that lit signal fires announcing the new moon during the Second Temple Period. The elevated city didn't gain religious notoriety until it was settled by Jews who had fled from Spain after the expulsion in 1492. Sephardim didn't have much to their name in possessions when they arrived in Safed, but they did import a form of mystical Judaism called Kabbalah. Safed produced some of the most influential kabbalistic teachers like Rabbi Isaac Ben Solomon Luria. Safed, in the sixteenth century AD and onward, has remained home to a vibrant Jewish community.

Jews were permitted to return to Jerusalem by the end of the second century AD. During the Middle Ages, the Jewish population of the city saw a drastic decline; however, the numbers increased again during the reign of the Ottoman Empire starting in 1517. Jewish immigration to the Holy Land continued to grow by the mid-nineteenth century AD. Ashkenazim also immigrated from eastern Europe making Jerusalem their home. Eventually, the Jewish population outnumbered the Muslim and Christian populations in the Holy City.

As the Jewish people were scattered, they adapted to the cultures around them and yet they maintained their unique identity. Despite the differences that separated Ashkenazim, Sephardim, and Mizrahi over the centuries, one attribute that linked them together was the hope of returning to their homeland. Jewry stretching from Spain all the way to China all prayed the same prayer at the conclusion of Passover: "Next year in Jerusalem!"

CHAPTER 7

THE MODERN
FOUNDERS OF ISRAEL

"We have preserved the Book, and the Book has preserved us."[1]

DAVID BEN-GURION

A monument of courage, hope, conviction, and destiny is planted in a field just outside of Tel Aviv, abutting a highway that takes you up to Jerusalem. Motorists speed past this modern sacred destination often without noticing it—blink and you wouldn't even know it's there. The monument marks the spot where a transitional moment in time occurred, when a humble Jewish journalist from Vienna became known as the face of modern Zionism by speaking with one of the world's most powerful leaders.

The statue in Mikveh, Israel, marks the spot where Theodor Herzl—the George Washington of the Jewish people—met with German emperor (kaiser) Wilhelm II on October 28, 1898, urging Wilhelm to use his position of power to convince the Turkish sultan to grant the Jewish people a state in Palestine. The encounter marks Herzl's first and final visit to Israel.

The larger-than-life sculpture designed by Israeli Motti Mizrachi has Herzl standing before Wilhelm, who is mounted on a horse, just as the event plays out in photographs taken from that day in 1898. Viewing the statue from either side, there doesn't appear to be any special features, but if you stand in Herzl's place, gazing at the kaiser and his horse, they are split in two with a perfect view of Israel in between the halves. Quotes from the emperor and Herzl are carved on the inside of the two halves. On one side is Herzl's famous statement, "If you wish for it, it is not a dream." On the other side, the emperor is quoted: "There is a future to this country." Herzl knew there was no future Jewish state without the support of world leaders; he had to go through them to get to his prize.

Don't be deceived by the image of Herzl standing before Wilhelm alone; he isn't the only modern founder of Israel. The sculpture of Herzl represents countless humble men and women who didn't come from a lineage of nobility, but they did share the same courage, hope, and conviction that Herzl had to see Israel reborn.

Motti Mizrachi sculpture of Herzl and Kaiser Wilhelm II meeting in Mikveh, Israel.

ELIEZER BEN-YEHUDA
AND THE RESURRECTION OF
THE HEBREW LANGUAGE

The modern Hebrew language is a miracle story in the rebirth of Israel. The tongue once spoken by prophets and kings sat dormant for nearly 1,700 years during the diaspora, where Hebrew was reserved for prayer at home and in the synagogue. Today, Hebrew is the official language of the Israeli people: spoken in government, commerce, courts, and schools thanks to the determination of one man's desire to unify the Jewish people returning to the Promised Land.

In 1881, Lithuanian-born Eliezer Ben-Yehuda immigrated to Jerusalem with his family. Jewish nationalism flowed through his veins; he was inspired by Bulgaria's struggle for independence from the Ottoman Empire. If the Bulgarians could carve out their own independence from the Turks, surely the Jewish people could too. Ben-Yehuda credits the novel *Daniel Deronda* for following the impulse to leave Lithuania for Jerusalem. The novel, written by British author George Eliot (pen name of Mary Ann Evans)—who was sensitive to Jewish nationalism—centers on Daniel, who discovers his Jewish roots and emigrates to the Holy Land to help establish a Jewish homeland.[2]

Ben-Yehuda believed a Jewish homeland required a single language to unify the diaspora into a nation of one. He could have made this endeavor easier by choosing English, German, French, or Russian, but Hebrew was his choice to bind the Jewish people together. The task at hand almost seemed impossible, but for Ben-Yehuda, Hebrew was the language of a shared Jewish heritage.

While still aboard the ship headed to the Holy Land, Ben-Yehuda told his wife they would speak only in Hebrew. She knew no Hebrew. This Hebrew experiment would start in their home, and Eliezer's son, Itamar, was the test subject. If he could speak fluent Hebrew, then there would be no linguistic argument against reviving Hebrew.

Ben-Yehuda started with a base of 8,000 Hebrew words from the Bible, the Talmud, and other ancient writings. He would spend the rest of his life compiling a Hebrew dictionary, the *Complete Dictionary of Ancient and Modern Hebrew*, which was not fully finished until after his death.

Hebrew purity was of the utmost importance. Itamar became the first Jew in centuries to hear only Hebrew spoken between both parents. The boy was isolated from friends who didn't speak Hebrew. Anytime a guest came who spoke a different language, Itamar was asked to leave the room. He would grow to become the first native speaker of Hebrew in the modern era.

Ironically, the Orthodox shunned Ben-Yehuda for attempting to turn the holy language into common speech. That did not deter the Hebrew lexicographer. He was invited to teach Hebrew in Jewish schools in 1882, influencing other teachers to do the same. By 1898, the first Hebrew kindergarten opened in Rishon LeZion.[3]

Ben-Yehuda also published his personal newspaper, *Ha-Zvi*, in 1884. The Hebrew publication used modern journalism to write about nonreligious issues. The Ottoman Empire temporarily banned the newspaper during World War I because it encouraged Jewish nationalism.

Ben-Yehuda died in 1922, but his legacy lives on in the language of the Israeli people. By 1948, when Israel declared independence, nearly 81 percent of Jewish people that had been born there spoke Hebrew as their only language in daily life.

Every year, Israelis celebrate Hebrew Language Day on Eliezer Ben-Yehuda's birthday.

Ben-Yehuda didn't start a political movement in eastern Europe. He didn't try to convince world leaders to approve a future Jewish state. Instead, he laid a foundation of unity that the future founders could build upon, and he and his wife started right in their own home.

PLACES TO VISIT: **BEN YEHUDA STREET**

You can't leave Jerusalem without a visit to Ben Yehuda Street. Along with the Via Dolorosa, Ben Yehuda Street is one of the most popular walks in the city of Jerusalem. It's named after the Hebrew language hero Eliezer Ben-Yehuda, but unlike the Via Dolorosa, nothing of significance happened there. The bustling street is simply a great place to get ice cream, shop for souvenirs, hang out with friends, and hear some Israeli street performers.

THEODOR HERZL— THE FATHER OF MODERN ZIONISM

Mount Herzl is Israel's national cemetery, a special place for Israelis to pay their respects to the past founders, leaders, and military men and women who sacrificed their lives defending their state. Israel's most influential leaders lay in repose here on the west side of Jerusalem—luminaries like Levi Eshkol, Golda Meir, Yitzhak Rabin, Yitzhak Shamir, Shimon Peres, and the father of modern Zionism himself, Theodor Herzl.

DID YOU KNOW?

Golda Meir is one of Israel's founding mothers and a signatory on Israel's Declaration of Independence. Before statehood, Meir raised $50 million to help Israel during the War of Independence. David Ben-Gurion said of Golda, "Someday when history will be written, it will be said that there was a Jewish woman who got the money which made the state possible."[4] She served as Israel's fourth prime minister during the Yom Kippur War.

Herzl is honored in the national memorial that bears his name for his part in founding, organizing, and advancing Zionism. For nearly two millennia, Jewish religious leaders prayed to one day return to the land, and Herzl put those prayers into action.

Mount Herzl isn't the only reminder of modern Israel's political forerunner. Herzliya, a prosperous start-up city on the Mediterranean coast, is named after Herzl. Also, Israeli politicians are reminded of him as they are working in the Knesset, where a portrait of Herzl looks down upon those who are present there.

So, who was this man? What could he have possibly done to become an image of Israeli national pride, to have a memorial named in his honor, to have streets that bear his name, to have a city named after him, and to have a steady view of Israel's ever-changing political landscape?

Theodor Herzl was born in May of 1860 to German-speaking Jewish parents in what is now Budapest, Hungary. A synagogue was a stone's throw away from his childhood home, but he never considered himself a religious man. The Herzl family moved to Vienna, where he earned a law degree from the University of Vienna, but while he was there, he honed his passion for writing, which led to his career as a journalist for the *Neue Freie Presse*.

In his early life, Herzl gave little thought to his Jewish ancestry. He was educated in the spirit of the German-Jewish Enlightenment of the time; he was taught to appreciate secular culture. He doffed his Jewish identity to look, sound, dress, and think like his surroundings. He believed assimilation would ease the pain of antisemitism.

In 1894, French captain Alfred Dreyfus was accused of treason; he was found guilty of giving the German government French military information. Evidence emerged proving Dreyfus, a Jewish man, was innocent, but leaders in the French military acquitted the real criminal and Dreyfus remained in jail.[5]

Herzl was on assignment as a correspondent covering the Dreyfus affair. France was divided; protestors at antisemitic riots proclaimed that Jewish people had no allegiance to their home country.

Herzl's philosophy of Jewish assimilation did an about-face in Paris. The Jewish journalist from Vienna struggled to reconcile his assimilation philosophy with what he witnessed. Dreyfus was the definition of Jewish assimilation: he donned the regalia of the French army, he embraced French culture, he defended the French way of life, and yet he was still targeted for being Jewish. When Herzl heard the crowds scream, "Death to the Jews," it was enough to unravel his theory that Jews were to blame for their own persecution. According to Herzl, that's when he knew Jewish people needed to leave Europe.

In 1896, Herzl published a pamphlet *Der Judenstaat*, "The Jewish State." In it he shared his vision for creating an independent Jewish state in the twentieth century. He argued the only way to circumvent antisemitism was with the creation of an independent Jewish state. "The Jewish State" is considered one of the crucial texts of early Zionism.

In 1897, Herzl swore in the First Zionist Congress in Basel, Switzerland; 200 were in attendance from 17 countries. *Hatikvah*, "The Hope," was adopted as their anthem, and

Theodor Herzl leaning over the balcony of the Hotel Les Trois Rois in Basel, Switzerland.

the song would eventually become Israel's national anthem. This was a momentous occasion; the dreams and aspirations of the Jewish people were transforming into a political movement.

Herzl spread his message of Zionism all over Europe. He reached the highest levels of power, petitioning German kaiser Wilhelm II and Turkish sultan Abdul Hamid II to permit the opening of land for a Jewish state. Both leaders denied his requests, but nonetheless, Herzl made it abundantly clear Zionism was here to stay.

In his diary, Herzl wrote, "At Basel, I founded the Jewish State. If I said this out loud today, I would be answered by universal laughter. If not in 5 years, certainly in 50, everyone will know it."[6] Herzl's personal prophecy was later realized; nearly 50 years after writing that statement, Israel would declare itself an independent Jewish state.

Herzl concluded *Der Judenstaat* by saying:

> Therefore I believe that a wondrous generation of Jews will spring into existence. The Maccabeans will rise again. Let

me repeat once more my opening words: The Jews who wish for a State will have it. We shall live at last as free men on our own soil, and die peacefully in our own homes. The world will be freed by our liberty, enriched by our wealth, magnified by our greatness. And whatever we attempt there to accomplish for our own welfare, will react powerfully and beneficially for the good of humanity.[7]

In 1904, Theodor Herzl died near Vienna of pneumonia coupled with a heart that was weakened by only a few years of stressful work advocating for a Jewish state; he was only 44 years old. In 1949, Theodor Herzl's remains were exhumed from Vienna and buried atop Mount Herzl. Theodor Herzl never saw the creation of the State of Israel, but his legacy of Zionism is woven into the fabric of Israel's modern history.

DAVID BEN-GURION—
ISRAEL'S FIRST PRIME MINISTER

David Gruen, a Russian Jew from Plonsk, was devastated when he heard of Theodor Herzl's death. The Gruen family were committed Zionists who idolized Herzl's vision of a future Jewish state. David later said of Herzl, "Only once in thousands of years is such an incredible man born,"[8] yet little did the young Zionist know that he would be the one to lead the Israelis across the Jordan River into the Promised Land, so to speak. Forty-four years after the passing of Herzl, David Gruen (Ben-Gurion) had the honor of proclaiming Israeli independence as Israel's first prime minister, recognizing Herzl's dream.

Gruen changed his last name to Ben-Gurion after he immigrated to Ottoman Palestine in 1906. Originally, Ben-Gurion supported the Ottoman Empire during World War I; he was adamant the Turks would grant Jewish independence. After the Allied forces defeated the Ottomans and took control of the empire, Ben-Gurion's alliances shifted to the West. In 1917, British foreign minister Lord Arthur Balfour declared the United Kingdom's intentions to aid the Jewish vision of establishing a homeland in Palestine.

DID YOU KNOW?

David Ben-Gurion met his wife Paula during a stint in the United States. Paula was an anarchist who ironically had no interest in state-building, Zionism, or Israel. She saw no need for a Jewish state and, according to Ben-Gurion, considered America better. However, she followed her husband from the United States to Tel Aviv and then, decades later, to Israel's desert. Ben-Gurion would say of his wife that she was a remarkable woman.

Ben-Gurion was a natural politician and military strategist who rose to prominence in the *Yishuv*, the prestate Jewish community of Palestine. He organized what was the most influential political party at the time, which would later evolve into Israel's Labor Party. He formed the first trade union that managed the well-being of Jewish workers, called *Histadrut*. As secretary-general of the union, representing nearly 75 percent of the Yishuv workforce in 1927, his name recognition soared.[9]

He was appointed the head of the People's Administration in

Israel's first prime minister, David Ben-Gurion.

April 1948, and he was also put in charge of security matters for the Yishuv. Less than one month later, on May 14, 1948, David Ben-Gurion announced Israeli independence. He was installed as the first prime minister, leading the brand new nation through their war of survival.

Ben-Gurion served as prime minister twice, first from 1948–1953, and then again between 1955–1963. Only recently has former prime minister Benjamin Netanyahu unseated Ben-Gurion as the longest-serving leader of Israel. The first prime minister is remembered for unifying the country under the banner of Israeli patriotism, establishing the Israel Defense Forces (IDF), and brokering Holocaust reparations with West Germany, which aided Israel financially through its infancy years.

Israel's cardinal leader is a national treasure and international travelers pay homage to him when they touch down at Ben Gurion International Airport. *Time* magazine considered Ben-Gurion one of the most influential people of the twentieth century, but he's also fondly remembered for his special exercise routine on the beaches of Tel Aviv, where he would perform headstands in his bathing suit.

PLACES TO VISIT: **BEN-GURION HOUSE**

While you're in Tel Aviv, be sure to stop by and visit Ben-Gurion's house. Here's the address: 17 Ben Gurion Boulevard. He's keen for you to pop in, in fact, the original prime minister entrusted his home to the State of Israel for that very reason. Ben-Gurion lived and worked in his Tel Aviv home until his death in 1973. It was open to the public by 1974.

CHAIM WEIZMANN— ISRAEL'S FIRST PRESIDENT

In the early stages of World War I, a shortage of acetone plagued Great Britain; the British had been accustomed to importing the solvent from the countries that became their enemies during the war, Germany and Austria–Hungary. Acetone was used to create cordite, the propellant used to fire artillery shells. Chaim Weizmann, a Russian-born chemist and ardent Zionist, had immigrated to Great Britain to do research at the University of Manchester, where he later developed a synthetic version of acetone.[10] When Winston Churchill became Minister of Munitions, he requested Weizmann manufacture 30,000 tons of his synthetic acetone, an act that saved Great Britain and kept them fighting in World War I.

Weizmann's scientific discovery made him famous, and it opened doors to create relationships with some of Britain's most influential leaders—one of them being Lord Arthur Balfour. Weizmann was the leading voice for the Zionist movement in Britain. He worked alongside Lord Balfour aiding in the historic statement that would become the Balfour Declaration (1917). The declaration became the first official document issued by the British government promising a Jewish national homeland in Palestine. The World Zionist Organization elected Weizmann as their president in 1920 and, in 1929, he led the newly formed Jewish Agency.

DID YOU KNOW?

Albert Einstein was offered the position of president of Israel in 1952, but he turned it down.

Weizmann was a pioneer in establishing a prestate university. He believed the sciences would propel a future Jewish state forward, providing peace and prosperity. He founded the Daniel Sieff Research Institute in Rehovot in 1934, and it was later renamed the Weizmann Institute of Science.[11] It ranks globally as one of the best research institutes in the world. Weizmann also helped establish the Hebrew University; he sat on the original board of the university with Albert Einstein and Sigmund Freud. He also had his hands in the creation of the Technion, one of Israel's prominent universities.

Weizmann was installed as Israel's first president in 1949, less a political title and more a ceremonial one—one he wished was more official. He served his country in that role until his death in 1952.

The truth is, there are also numerous more modern founders of the State of Israel who risked their lives and embarked on a journey to fulfill a dream to see an independent Jewish state become a reality. Some of the leaders are remembered fondly in the annals of Israeli history. They are the George Washingtons, the Ben Franklins, and the John Adamses in the story of Israel. However, there are also those Jewish people who remain known, but nameless. Pioneers who also looked for a better life in the Holy Land. They tilled the malaria-infested swamps into productive farmland. They also grew the Jewish communities where they settled.

Israel doesn't exist because of just one person. Israel lives today because of the aspirations of many Jewish people who gave everything to see their ancient homeland become their modern state.

CHAPTER 8

THE HOLOCAUST

"To forget the dead would be akin
to killing them a second time."[1]

ELIE WIESEL

Sobering is the only way to describe *Yad Vashem*, Israel's Holocaust
memorial. The memorial is purposefully situated adjacent to Israel's national cemetery on Mount Herzl, located on the west side of
Jerusalem. The site has no connection to a biblical event; nevertheless,
it is still hallowed ground in the Holy Land. Anyone who enters Yad
Vashem should be ready for introspection as they honor those six million innocent Jewish lives taken without cause. You will leave Israel's
Holocaust memorial with more questions than answers.

In 2005, Yad Vashem opened a modern museum to educate about
the perils of the Holocaust. The elongated triangular structure cuts into
the western slope of Mount Herzl; it's 600 feet long and 54 feet high.
The walls are constructed of industrial concrete, settling you into the
reality that you're no longer at home. The peak of the triangle-shaped
museum is a long skylight. When you're surrounded by concrete, the
design gives you the feeling that the only way out is from the sliver of
light high above your head.

Walking from one end of the corridor to the other should be an easy
task, but Canadian-American-Israeli architect Moshe Safdie designed
the museum to be anything but easy. Obstacles, similar to the ones

Jewish people encountered on a daily basis during the Holocaust, were strategically placed in the middle of the museum corridor, forcing you through ten exhibit rooms that detail Adolf Hitler's plans to exterminate the Jews.

The first visual you see entering the museum is an eerie black-and-white film depicting vibrant Jewish life in pre-Nazi Europe. The footage, from the early 1930s, features hundreds of little children singing *Hatikvah*, "The Hope," in what was then Czechoslovakia. The song would come to be Israel's national anthem.

The sights and sounds of the pre-Holocaust film footage are chilling. The children innocently singing about the Jewish hope to one day return to the land of Israel would fall victim to Hitler's genocidal scheme. On this side of history, you're cognizant of the destiny that befell these little ones, and yet, the only way forward for you from there is to stare down the long narrow hall that represents the darkest moment of our modern era and begin your journey.

DID YOU KNOW?

Yom Hashoah—Holocaust Remembrance Day—is a national memorial added to the Hebrew calendar after Israeli statehood. In the morning, a siren blast is heard throughout the land, and Israelis stop for two minutes wherever they are to remember the six million Jewish people who lost their lives during the Holocaust.

HOW DID IT GET SO BAD?

Intuitively, you would probably expect to see Adolf Hitler's upbringing and rise to power in one of the first exhibit rooms of Yad Vashem; he was the one who spearheaded the "Final Solution," systematically exterminating six million Jewish people. However the museum was not designed that way. Holocaust education doesn't begin or end with Adolf Hitler because he was not the one who invented European antisemitism. He utilized and ignited the intolerance and antisemitism that had already existed in European culture for hundreds of years.

The pictures you see in the first exhibit hall are faces of church fathers and theologians whose sermons and teachings promoted hatred toward the Jews.

The *Epistle to Barnabas*, written in the second century AD, stressed that the promises made to Israel in the Old Testament were handed over to the church through Christ, unhitching Israel from their unique covenantal relationship with God. Essentially, the church supersedes and replaces Old Testament Israel, ultimately conveying that Jewish people are inferior or subservient to the church.

Justin Martyr (AD 100–165) wrote that the church is the "true Israelitic race,"[2] dehumanizing the Jewish race. *Adversus Judaeos*, "Against the Jews," was a series of sermons preached by John Chrysostom (AD 349–407), who was critical of Christians who honored the Jewish festivals. Even the most notable figurehead of the Protestant Reformation, Martin Luther, wrote some of the most vitriolic antisemitic rants on the Jewish people toward the end of his life. In his *On The Jews and Their Lies*, he wrote:

> I had made up my mind to write no more either about the Jews or against them. But since I learned that these miserable and accursed people do not cease to lure to themselves even us, that is, the Christians, I have published this little book, so that I might be found among those who opposed such poisonous activities of the Jews who warned the Christians to be on their guard against them. I would not have believed that a Christian could be duped by the Jews into taking their exile and wretchedness upon himself. However, the devil is the god of the world, and wherever God's word is absent he has an easy task, not only with the weak but also with the strong. May God help us. Amen.[3]

Hans Schemm, the head of the Nazi Teachers' League, was known for drawing comparisons between Luther and Hitler. At the 450th anniversary of Luther's birth, Schemm publicly stated:

The older and more experienced [Luther] became, the less
he could understand one particular type of person: this was
the Jew. His engagement against the decomposing Jewish
spirit is clearly evident not only from his writing against
the Jews; his life too was idealistically, philosophically antisemitic. Now we Germans of today have a duty to recognize and acknowledge this.[4]

Dietrich Eckart, a personal friend and influence on Hitler, wrote in
a poem, "The New Testament broke away from the Old/ as you once
released yourself from the world/ And as you are freed from your past
delusions/ so did Jesus Christ reject his Jewishness."[5] It should be noted
that Hitler dedicated the first volume of his work *Mein Kampf* to Eckart and considered him a fatherly friend.

In *Mein Kampf,* Hitler wrote, "I believe that I am acting in accordance with the will of the Almighty Creator: by defending myself
against the Jew, I am fighting for the work of the Lord."[6]

Again, Hitler didn't invent antisemitism. He simply tapped into
the hostility and prejudice against the Jewish people that was already
present in the culture both religiously and socially. Remember, just
before the end of the nineteenth century—preceding the Holocaust—
Theodor Herzl saw Europe as a tinderbox of anti-Jewish activity. He
believed he and his kinsman needed to get out before it was too late.

NAZI PROPAGANDA—MOVING FROM
RELIGIOUS TO RACIAL PERSECUTION

The Holocaust didn't start with mass murder; it started with words
and lies. *Der Giftpilz,* "The Poisonous Mushroom," a German children's book, was published in 1938 to indoctrinate kids to treat Jewish
people as subhuman; they were seen as criminals, cheats, communists,
and Christ-killers. The moral of the propaganda likened Jewish people
to poisonous mushrooms, just as hard as it is to determine a poisonous
mushroom from an edible one, it is difficult to recognize that a Jewish
person is a swindler or a criminal.

An illustrated sulking mushroom sat front and center on the cover of *Der Giftpilz*. The face of a depressed man protrudes from the mushroom stalk; his nose is bulbous, he has a beard, and on his belly is a Star of David. All of these images were typical markers of Hitler's antisemitic propaganda machine.

In the late nineteenth century, antisemitism took on a new form with the rise of social Darwinism, a theory where cultural survival and advancement is based on competition against one another. Antisemitism was no longer about the Jewish religion, but about genetics. Hitler pitted what he considered to be the perfect Aryan race against the dodgy Jewish race who could never be trusted; their flaws were inherent to their genetic design.

Nazi propaganda marked Jewish people with abnormally large, crooked noses, a genetic marker to distinguish the Jew from everyone else. Even though it's been scientifically proven that Jewish noses are no different than their Gentile counterparts, sadly, that Nazi-era antisemitic trope lingers even to this very day.

In 1933, Hitler tapped Joseph Goebbels to head Germany's Ministry of Propaganda and Public Enlightenment. The country's news and editorial content that was broadcast over all different types of media fell under Goebbels's control. In films, Jewish people were depicted as villains guided by no moral compass and the films lauded all of Hitler's accomplishments.

DID YOU KNOW?

Corrie ten Boom has a tree planted along the Avenue of the Righteous Among the Nations at Yad Vashem. Corrie and her Christian family risked their lives hiding Jewish people during the Holocaust. Thousands of trees are planted in honor of the non-Jews who defended, rescued, and supported the Jewish people during their darkest time.

The walls of Yad Vashem are covered with Nazi propaganda to stand as a testament to the dangers of this form of psychological manipulation. The average German was conned into believing that Jewish people were parasitic; Jews would infest their host countries and scheme to provoke war among the nations with the goal of financially enriching themselves.

The Jewish people were Hitler's scapegoat to explain the struggles Germans faced in the aftermath of World War I. Every economic, social, and cultural problem facing the average German could be blamed on the Jew. Hitler and his leadership deceived millions into justifying persecution and even genocide.

ISOLATION AND SEGREGATION
OF THE JEWISH PEOPLE

Hitler used his manufactured fear to justify the isolation and segregation of Jews from German life. In April 1933, the Nazis instituted the boycott of Jewish businesses. Later in the same month, the German government introduced a law barring Jews or any opponent of the Nazi party from serving in positions of government. This included roles in civic government, public safety, legislation, law, and education.

Especially notable was the effect on German academia. Albert Einstein was one of those academics. He was both Jewish and a vocal critic of Hitler and the Nazi party. Einstein left Germany for a two-month stint as visiting professor at the California Institute of Technology in Pasadena at the end of 1932. In the following month, Adolf Hitler took power as Germany's chancellor, leaving the theoretical physicist to question his return to Berlin.

At the time, Germany was considered the center of liberal education. But after the shift of government control to the Nazi party, numerous Jewish academics were exiled, forced to flee to the United Kingdom or the United States or elsewhere. A 2016 study shows, the 15 percent of physicists who were banned from German universities accounted for 64 percent of all German physics citations found in scientific publications.[7]

At a public book burning in Berlin, in May 1933, propaganda minister Joseph Goebbels told nearly 40,000 Germans, "Jewish intellectualism is dead," and "The German soul can again express itself."[8]

The psychological distinctions created through the spread of propaganda rapidly spiraled downward into the application of physical segregation in German society. Einstein was able to take a position at Princeton University and he later became a citizen of the United States; however, the Jewish people who remained in Germany and other parts of Europe weren't as fortunate. In the span of just a few years, Jewish academics, lawmakers, public servants, educators, court members, and civic leaders who were ripped from their professional positions would soon be stripped of all their human dignity.

JEWISH GHETTOS

On January 23, 2020, the Warsaw Ghetto Square at Yad Vashem was center stage for the largest diplomatic event in the history of the State of Israel. Presidents, prime ministers, royalty, and politicians from North America, Europe, and Australia attended the Fifth World Holocaust Forum, entitled "Remembering the Holocaust, Fighting Antisemitism."[9]

Two bronze monuments that line the square served as the backdrop to the international gathering. Sculptor Nathan Rapoport, who was born in Warsaw, created "The Warsaw Ghetto Uprising" and "The Last March" sculptures. Cast into the bronze are both the emotions of Jewish dehumanization and the expressions of Jewish heroism for visitors to admire. That evening, former US vice president Michael Pence stood in front of Rapoport's work and said, "Today we remember what happens when the powerless cry for help and the powerful refuse to answer."[10]

After Hitler's invasion of Poland in 1939, three million Jewish people came under his authority. In order to preserve the Nazi vision of a pure Aryan race in German-controlled land, Jewish people were segregated into temporary holding neighborhoods called ghettos until a plan could be constructed to answer the "Jewish Question." After the start of World War II, more than 1,000 ghettos were created; some functioned for days, while others imprisoned Jewish people for years.

The Warsaw ghetto was the largest in occupied Poland. More than

400,000 Jewish people were sealed into an area spanning 1.3 square miles. Ten-foot-high walls separated the ghetto from the rest of Warsaw. An average room in the buildings inside the walls would sleep seven people. Food allotments in 1941 limited the average Jew in the ghetto to 1,125 calories a day. Photos from the era of emaciated men, women, and children show the severity of their plight; they were dying in the streets due to starvation.

Hitler's Jewish Question was, What to do with all of the Jews in the territories under his control? His ultimate goal was the complete removal of the Jews altogether. Hitler initially approved of the resettlement of millions of Jewish people to the island of Madagascar, located off of the coast of Africa. However, the Madagascar Plan could not be implemented after Germany was defeated in the Battle of Britain. The Third Reich had anticipated being able to confiscate British navy vessels and using them to transport the Jewish people out of Europe. Also, to Hitler's dismay, Madagascar fell under Allied control in 1942. The destiny of the Jewish people under the Nazi government still rested in Hitler's hands. Less than a year after tabling the Madagascar Plan, deportations from the Warsaw ghetto to Treblinka extermination camp ensued. The Final Solution—Hitler's answer to the Jewish Question—had begun.

DID YOU KNOW?

A 2020 survey found that 63 percent of Millennials and Generation Z in the United States did not know six million Jews were murdered during the Holocaust. A staggering 11 percent of the respondents believe Jews caused the Holocaust.

THE FINAL SOLUTION

The Hall of Remembrance was the first memorial built at Yad Vashem in honor of the six million Jewish people who perished in the

Holocaust. The tombstone-like structure opened in 1961. Its walls are made of black basalt stone cut from the land around the Sea of Galilee. Reverently, visitors enter the building staying to the path that runs along the wall. On the floor are the names of 22 camps and places where Jewish people were murdered. The names surround smoke that rises from the Eternal Flame and a long flat tomb where the ashes of Jewish victims, brought from extermination camps, were laid to rest.

In June 1941, Hitler launched Operation Barbarossa, a military campaign tasked with the objective to topple the Soviet Union. To this day, it is considered the largest land invasion in the history of warfare. Hitler's aims were to seize Soviet land to maximize German *Lebensraum*, "living space," and to stamp out communism.

Operation Barbarossa also brought clarity to the Jewish Question for Hitler. As millions of German soldiers marched toward Moscow, Leningrad, and Kiev, a special task force dubbed *Einsatzgruppen* (the SS) followed closely behind ensuring that seized territory was secure from any potential threats—high on that list of threats were Jewish people.

The Einsatzgruppen and other conspirators began the systematic murder of Soviet Jews, eradicating entire Jewish villages through mass shootings and gas vans. It is estimated between 1.5 to 2 million Jewish people were murdered in the wake of the advancement of Operation Barbarossa.

Initially, Hitler was unsure of the German people's willingness to kill women and children in large numbers, but after Barbarossa, he pushed genocide to what Philipp Bouhler said were the "furthest extremes"—Bouhler was the senior Nazi official that was responsible for the deaths of more than 70,000 handicapped German people.[11]

The Nazis established a killing machine. Death camps could kill several thousand Jewish people in a matter of hours, and they continuously advanced their methods of efficiency.

Operation Reinhard was a code name for the annihilation of the Jews living in the General Government—an administrative region in occupied Poland—which consisted of mostly Polish Jews. The killing centers Belzec, Sobibor, and Treblinka were brought online as

The railroad that carried Jewish people into the Auschwitz-Birkenau death camp.

early as March 1942. Prisoners were transported by train to the camps and, upon their arrival, they were stripped of their possessions and immediately forced into gas chambers. At the height of their killing, between August and October of 1942, German forces and their allies in Poland killed at least 1.32 million Jews through carrying out Operation Reinhard.

Auschwitz-Birkenau is probably the most recognized extermination camp; it functioned as both a labor camp and a death camp. In contrast to the Operation Reinhard killing centers, Auschwitz-Birkenau used Zyklon-B in its gas chambers. At its peak, Auschwitz-Birkenau could systematically murder 6,000 Jews a day. In total, 1.1 million Jewish people were killed at Auschwitz-Birkenau between 1942 and 1945.

The Holocaust decimated the Jewish communities in Europe. Prior to Nazi control in 1933, 9.5 million Jewish people considered Europe home. However, after the end of the war, the Final Solution had claimed nearly six million Jewish lives, leaving Europe with only 3.5 million Jews by 1950. And today, the numbers remain in steady decline.

"There is no answer to Auschwitz...To try to answer is to commit a supreme blasphemy. Israel enables us to bear the agony of Auschwitz without radical despair, to sense a ray of God's radiance in the jungles of history."[12]

Abraham Joshua Heschel

AM YISRAEL CHAI— "THE PEOPLE OF ISRAEL LIVE"

As you complete the tour at the Holocaust Museum at Yad Vashem, the floor of the building begins to slant slightly upward. The darkness and despair of the Holocaust are now behind you, but you also know you'll never forget what you saw. Continuing forward, the triangle-shaped structure begins to expand before you; a glass wall separates you from the outdoors, and all that can be seen is the beautiful blue sky. If you could keep walking upwards, it feels like you would step straight into heaven.

Exiting the glass doors, you find yourself out on a large balcony, and before you are the Judean Mountains as far as you can see. Hitler and his followers tried to write the end to the Jewish story, but God had a different plan. At Yad Vashem, it certainly means something when you move forward from the sadness, despair, and death of the Holocaust and you step out to an endless view of the only sovereign Jewish state in the world—Israel.

PLACES TO VISIT: **YAD VASHEM**

The World Holocaust Remembrance Center in Jerusalem was built in memory of the six million Jewish people murdered by the Nazis. Yad Vashem honors the victims, educates the public, and is a leader in research on the Holocaust. The name *Yad Vashem,* "a memorial and a name," comes from the prophecy in Isaiah 56:5. It's never the easiest site to visit as it exposes the monstrous, vile side of humanity. But the museum will leave you with a greater understanding of the history and atrocity of the Holocaust, and even more, the need for a Jewish state will make more sense.

CHAPTER 9

THE REBIRTH
OF ISRAEL

*"I will plant Israel in their own land,
never again to be uprooted from the land I have
given them,' says the LORD your God."*

AMOS 9:15

s your international flight descends into Israel, your first glimpse
is of the skyline and surrounding suburbs of Tel Aviv. A Mediterranean version of New York City, Tel Aviv has all the trappings
of a modern city with a mixture of Middle Eastern, European, and
North American influences. Now, if you're flipping through the index
of your Bible trying to locate Tel Aviv in the Scriptures, you won't find
it, because the city was founded in 1909. Tel Aviv was considered the
first all-Jewish city in the early-twentieth century as those who were in
the diaspora continued to immigrate to what was then Palestine under
the Ottomans, and then the British.

Tel Aviv's name is a tip of the hat to Theodor Herzl. In 1902, Herzl
published his second work, *Altneuland*, "The Old New Land," a utopian novel detailing Herzl's vision of a future Jewish state. The Hebrew
translation of the title *Altneuland* was *Tel Aviv*. A *tel*, remember, is a
hill with layers of ancient civilizations buried beneath the surface, representing the past. *Aviv*, on the other hand, is "spring" in Hebrew. It

represents something recent, like spring water that bubbles to the surface; it's always fresh and new.

Tel Aviv is the Old New City, and modern Tel Aviv has come to embody the ethos of Herzl's vision better than any other city in Israel. The founders valued their Jewish heritage; it's the reason they fought to establish a homeland in Israel. However, like Herzl, they knew Israel's past wouldn't limit the potential for their future as they embarked on creating something new.

PLACES TO VISIT: TEL AVIV

Tel Aviv is a modern Jewish city on the coast of the Mediterranean Sea. The *New York Times* dubbed it "The Capital of Mediterranean Cool." It has everything going for it: history, culture, and great food. Plus, there is never a bad view of the sunset from a beach in Tel Aviv.

In little time, Tel Aviv grew to become the hub of prestate Jewish governance. By 1947, the time was ripe; the British announced they were determined to leave Mandatory Palestine on May 15, 1948. A new day was dawning, and the pieces of the puzzle were falling into place.

The prophets' visions of a resurrected Israel—a sovereign Jewish state—was rapidly becoming a reality.

ARAB HOSTILITY TO A JEWISH STATE

Jewish immigrants flooded into British Palestine between 1933 and 1936. In those three years, the population surged from 235,000 to 384,000 people.[1] The uptick in immigration added fuel to the already-tense relationship between the Jews and Arabs who were living in close proximity to one another.

Arab violence against the Jews escalated, homes were set ablaze, businesses were devastated, farms and orchards were destroyed, and innocent Jews were murdered in cold blood when traveling between towns. In response to the murders, the Irgun, a small recusant Jewish group, repaid the violence, murdering innocent Arabs.

Arab leadership called on the British to put a stop to Jewish immigration and end the ability of Jewish people to purchase land. The British were sandwiched in the middle of the unrest; in an effort to bring stability to the region, they vowed retribution would be made. Jewish communities continued to suffer as the oversight of British security proved ineffective.

A royal investigation into tumult in the land was commissioned by the British government and became known as the Peel Commission. British sentiments toward a sovereign Jewish homeland waned between the Balfour Declaration of 1917 and the Peel Commission in 1937. In the early 1920s, the League of Nations set the framework for the establishment of a Jewish homeland in an area that included all of British Palestine and what became Transjordan (modern-day Jordan). However, subsequent conflict and ratifications of the agreements meant that by the time of the Peel Commission's recommendations, the space was whittled down to a sliver of land along the Mediterranean coast and areas around the west side of the Sea of Galilee.

The commission published its findings in the summer of 1937, recommending the first two-state solution for the region proposing: a Jewish state, an Arab state, and that the holy places would be neutral territory. Zionist leaders were frustrated by the outcome of the report, but they still saw an opportunity amidst the obstacles.[2] In response to the report's proposals, Jewish representatives agreed to move forward on the basis of border negotiations. On the other side of the table, the Arab representatives outright rejected the proposal. The British government abandoned the Peel report in 1938 as they deemed it impractical for creating a Jewish state and Arab state in British Palestine.

DID YOU KNOW?

Israel is the only democracy in the Middle East. Egypt and Iraq are considered partially democratic, while the remaining Middle Eastern countries are authoritarian. Authoritarian countries tend to neglect or even abuse minorities. In contrast, the equal rights of minorities in Israel are guaranteed under law. These same minorities are also represented in Israel's government, in their legislature—the Knesset.

UNITED NATIONS RESOLUTION 181

At the conclusion of World War II, the British government was left to decide whether to embrace a two-state solution dividing the land or to create a single state with special rights for a Jewish minority. The British chose a third option: to hand over their Middle East problem to the United Nations. A United Nations Special Committee on Palestine (UNSCOP) was formed in July 1947. The special envoy traveled to the Middle East to construct a future for the Jews and Arabs in the land.

Meanwhile, the Royal Navy was directed to seize boats that were carrying Holocaust survivors who were bound for British Palestine with the aim to start new lives for themselves. The boats were redirected to Cyprus, where nearly 50,000 Jews were held in displaced-person camps. The British enforced strict limits on Jewish immigration to quell an Arab uprising.

One of those boats, the *SS Exodus 1947*, carrying 4,500 German and Polish refugees, arrived from France into the port of Haifa; it had been intercepted by the Royal Navy. New orders to return the refugees back to Europe came from the British government. The United Nations envoy traveled to Haifa only to witness British sailors forcibly transferring these fragile refugees from the *Exodus* onto three ships that were bound for France. The members of the committee watched as Jewish refugees, who narrowly escaped Hitler's grip, were beaten back onto a boat and shoved into cages.

When the return ships arrived in Europe, the refugees did not disembark in France as originally planned, but ended up in Germany, the place that occupied the refugees' nightmares. Members of the UNSCOP committee were deeply affected by the events that unfolded that day in Haifa and in the coming weeks. Historian Martin Gilbert tells us, one UNSCOP member said the *Exodus* "'is the best possible evidence we have' for allowing the Jews into Palestine."[3]

On November 29, 1947, only a few months later, the United Nations General Assembly adopted a resolution to partition British Palestine: 33 nations voted in favor, 13 against, ten abstentions, and one absent. Similar to the Peel Commission, UN Resolution 181 divided the land into two states, but this time more land was allocated to the Jewish community. To be exact, 56 percent of the land would be for a Jewish state. The majority of that land was the Negev desert in the south.

The passing of the United Nations partition plan proved to be the legal basis for a sovereign Jewish state. The provisional government representing Jews in Palestine, *Va'ad Leumi*, embraced the terms of the UN resolution despite the allotment of land they received and the treatment of Jerusalem as an international city under the administrative control of the United Nations. The entire Arab League, on the other hand, rejected the resolution and launched a terrorist campaign against their Jewish neighbors.

Recall, in 1897, Theodor Herzl wrote, "At Basel, I founded the Jewish State. If I said this out loud today, I would be answered by universal laughter. If not in 5 years perhaps, certainly in 50, everyone will know it."[4] And Herzl's prognostication was as good as his writing; nearly 50 years after his prediction, the world, through the United Nations, approved the establishment of a Jewish state in their ancient homeland.

The 600,000 Jews of British Palestine celebrated and danced in the streets; synagogues in the diaspora were full of worshippers offering up a prayer of thanksgiving. An independent Jewish state was mere months away from becoming a reality.

"This is the land of our forefathers, the Land of Israel, to which Abraham brought the idea of one God, where David set out to confront Goliath, and where Isaiah saw a vision of eternal peace. No distortion of history can deny the four-thousand-year-old bond, between the Jewish people and the Jewish land."[5]

Benjamin Netanyahu

INDEPENDENCE DAY

Attention turned toward 16 Rothschild Boulevard in the center of Tel Aviv on May 14, 1948. The address was once home to the city's beloved mayor, Meir Dizengoff, a devout Zionist with a big vision for his city. After the death of his wife, Zina, in 1930, he converted his home into the Tel Aviv Museum (later to be known as the Tel Aviv Museum of Art) in her honor.

He was one of the original 66 Jewish families who moved north from Jaffa to divide plots of land on the sand dunes that would become modern Tel Aviv. At his death in 1936, Tel Aviv had nearly 160,000 residents. Dizengoff probably could have never imagined the home he built would later become the epicenter of the unfolding story of Israel's rebirth.

On the morning of May 14, 1948, the Provisional Government of Israel had invited 350 select individuals to witness David Ben-Gurion declare independence for a new state. Invitations requested that the event be kept secret to prevent the possibility of a preemptive invasion by Arab forces or any obstruction by the British. But, the secret was leaked and, by that afternoon, well-wishers were singing "Hatikvah" in the streets. Soon the Tel Aviv Museum was surrounded by future Israeli citizens anxiously waiting to hear Ben-Gurion's announcement.

DID YOU KNOW?

On the heels of independence, the Jewish state still didn't have an official name. The name *Israel* was elected by a vote of 7-3, but other suggestions included Zion, Judah, and Tzabar (Sabra).

The Tel Aviv Museum was strategically chosen to host the event. The building was formal enough for the pomp of the makeshift ceremony, but more importantly, the thick walls of the first floor, which were partially underground, provided a sense of safety from potential attack.

Ben-Gurion was at a long table flanked by the community leaders whose signatures were inked on the declaration, many of whom would go on to play major roles in Israeli politics. Behind him, draped on his left and on his right, were two elongated Israeli flags, and in the center, positioned directly above Ben-Gurion, was a large framed photo of Theodor Herzl.

Time was of the essence; the British Mandate was set to expire on Saturday, May 15. To avoid declaring independence on Shabbat, the ceremony was held at 4:00 p.m. on Friday, May 14. Ben-Gurion read the entire document in just under 20 minutes and the ceremony lasted only 32 minutes.

David Ben-Gurion spoke these words to a watching world:

> *Eretz-Israel* [(Hebrew)—the Land of Israel] was the birth-
> place of the Jewish people…Impelled by this historic and
> traditional attachment, Jews strove in every successive gener-
> ation to re-establish themselves in their ancient homeland…
> This right is the natural right of the Jewish people to be mas-
> ters of their own fate, like all other nations, in their own

David Ben-Gurion reads the Declaration of Independence on May 14, 1948, at the Tel Aviv Museum.

sovereign State. Accordingly we, members of the People's
Council, representatives of the Jewish Community of Eretz-
Israel and of the Zionist Movement, are here assembled on
the day of the termination of the British Mandate over Eretz-
Israel and, by virtue of our natural and historic right and on
the strength of the resolution of the United Nations General
Assembly, hereby declare the establishment of a Jewish state
in Eretz-Israel, to be known as the State of Israel...[6]

Four hours later, Egypt attacked. Israel was in a fight to preserve
and protect its newly found state. Five Arab countries—Egypt, Lebanon, Syria, Transjordan, and Iraq—plus the local Arab community
attacked the nation only just reborn. The War of Independence was
fought for more than a year and ended in 1949.

PLACES TO VISIT:
INDEPENDENCE HALL AND THE TAYELET

When you're in Tel Aviv, be sure to tour Israel's Independence Hall
(formerly, the Dizengoff home and the Tel Aviv Museum) on the
iconic Rothschild Boulevard to see where it all happened on May
14, 1948. Afterward, take a stroll down the *Tayelet* (promenade) in
Tel Aviv that connects Jaffa port to Tel Aviv port. Enjoy a 5 kilome-
ter stretch of shopping, food, and beautiful Mediterranean beaches.

Tel Aviv continued to serve as the temporary seat of Israeli government until the end of the war. As influential as the city became to modern Israelis, it was never intended to have a permanent place as Israel's
capital. The heart of Jewish life was and will always be Jerusalem, which
is mentioned more than 800 times in the Bible. Jerusalem was established as the capital city of the State of Israel in December of 1949.

When one considers how Israel attained its status as a state, it's easy
to point to the Holocaust as being the sole reason. There's no doubt

Hitler's systematic extermination of six million Jewish people aroused global sympathy to see a national homeland for the Jewish people and a place provided for those who survived the Holocaust. However, as Israel's Declaration of Independence read by Ben-Gurion stated, "Jews strove in every successive generation to re-establish themselves in their ancient homeland"[7]—a desire we read in the prophets of old.

Israel's rebirth is connected to the prayers of generations of Jews who hoped that God would be faithful to His chosen people. The nation was made up of those who revived the Hebrew language, influenced world leaders to draft vital documents like the Balfour Declaration, and Jewish pioneers who toiled to transform the forsaken ground of Israel back into a land flowing with milk and honey.

The Holocaust became a testimony to the world, for them to see what Theodor Herzl saw: the Jewish people's need for a national homeland, where their self-determination, livelihood, and protection were no longer dependent on foreign nations, but instead were dependent on themselves. And also, all of the prayers, suffering, hard work, determination, striving, and patience of the Jews, over many centuries, led them to a moment when the world recognized an independent Jewish state. Their hope was finally realized.

CHAPTER 10

HANGING ON BY A THREAD: THE EARLY YEARS OF THE STATE OF ISRAEL

*"Israel will endure and flourish. It is the child
of hope and the home of the brave."*[1]

JOHN F. KENNEDY

Levi Eden, a young Hungarian Jew, immigrated to Israel in 1948 after surviving the brutality of the Holocaust. Eden and 700,000 other Jewish refugees flooded Israel's shores, doubling Israel's population in just three and a half years. The mass-influx left very little room for planning or infrastructure that could absorb and accommodate the waves of immigrants, forcing the infant country into adolescent growing pains and maturity.

Jewish immigrants would not be deterred from coming to Israel by the state; instead of turning away the masses, Israel scrambled to provide lodging, food, and for the basic needs of its new citizens. Former Israeli president Chaim Herzog observed, "Absorbing these immigrants would have been beyond the ability of a well-established, prosperous country, let alone one newly born and struggling to defend itself."[2]

Austerity is the only way to describe the mid-twentieth-century way of life in Israel. During its first ten years, the government would tackle large waves of immigration, housing shortages, food and clothing rations, and an economic crisis. Life as an immigrant was penniless and deprived, but a difficulty faced in Israel could never compare to Hitler's genocide or oppression in Arab lands.

WAVES OF IMMIGRATION

When David Ben-Gurion read the Declaration of Independence, he vowed Israel would be a home to all worldwide Jewry wherever they come from: "The catastrophe which recently befell the Jewish people—the massacre of millions of Jews in Europe—was another clear demonstration of the urgency of solving the problem of its homelessness by re-establishing in Eretz-Israel the Jewish State, which would open the gates of the homeland wide to every Jew and confer upon the Jewish people the status of a fully privileged member of the comity of nations."[3]

After World War II, more than 250,000 Jewish displaced persons lived in camps located in Germany, Austria, and Italy over the span of nearly seven years (1945–1952). After the Holocaust, Zionism was a hot topic among the refugees; they wanted to live in a Jewish state. The problem was, the British government severely limited Jewish immigration into the land based on their White Paper published in 1939. When the gates of immigration opened, after the British Mandate ended and Israel became a state, 140,000 Holocaust survivors made *Aliyah*, or "ascent," to Israel.

At the same time, the Middle Eastern and North African Jewish communities were dealing with their own forms of persecution and antisemitism. The plight of the Jews in these Muslim countries during and after the Holocaust is a tragedy of epic proportions that is rarely taught in any history lessons. The Middle East and North Africa were home to communities of Jewish people since the Babylonian exile recorded in the Old Testament, dating back some 2,600 years.

"I am not a Jew with trembling knees. I am a proud Jew with 3,700 years of civilized history. Nobody came to our aid when we were dying in the gas chambers and ovens. Nobody came to our aid when we were striving to create our country. We paid for it. We fought for it. We died for it. We will stand by our principles. We will defend them. And, when necessary, we will die for them again, with or without your aid."[4]

Former Israeli Prime Minister Menachem Begin

A violent pogrom targeting Jewry in Baghdad started in June 1941 and was known in Arabic as the *Farhud*. Nearly 180 Jews were killed and thousands were injured in this act of antisemitism that was influenced by Nazi propaganda. By this point in history, *Mein Kampf* had been translated into Arabic and published in an Arabic newspaper.

Zionism was soon banned in Iraq; Jews with seats of power in the government were barred from their positions. The Farhud, coupled with anti-Zionism laws, sparked a mass Iraqi-Jewish emigration between 1948–1951. An estimated 120,000 Jews fled Iraq for Israel.

When Jewish immigrants arrived in Israel, many were forced to live in tent cities called *ma'abarot*. The absorption camps were scattered throughout the land, and despite their temporary nature, they remained vital communities for the first decade of Israel's modern history.

Levi Eden policed the ma'abarot after his service in the Israeli army concluded. He spent most of his days apprehending youngsters who were stealing food to feed their families. As an immigrant in law enforcement, he was sympathetic to the plight of these immigrant families, but he was firm with the little culprits. Flashbacks of the Holocaust would overtake Eden when he would catch those kids pilfering food; he would relive moments of stealing food just to survive the Nazi ghettos.

In the camps, parents would encourage their children to commit crimes. It sounds cruel and irresponsible, but they did this because they

A Yemenite family trek through the desert to immigrate to Israel.

knew that the fourth time their kids got caught, they would be sentenced into a home with lodging, food, and an education. It was a better life than the one they were living in the ma'abarot.

When Eden patrolled the absorption camps, Iraqi Jews were the new tenants of the tent cities. European Jews had already moved through the temporary housing into more stable accommodations. Moroccan Jews replaced the Iraqis, then Yemenites followed them, and finally Persians. Scholars estimate somewhere between 850,000 to one million Jews were forcibly removed from their homes in the Middle East and North Africa, and Israel was the only place for many of them to go.

On July 5, 1950, the Israeli government honored the forty-sixth anniversary of Theodor Herzl's death by passing the Law of Return, which guaranteed any Jewish person the right to immediate Israeli citizenship upon their arrival. This was momentous legislation that further solidified Israel's identity and position as a state where the diaspora was welcome.

HOUSING SHORTAGES

Under British rule (1917–1948), modern and sophisticated cities like Tel Aviv were developed, and the prestate Jewish government managed to provide adequate housing, food distribution, and work. But nothing could have prepared them to handle the numbers of Jewish refugees that arrived after statehood.

Immediately, a housing-development crisis developed; there were too many people and not enough homes. And, many of those in need of shelter couldn't afford a home to begin with. To make matters worse, Israel lacked the basic building materials for construction such as lumber, steel, and plumbing, or even the currency to purchase them.[5]

Housing developments materialized; these were one- and two-bedroom apartments averaging 150 to 300 square feet in size. Amenities included a cold-water kitchen and an outhouse.

DID YOU KNOW?

Another type of settlement that developed in Israel was the *kibbutz*. These communities can be seen scattered all throughout Israel. They are known for collective property ownership, labor practices focused on serving the community, and communal child care—they are little pocket settlements practicing socialism. In modern Israel's formative years, the kibbutz played a role in the settlement, development, employment, and defense of the new Israeli citizens. Over time, with the growth of capitalism in Israel, the *kibbutzniks* (people that live in kibbutz) shifted their practices and embraced new economic paths.

Golda Meir, who would later become Israel's fourth prime minister, was tasked with the role of labor minister, to oversee the transition of immigrants from the ma'abarot to permanent housing. Building contractors feared the woman when she would arrive on-site because she was opinionated about every detail of construction.

Once, Golda was touring the construction of new housing in Tiberias, a city that sits on the shores of the Sea of Galilee. When she walked into one of the apartments, she stared at the kitchen window. Meir called the contractor and lectured him on the placement of the window; it was too high. She scolded him, saying, "A woman stands in the kitchen five hours cooking, and you are forcing her to see the wall and not the Kinneret [Sea of Galilee]?" Immediately, blueprints were altered, the window was lowered, and even to this day they are called "Golda Windows."[6]

Meir pushed for a modern standard of living out of fear that neighborhoods would crumble into slums. The cost was always an issue; most immigrants arrived with nothing to their name.

Apartments were barely large enough to house a family, let alone a place to host guests. Small spaces didn't stop Israelis from socializing. Local cafés were always bustling with activity and conversations. And they came to serve as extended living and dining room spaces.

Israel investigated the building of prefabricated homes, affordable living spaces constructed in little time. The Jewish Agency and American real-estate developer Levitt & Sons were in talks to invest $25 million into developing a Levittown, Israel. William Levitt, a Jewish man himself, is considered one of the most influential people of the twentieth century for creating the American suburban culture and lifestyle. He mass-produced homes like Henry Ford mass-produced cars.

Levitt proposed 600-square-foot dwellings that were double the size of the Israeli homes that were being built, furnished with American-style kitchens. The Levitts and the Jewish Agency were overwhelmed with the response. Israelis with cash in hand were ready to buy into the American-Israeli dream, but the agreement never got off the ground.

New housing, jobs, and assimilation helped the process of absorption into Israeli culture by new immigrants move more effectively. The numbers of immigrants living in temporary housing drastically declined by the mid-1950s. Some of the ma'abarot developed into *moshavim*, cooperative communities of farmers, while other camps were converted into suburban neighborhoods, and the rest were simply taken down. Rosh Ha'Ayin, for instance, was originally an immigrant absorption center, the home to a community of Yemenese Jews. The town was converted into a permanent settlement in 1951, and then incorporated in 1955, receiving municipal council status.

The housing crisis lingered for a decade. By 1963, 15,000 immigrants remained in temporary housing.[7]

PLACES TO VISIT: KIBBUTZ EIN GEV

Kibbutz Ein Gev is one of my favorite places to stay while touring Israel. This kibbutz was founded in the mid-1930s and is located on the eastern shores of the Sea of Galilee. Today, it is one of the largest and most prosperous kibbutzim in Israel, having a focus on the agricultural and tourism industries.

RATIONS AND ECONOMIC CRISIS

Israeli couscous can be found on grocery store shelves all over the world—it's a staple in the Israeli diet and cuisine. But it didn't originate from a Jewish mother cooking in a Jerusalem kitchen. Israeli couscous are small, pearl-shaped spheres made of baked wheat and the food has a litany of monikers like *ptitim* and "Ben-Gurion's rice." What's funny is that only non-Israelis dub the small orbs Israeli couscous, and what's even funnier is that it's not made of either couscous or rice at all.

The dust had barely cleared after the War of Independence in 1949 when the Israeli government was presented with another crisis: the state had no line of credit and was on the cusp of bankruptcy. The government initiated a strict austerity program it called *Tzena*, "austerity," in order to feed the rapidly growing population and kickstart economic growth. Dov Yosef was head of the Ministry of Rationing and Supply, and his reputation among Israelis went from that of a respectable lawyer and one of the state's founding fathers to scum overnight.

"Pessimism is a luxury that Jews cannot afford."[8]

Golda Meir

Every Israeli felt the pinch, or better yet—the stranglehold, on basic goods needed to survive. It didn't matter if you were a veteran who had lived through the British Mandate and fought in the War of Independence, or an immigrant who had just arrived at the conclusion of the war; everyone received the same rations for the betterment of the whole Jewish state.

Grocery stores functioned more like Department of Motor Vechiles offices; citizens were assigned to an authorized grocery store where they received a coupon book. If you didn't have your coupons you couldn't purchase your food. Lines of people formed outside of grocery stores waiting to receive their rations of food and basic necessities. Some waited hours, only to hear nothing was left when it was their turn.

Dietitians and medical experts determined 1,600 calories per day

Israelis in Tel Aviv standing in line to purchase food rations with coupons issued by the government.

was enough to feed an individual without starvation occurring; this included a half-loaf of bread per person, per day, 60 grams of corn, rice, and legumes, while meat was only 0.75 grams per month, given its high cost.[9] Food controllers were stationed at grocery stores to handle rationing issues, complaints, and questions. Broth cubes replaced chicken soup, coffee companies converted to using chicory, and both powdered eggs and powdered milk were swapped in for the real stuff.

It was at this time Ben-Gurion spoke with Eugen Propper, co-founder of the Osem food company, to develop an inexpensive replacement for rice, an essential grain in the traditional meals of the Middle Eastern and North African immigrants. The product that was developed from this project was a rice-shaped wheat pasta that was dried and toasted. It was so popular with customers that Osem developed an orb-shaped replacement for rice, and since then, Israeli couscous has remained a mainstay in Israeli cuisine.

DID YOU KNOW?

During the era of austerity in Israel, clothing companies would take rationing coupons in exchange for new clothes. This heavily influenced the fashion trends that developed in Israel during this time period.

The government agency would go on to expand rationing to clothing, shoes, and furniture. The restrictions caused many Israelis to look to the underground to buy luxuries that were limited for the masses. The Israeli government fought profiteering to stifle the influence of the black market. Police raided homes, vehicles were stopped and searched, and businesses were closed down. By the beginning of 1950, nearly 5,000 charges were brought against law offenders.[10]

Israel's government officially ended the era of austerity in 1959, and by then Dov Yosef's Tzena Plan was considered nostalgic. However, Yosef's reputation remained stained for the rest of his political career.

Israel was in desperate need for financial assistance in the early years. Ben-Gurion commissioned Golda Meir to raise significant funds among diaspora Jewish communities. She returned with tens of millions of dollars in support. Additionally, Germany agreed to Holocaust reparations, money that financed Israel's electrical development, railways, mining equipment, and port development. Holocaust reparations, according to The Bank of Israel, accounted for about 15 percent of Gross National Product growth, creating 45,000 jobs during the 12-year period.[11] Financial help from the United States also helped jump-start the Israeli economy into the 1960s.

Austerity measures defined Israel's first decade of modern statehood. The government's decision to embrace mass immigration in the early stages of the state was difficult. The immigrant influx was very costly and weighed heavily on Israel's economy. However, it was the right choice for the country's future. The human capital gained during this time alone would prove to be most beneficial to Israel's growth in the long term.

Mentioned at the beginning of this chapter, remember what Chaim Herzog said: that Israel's absorption of the immigrants coming from Europe and the Middle East would put stress on a prosperous country, let alone a country just born. From a human perspective, the financial and social pressures placed on Israel should have caused the Jewish state to crumble early on in its existence. But once again, we see that God's promise to Abraham of a land, descendants, and blessing carried them through even the most difficult times.

CHAPTER 11

OUTNUMBERED: FROM THE WAR OF INDEPENDENCE TO THE YOM KIPPUR WAR

"It is true we have won all our wars,
but we have paid for them."[1]

GOLDA MEIR

I n 1937, the British imposed a new law stating that anyone caught of being in possession of unauthorized weapons, ammunition, or explosives in the British Mandate could be sentenced with the death penalty. As Arab hostilities intensified around the Yishuv, Zionist leaders were well aware that they would need to fight for their independence if the dream of statehood was ever to be realized. This put Zionists in a precarious position. How do they prepare for war without starting a revolt against the British Empire?

Yosef Avidar, a senior military commander for Israel's prestate military, the *Haganah*, devised a plan to help the Jewish people who were outgunned and outnumbered in the years leading up to their independence. It was so ambitious, you'd think it had come straight from an action movie.

Avidar turned to the Kibbutz Hill community, a training ground

for young Zionist pioneers who were learning the skills and trades
of the kibbutz lifestyle. These young pioneers had everything Avidar
needed to make his plan work: drive, ambition, purpose, and mission.

The Haganah had already had success in smuggling weapons and
establishing arms factories, where they covertly manufactured the Sten
submachine gun, but they still had a hard time obtaining the 9mm bullets they needed to fire their weapons.

Avidar gathered 45 unsuspecting twentysomethings from Kibbutz
Hill and he offered them a life-threatening mission, not for the faint-
at-heart. He tasked them to manufacture ammunition in a top-secret
underground bunker below the kibbutz, right under the nose of the
British military.

If the British caught them, they could be executed on the spot. The
45 recruits were sworn to secrecy; not even the other residents of Kibbutz Hill were aware of what was going on right below their feet. The
military code name for the clandestine ammunition factory was Ayalon Institute.

The Haganah dug out a 2,700-square-foot factory that was 13 feet
underground, and that had walls and a ceiling that were two feet thick.
Directly overhead was the kibbutz laundry room, masking the smells
and the sounds of the machinery operating in the factory below. The
entrance to the factory was in a secret passageway that was covered
by a large washing machine that could pivot open and shut over the
opening.

PLACES TO VISIT: AYALON INSTITUTE
(WAR OF INDEPENDENCE)

The Ayalon Institute in Rehovot was a prestate secret underground factory, covertly manufacturing bullets for the Haganah.
The ammunition would be used later in the fight for Israeli independence. Walk through the underground factory for yourself and
experience firsthand the strategic role that young Zionists played
in helping modern Israel win their first war.

British soldiers were stationed close to the kibbutz, so they would use the laundry services of the community to wash their uniforms. To keep the British at a distance, kibbutzniks offered to pick up and drop off the soldiers' clothes, so as not to be caught. Large amounts of copper would arrive at the kibbutz to be used for making the bullet casings. The British were told the metal was being used to make kosher lipstick cases.

The manufacturing, testing, and packaging of the 9mm bullets was a round-the-clock operation. It's estimated that between 1945 and 1948, the 45 young recruits manufactured some two million bullets that were used to defend Israel from its enemies.[2] Each casing was stamped with the initials "E.A.," which stands for *Eretz Israel/Ayalon*.

WAR OF INDEPENDENCE

The Jewish Telegraphic Agency (JTA) reported on May 30, 1948, just a few weeks after Israel declared its independence, that the Old City of Jerusalem had fallen to Transjordanian King Abdullah's Arab Legion after 11 days of fighting. The Israelis did all they could to push back their enemies, but as the JTA reported, they were "outnumbered and outgunned,"[3] a theme that will define Israel's fight for survival as five Arab-Muslim countries simultaneously attacked the one Jewish state.

The Israeli government summarizes the War of Independence as happening in four phases:[4]

The first phase started after the United Nations approved the UNSCOP partition plan in November 1947. As Jews were celebrating in the streets, terror broke out in Jerusalem. The "City of Peace" had been determined by the UN to be under international control; however, Arabs and Jews fought to claim ownership of the city.

Immediately, local Arab forces went on the offensive with help from their surrounding allies, who would join the war in the following months, forcing the Yishuv into a defensive posture. The partition plan was already disintegrating; the Jewish people suffered severe casualties and roadways between their settlements were cut off.

Arab forces cut off the only road traveling between Tel Aviv and

Jerusalem, isolating the 100,000 Jewish residents of Jerusalem from all other Jewish cities. Their water supply to the city was also cut off. Only armored vehicles were successful in breaking through the Arab barricades, bringing needed supplies to the Jews living in Jerusalem.

The Haganah was the largest prestate Jewish defense group, and it developed into an organized army after the adoption of the United Nations partition plan.

Phase two started on April 1, 1948, when the Jews positioned themselves offensively toward the Arab onslaught. In a period of six weeks, the Haganah temporarily opened the road to Jerusalem and captured the cities of Tiberias, Safed, Acre, and Haifa, and secured the land allotted to them under the UN resolution.

Days before May 14, 1948, Golda Meir, in the dark of night, covertly crossed the border into Transjordan in a valiant attempt to prevent war with their neighbor. King Abdullah, who had once preached for peace, changed his tune because Egypt, Iraq, Syria, and Lebanon had become involved. Abdullah said to Meir, "Why are you in such a hurry to proclaim your State?…You are so impatient!" Meir responded that she didn't think "people who had waited 2,000 years should be described as being 'in a hurry.'"[5]

Phase three began on May 15, 1948, the day after David Ben-Gurion declared independence. Five Arab states had been waiting in the wings to launch an attack on the single Jewish state. On May 31, 1948, the Haganah was transformed into Israel's national army and renamed the Israel Defense Forces.

DID YOU KNOW?

What Israelis call Independence Day, Palestinians dubbed Nakba Day (Catastrophe Day): a solemn day to protest when Israel was established. Nakba Day has been unofficially celebrated since 1949. In 1998, coinciding with Israel's 50th-anniversary celebrations, former Palestinian leader Yasser Arafat officially established Nakba Day to be observed on May 15.

The first month of the war for the new nation was concentrated in Jerusalem, fighting against Transjordan's Arab Legion. By the end of May, the Transjordanians had taken control of the Old City and expelled its Jewish inhabitants.

Lebanon attacked from the north, capturing the border crossing at Malkia. Syria advanced from the east, moving toward the Sea of Galilee and attacked Kibbutz Degania on the south end of the lake. If Degania fell, that would have spelled disaster for the entire north. Reluctantly, Ben-Gurion sent two 65mm guns from Tel Aviv to the lakeside town, and they arrived just in time to destroy Syrian tanks, frightening the infantry and sending them into retreat. The Syrian defeat gave a boost of confidence that was felt by all Israelis throughout the land.

Iraq crossed the Jordan River toward Beit She'an. Israeli forces successfully defended the area and then moved toward Samaria.

Egypt entered Israel with a two-pronged approach. First, they maneuvered through the Negev desert to the hills around Hebron, advancing north into Jerusalem, where they were stopped by Jewish defenders at Ramat Rachel. Egypt's second offensive followed the coastal road from Gaza toward Tel Aviv. When the Egyptian army arrived in Ashdod, they were met by the few fighter planes Israel had in their arsenal. Bombs were dropped from the Israeli planes, causing thousands of Egyptian soldiers to flee.

The Jewish fighters were able to defend the west side of Jerusalem, but they remained under constant attack. A secondary road, dubbed the "Burma Road," provided for the desperate need to resupply and rearm those who were trapped in Jerusalem.

Transjordan took the east side of Jerusalem, which contained the Temple Mount, the Western Wall, and the Old City. Mount Scopus, which was home to Hadassah Hospital and the Hebrew University, remained under Israeli control, even though it was in the eastern part of Jerusalem. For the next 19 years, Jerusalem was divided between the Israelis and Jordanians.

The fourth phase started on July 19, 1948; by this point, the United States was confident that Israel would win the war. The IDF sealed up loose ends, capturing the Negev and Upper Galilee, land that was promised to them by the UN.

Fighting would continue through the winter of 1948 into the spring of 1949, but Israel would remain in control of the war. One by one, Arab states entered a cease-fire with Israel: Egypt (February 24, 1949), Lebanon (March 23, 1949), Transjordan (April 3, 1949), and Syria (July 20, 1949).

According to historian Benny Morris, Israel was outnumbered two-to-one by the Palestinian Arabs in the land, and the surrounding Arab states had a combined population of 40 million, compared to the 650,000 Jews in the Yishuv.[6] Against all odds, Israel gained land previously granted to the Palestinian Arabs. At the end of the war, Egypt occupied Gaza and Transjordan occupied the West Bank—which included East Jerusalem and the Old City of Jerusalem. The secret mission of the Ayalon Institute, and other brave undertakings by the people in the Yishuv, had a profound impact on the War of Independence. Without them, the war could have been lost.

SIX-DAY WAR

They say that a picture is worth a thousand words. That's true, but David Rubinger's photo of three IDF paratroopers standing at the Western Wall, moments after Israel had recaptured the Old City of Jerusalem in 1967, could fill volumes. The faces of Yitzhak Yifat, Tzion Karasenti, and Chaim Oshri define the moment impeccably; their countenances express the emotions of wonder, loss, and triumph all in one glance.

Wonderment, because after more than 2,000 years, the Jewish people had control of their ancient capital and the Temple Mount. Yifat, Karasenti, Oshri, and the whole army were well aware of the significance of the moment. Their thoughts probably wandered to realms of astonishment as they contemplated their historic role in Jerusalem's liberation—fulfilling prayers offered up by their ancestors.

What seemed like an age-old dream was now a reality.

The three young soldiers are noticeably exhausted, tired from three days of fighting. From their vantage point, they don't know that there are still three days left in the Six-Day War, but their fatigue is visible. Brothers were lost during the battle; nearly 100 Israeli paratroopers were killed and 400 were wounded that day.[7]

Rabbi Shlomo Goren, who would later become Israel's chief rabbi, recited the memorial prayer and blew the shofar. The *Voice of Israel* radio broadcast captured the moment for the whole nation to hear; in the background, soldiers could be heard weeping over the loss of friends killed in combat.

Army chief chaplain Rabbi Shlomo Goren blows the shofar in front of the Western Wall in Jerusalem after Israel captured East Jerusalem from Jordan.

And through the wonder, tears, and fatigue, a new day was seen dawning for the tiny Jewish state. June 7, 1967, was a major symbol of victory. From the human perspective, the odds were against Israel, but with God on their side, the planned attack that was staged by the Arab coalition, who wished to push Israel into the sea, backfired. In just six days, Israel had tripled its size, and on the seventh day, the IDF rested.

DID YOU KNOW?

To this day, the walls and gates of the Old City of Jerusalem remain covered in bullet holes from the battles fought during the War of Independence (1949) and the Six-Day War (1967).

Two years prior to the war, Arab leaders had convened in Morocco to gauge whether another major conflict with Israel was feasible. King

Hassan II, Morocco's monarch, was suspicious of his guests and their motives; he recorded the meeting and, shockingly, handed over the audio recording to Israeli intelligence. The tapes indicated an attack on Israel was imminent, but they also revealed the Arab nations were disorganized and incohesive.

On May 27, 1967, mere days before the start of the war, the Egyptian president, Gamal Abdel Nasser, publicly stated, "Our basic objective will be the destruction of Israel. The Arab people want to fight."[8] Israel called reserve forces into action after Jordan, Syria, Lebanon, Iraq, and Saudi Arabia advanced their armies to Israel's borders. The Arab rhetoric was matched by the mobilization of the Arab forces. Approximately 547,000 troops, more than 2,504 tanks, and 957 aircraft encircled Israel.[9]

Israel found itself surrounded and alone. On June 5, 1967, desperation forced Israel's military commanders to think strategically; they opted to go on the offensive and preemptively strike the amassing Arab military units, using the full force of the Israeli Air Force (IAF). The plan was to bomb Egyptian airfields while the Egyptian pilots were eating their breakfast. Prior to the strike, chief of staff of the IDF at the time, Yitzhak Rabin, addressed Israeli pilots, "Remember: your mission is one of life or death. If you succeed—we win the war; if you fail—God help us."[10]

The Israeli Air Force managed to destroy 302 fighter planes, obliterating the Egyptian Air Force, and several Syrian and Jordanian aircraft. Then the fight moved from the air to the ground. Some of history's most famous tank battles were fought in Egypt as the IDF blazed across the Sinai Peninsula, reaching the Suez Canal by June 9, 1967.

Israeli prime minister Levi Eshkol informed Jordan's King Hussein on the first day of the war that Israel had no interest in fighting with their eastern neighbor. However, they would retaliate if instigated to war. Later that day, Israel's capital, West Jerusalem, was under siege as Jordanian mortars fell upon the Knesset.

King Hussein's decision to fight changed the course of Middle Eastern history. Within just two days, the Temple Mount, the Old City of Jerusalem, East Jerusalem, and the entire West Bank were under Israeli control as they responded to the siege.

With the threats from Egypt and Jordan contained, the IDF's energy was directed toward the north, to Syria. The Syrian Army had the strategic high ground in the Golan Heights, but after two days of Israeli airstrikes, the IDF penetrated Syrian lines.

In the span of just six days, Israel's armies were militarily positioned to be able to take the capital cities of their enemies: Cairo, Amman, and Damascus. Israel had seized control of the Sinai Peninsula (Egypt), the Gaza Strip (Egypt), the West Bank (Jordan), and the Golan Heights (Syria). Jordan and Egypt agreed to a cease-fire on June 8, and Syria followed a day later on June 9. The agreements were signed on June 11, 1967.

PLACES TO VISIT:
AMMUNITION HILL (SIX-DAY WAR)

Ammunition Hill in Jerusalem was the location of one of the deadliest battles during the Six-Day War. Today it's a memorial for the soldiers who died in the campaign for Jerusalem. It also houses a museum that will open your eyes to the military strategy and the events that unified Jerusalem in 1967.

YOM KIPPUR WAR

A burned-out, rusted Syrian T-62 tank sits front and center at the Oz 77 memorial, overlooking the Valley of Tears, near the border of Syria and Israel. The dilapidated tank is a totem, representing the 700 Syrian tanks that well outnumbered Israeli tanks during a decisive battle, when Israel put a stop to the Syrian advance during the Yom Kippur War in 1973.

The Arab world was still reeling from the stinging loss of the Six-Day War. King Hussein of Jordan learned his lesson. He would avoid any future conflict with Israel out of fear that Israel would move further into his country.

Egypt and Syria, however, were resolute to reclaim their dignity and take back land.

Israeli intelligence knew that another war was imminent, but there were false alarms that produced uncertainty about when it could occur. Israeli prime minister Golda Meir was advised by the United States not to repeat actions taken during the Six-Day War by striking first. This only added pressure to the situation for Israel's first female leader.

On October 6, 1973, Israelis were honoring Yom Kippur, a day of rest, fasting, and prayer—it's a sacred Jewish holy day. Israel was completely shut down; businesses and schools were closed and roads were empty.

At 8:00 a.m., six hours before the start of the war, Golda Meir gathered with defense minister Moshe Dayan and chief of staff David Elazar. Dayan believed that too much uncertainty clouded their ability to choose to attack, but Elazar argued to execute a preemptive attack. Meir sided with Dayan, fearing the United States would pull their support. She knew Israel couldn't go it alone.

DID YOU KNOW?

Israeli military leader Moshe Dayan, famously known for his eyepatch, played a crucial role in four of Israel's wars, but he would later aid in peace negotiations between Israel and Egypt. Dayan was an IDF commander in Jerusalem in 1948–1949 and served as Defense Minister during the Six-Day War and the Yom Kippur War.

Striking on Yom Kippur gave Egypt and Syria the initial upper hand. Egypt moved swiftly into the Sinai Peninsula without any opposition, while Syria advanced into areas of the Israeli-controlled Golan Heights.

The numbers and the odds related to the opening battles of the war were staggering. In the Golan Heights, 180 Israeli tanks defended their state against a blitz of 1,400 Syrian tanks. Along the Suez Canal border, nearly 500 Israelis with only three tanks were attacked by 100,000 Egyptian soldiers, who were backed by 2,000 tanks and 550 aircraft.

By the next day, October 7, the Syrians moved within 800 meters of El Al, an Israeli moshav near the Sea of Galilee. Israel was on the back foot. However, by October 10, Israeli forces were reinforced in the north, driving the Syrians from the Golan Heights and forcing them back to the cease-fire line. Israeli forces then went on the offense into Syria. By October 12, they came within 18 miles of Damascus. To the south, following an intense three-day tank battle in the Sinai, Israel defeated the Egyptians. Israeli paratroops almost reached as far as Cairo.

PLACES TO VISIT: VALLEY OF TEARS (YOM KIPPUR WAR)

The Valley of Tears is where one of Israel's largest and most significant tank battles took place. Fought during the Yom Kippur War, the Valley of Tears sits between Mount Hermon and Mount Bental in the Golan Heights. Tour the site where the Israel Defense Forces blocked a substantial Syrian attack, keeping control of the Golan Heights.

In response, Saudi Arabia and Libya cut off oil supply to the United States, and the Soviets threatened to enter the fighting. US secretary of state Henry Kissinger went to the USSR to talk about restoring peace.

The Yom Kippur War was more than a battle between Israel and her neighbors. On a macro level, it was a battle between two global powers struggling for influence during the Cold War. The Soviets supplied arms and advanced weaponry to Egypt and Syria; the United States placed its support behind Israel. US President Nixon provided $2.2 billion in emergency aid through congressional approval to resupply Israel with military equipment in order to counterbalance the Soviet Union's massive resupply to Egypt.

On October 21, the UN Security Council adopted Resolution 338, calling for, among other things, a cease-fire, the posting of UN observers along the cease-fire lines, and the implementation of UN Resolution 242 on the ground. Resolution 242, adopted in 1967 after the Six-Day War, included a request for Israel to withdraw from territories that were gained during the Six-Day War.

Syria would accept Resolution 338 only if Israel withdrew from the land it won during the Six-Day War. At the same time, Egypt and Israel accused each other of cease-fire violations, and heavy fighting resumed on the Suez Canal front. So the war continued. Israeli forces pushed south and cut off the city of Suez and the Egyptian Third Army of 20,000 men. Israel was forced to accept a cease-fire just at the moment when it was capable of destroying the Egyptian army. On November 11, 1973, Israel and Egypt signed a cease-fire accord that was drawn up by Israel's ally, Kissinger, and Egyptian president Anwar el-Sadat.

Israel was outnumbered and lacking in firepower in three of its most influential wars with its surrounding neighbors. However, in every case, Israel was never outmaneuvered or divided in the fight. Every rank in their military was unified in their resolution to defend their state, and with God's help, they defeated their enemies.

In 1973, Golda Meir told then-US senator Joe Biden that Israel's secret weapon to war was "We have nowhere else to go."[11] The implications of Meir's statement are profound. It illuminates the drive and audacity that pushed Israel to fight for survival, knowing they were outnumbered on all sides. Israel was unified as a nation, with both a singular purpose and a fear that motivated the people to fight as one—it was the terror of a new Holocaust.[12] Unlike their brothers and sisters, who had their voices silenced during the Holocaust, Israel's existence is an affirmation that every Jew can have the sovereign right to defend themselves against their enemies.

There is no doubt God was protecting Israel during these strategic battles early in their history. Like Gideon's army, they were few, but remember, God promised Abraham and his descendants divine protection: "I will bless those who bless you, and whoever curses you I will curse" (Genesis 12:3).

PART 2:

TODAY

CHAPTER 12

THE LAND
AND THE PEOPLE

*"The world will be freed by our liberty, enriched by
our wealth, magnified by our greatness."* [1]

THEODOR HERZL

U niversities and colleges have become a hotbed of anti-Israel and antisemitic activity. Professors compare modern Israel to South Africa during apartheid, while university officials turn a blind eye to the left-leaning bias and politicization that fills their halls of academia—all under the guise of academic freedom.

Anti-Israel activists target college campuses, where they encourage students to engage in BDS: Boycott, Divestment, and Sanctions against Israel. BDS against Israel isn't original; it's modeled after the same anti-apartheid activism that forced South Africa to end its institutional racism and segregation.

Kenneth Meshoe, a South African member of parliament, is personally offended that anti-Israel activists would dare equate his country's racist history to Israel's vibrant democracy. Meshoe was raised in apartheid, and he experienced firsthand the discrimination of total racial segregation, where the majority non-whites were completely separated socially, politically, and economically from the minority whites.

Meshoe was prohibited from learning in the same schools as whites, entering into social contracts with other races, using the same public facilities, working the same jobs, and even living in the same areas. The South African parliamentarian publicly defended Israel, saying, "Those who know what real apartheid is, as I know, know that there is nothing in Israel that looks like apartheid."[2]

The South African politician is spot on. From Tel Aviv to Jerusalem and Nazareth to Eilat, Israeli people make up an eclectic blend of race, religion, politics, and culture. I've traveled all throughout the land, and in just one day I've had breakfast at a Druze restaurant in the Golan Heights, driven southwest toward Haifa for a traditional Arab lunch, and made it, just in time, to catch the sunset in Tel Aviv as I enjoyed kosher sushi for dinner from a Jewish restaurant.

There were no signs posted on the entrances of these restaurants declaring they would not serve Israelis based on their particular race, religion, gender, or sexual orientation.

To be an Israeli citizen doesn't mean you're Jewish. Yes, Israel is the only Jewish state in the world, but its citizenry is a tapestry of ethnicities from all over the world. Arab Muslims or Christians live right next to religious or secular Jews, who also serve in the army alongside Druze.

DID YOU KNOW?

Olim, immigrants to Israel, can claim financial benefits, rent subsidies, health coverage, tax deductions, tuition benefits, and free Hebrew courses from the Israeli government for immigrating.

According to recent census data, Israel's Jewish community makes up around 74 percent of the population, with 6,841,000 registered citizens. Arabs make up another 21 percent, at 1,946,000 citizens, and other ethnicities make up the remaining 5 percent.[3]

The best way to understand the land and the people is to hear the stories of Israel's citizens who come from various backgrounds. This chapter will encourage you to see that Israel is the furthest thing from an apartheid state.

RIVKA RAVITZ[4]

In the fall of 2019, former Israeli president Reuven Rivlin commented on Twitter: "Blessings and congratulations to the dear, dedicated Chief of Staff, beloved mother Rivka Ravitz and the dear father Yitzhak Ravitz, on the birth of a son. A new brother and uncle for the entire Ravitz family. Raise him in peace and with love, with G-d's help."[5]

Rivka Ravitz, an ultra-Orthodox Jewish woman and mother of 12, has spent two decades serving one of Israel's most influential statesmen. Since 1999, Ravitz has traveled the globe and stood beside many twenty-first-century world leaders like US presidents Biden, Trump, and Obama; Russian president Vladimir Putin; German chancellor Angela Merkel; Pope Francis; and more. It should be noted: Ravitz literally stood beside male leaders, but she never shook their hands. Not out of disrespect to them or their positions, but out of deference for God, in keeping with Jewish law and respect for her family.

Ravitz originally planned to be a part-time teacher, but the pay was a pittance. Her father-in-law, who was at the time head of the Knesset Finance Committee, hired her as a parliamentary assistant, which would make more money. After three years, a new Israeli law prohibited government officials from hiring their family members, which meant Rivka would transition to working for another member of the finance committee, Reuven Rivlin.

As an ultra-Orthodox Jewish woman, Ravitz was a boundary-breaker, entering the political world at a time when no other Orthodox women did. She would manage many of Rivlin's successful campaigns for Speaker of the Knesset and president of Israel, while also managing her family's religious life at home as the matriarch.

There is no full-time housekeeper to help Ravitz juggle life's responsibilities; she prepares meals the night before and has plenty of help from all of her children that still live at home. Ravitz honors the Sabbath day and celebrates the Jewish holidays whether she's at home or traveling abroad. She believes her high-profile position is a mission to sanctify God's name.

As one of Israel's most powerful women, a pioneer and trailblazer, Ravitz believes there is no such thing as a "normal" woman. Whether you are chief of staff or a busy housewife, you're always a full-time woman.

IMAD AND REEM YOUNIS[6]

Nazareth is called the Arab capital of Israel, with 69 percent of the population being Muslim and 31 percent being Christian. Imad and Reem Younis were both born and raised in Nazareth. The Arab-Christian couple met at Israel's prestigious institute of technology, Technion. Reem was studying civil engineering, while her husband, Imad, majored in electrical engineering.

In 1993, the husband-and-wife duo ventured out on their own, creating a new company on a shoestring budget. Alpha Omega was established to bring the high-tech industry to Nazareth and the Arab community. Arab-Israeli involvement in the field of technology is much lower than their Jewish counterparts. It's estimated that Arabs make up only 2 percent of the Israeli technology sector workforce. But thanks to the Younises, more Arab-Israelis are attending university and filling the engineering positions at the Israeli offices of Google, Cisco, Microsoft, and Intel.

Alpha Omega found its niche developing products for neurosurgery and neuroscience. Reem and Imad created a "GPS" system of the brain, which allows neurosurgeons to target the precise locations for implanting Deep Brain Stimulation (DBS) electrodes that energize neural tissue that provides relief to patients suffering from Parkinson's disease.

Today, Alpha Omega employs about 100 people, with offices in Israel, the United States, China, and Europe. Imad credits his company's diversity as the true driver of their success. They employ Muslims, Christians, and Jews, all from a plethora of backgrounds.

Reem invests much of her energy in encouraging the younger generations of Arab-Israelis to pursue their dreams. She sits on a variety of nonprofit boards, building bridges between private businesses and the Israeli government to create opportunities for the next generation of Arab-Israeli innovators.

"The State of Israel will be open for Jewish immigration and for the Ingathering of the Exiles; it will foster the development of the country for the benefit of all its inhabitants; it will be based on freedom, justice and peace as envisaged by the prophets of Israel; it will ensure complete equality of social and political rights to all its inhabitants irrespective of religion, race or sex; it will guarantee freedom of religion, conscience, language, education and culture; it will safeguard the Holy Places of all religions; and it will be faithful to the principles of the Charter of the United Nations."[7]

Israel's Declaration of Independence

FARES AND FIRAS MUHAMMAD[8]

As many high school graduates in the Western world prepare for college or university, Israelis gear up for basic training to serve in the Israel Defense Forces. The mandatory military draft dates back to Israel's founding; males at 18 years old serve their country for 32 months, and females of the same age, for 24 months.

Arab-Israelis are exempt from conscription even though they consist of 20 percent of the population. Statistically, only 1 percent of Arab-Israelis enlist in the army; however, within the past decade, a surge of Arab-Israelis have joined the ranks to serve and defend their country.

Fares and Firas Muhammad are a part of the 1 percent who chose to enlist, but their journey to the IDF wasn't easy. The Muslim-Arab twins, from the east side of Jerusalem, grew up in a broken home with an abusive father. Their mother enrolled them in a Jewish preschool, but as the abuse became unbearable, she left and moved to Haifa with her boys.

As the Muhammad twins grew older, they spent more time looking for trouble than running from it; their adolescence was filled with
police run-ins, violence, and crime. After being caught robbing a gas
station, Fares was sentenced to time in the Nirim Youth Village, a camp
for at-risk teens created by members of the Shayetet 13 command unit,
an elite navy unit that has played a role in most of Israel's major wars.

Fares's direction in life changed after camp counselors recommended
that he hike the Israel National Trail, a route that spans the entire country from its southernmost city in Eilat to Kibbutz Dan in the north. Fares
admits that the alone time forced him to think about his life and the
choices he had made in the past. Afterward, he decided to enlist in the IDF.

As Fares was hiking through Israel, his brother was moving in
and out of prison. Firas was going nowhere fast in life; every time he
appeared in court, his mother was there to bail him out. He grew tired
of his mother seeing him in handcuffs and he changed course by enlist-
ing in the army, like his brother.

Firas requested to serve in a combat unit, but with his past criminal
record, the IDF draft office wanted him instead placed in combat support. Firas wouldn't back down and he was insistent on joining a combat unit, a skill that would come to serve him well.

By age 18, both Fares and Firas entered into the Golani Brigade, an
infantry brigade assigned with defending Israel's northern borders. The
twins are valued and loved by their fellow soldiers; they know that the
Muhammad twins would risk their own lives to save their comrades,
and those comrades would do the same for the twins.

When asked why the brothers would go against the grain of the
Arab-Israeli culture and enlist in the IDF, they admit "military service is
their path to acceptance in mainstream Israeli society,"[9] and they wanted
to show appreciation to the country that had done so much for them.

ILAN RAMON

A geological phenomenon—many call the "Grand Canyon of
Israel"—cuts right through the heart of the Negev desert. At nearly
25 miles long, Makhtesh Ramon is the world's largest natural erosion

basin. The visitors center, which is perched on the edge of the "crater," as they call it, offers spectacular views of the Ramon Nature Reserve. In a unique way that only Israel can do, the visitors center is also home to the memorial and museum for Colonel Ilan Ramon—one of the IDF's finest fighter pilots and Israel's first astronaut.

Born Ilan Wolferman, he was the son of Holocaust survivors Tonya and Eliezer Wolferman. His father, Eliezer, fled Hitler's Germany in 1935, while Ilan's Polish mother barely escaped Auschwitz. The family immigrated to Israel in 1949 with the initial wave of Holocaust survivor immigration.

After Ilan graduated high school in 1972, he joined the Israeli Air Force. A broken hand kept him grounded during the Yom Kippur War. Ramon became a fighter pilot in 1974 and he was one of the first Israelis to fly in Israel's first F-16 squadron—the F-16 being the most modern and sophisticated fighter jet of its time.

Later on, leaving his position as the head of the Department of Operational Requirement for Weapon Development and Acquisition in 1998, he went to train with NASA to become the first Israeli astronaut to orbit earth as a payload specialist.

On January 16, 2003, STS-107 *Columbia* blasted off into space. Five years of training at the Johnson Space Center prepared Ramon for the speed, G-forces, and weightlessness of space travel. But, that time didn't prepare him for being a Jew in space. Prior to launch, Rabbi Zvi Konikov met with the Israeli maverick to train him on keeping kosher and celebrating Shabbat in space.

Like many secular Israelis, Ramon was a proud Jew, but he didn't practice Judaism. His assignment to the *Columbia* mission changed that. It's not that he became more religious, but he knew that in space, he was representing all Jewry.

As Ramon was hurled nearly 18,000 miles per hour into orbit, he traveled with significant memorabilia close to the heart of the Jewish people. Onboard *Columbia* was the "Moon Landscape" drawing, sketched by Petr Ginz, a 16-year-old Jewish boy who perished at Auschwitz; two Torahs: one in microfiche form, and the other, a tiny Torah scroll from the Holocaust; a barbed-wire mezuzah (chosen as a symbol of the Holocaust); and a dollar bill from the famed Rabbi Menachem Mendel Schneerson.[10]

Colonel Ilan Ramon logged 15 days, 22 hours, and 20 minutes in space; during that time he ate kosher food and kept the Sabbath. As Rabbi Yossie Denburg of Coral Springs, Florida, said, "This is one small step for Colonel Ramon, but a large step for Jews worldwide."[11]

As space shuttle *Columbia* was reentering the earth's atmosphere, the orbiter disintegrated in midair, just 16 minutes from its scheduled landing, killing Ramon and the other six crew members onboard. His death was a tragic loss for the Ramon family, Israel, NASA, and the United States.

The Israel Defense Ministry's archives released a rare video in 2021, 40 years after Operation Opera—an IAF mission that resulted in the destruction of Saddam Hussein's Osirak nuclear reactor in Iraq. In the video, Ilan Ramon shares about the fear that gripped him flying in this dangerous mission, knowing he may not return. He remembered what his mother experienced in the Auschwitz extermination camp and he shared, "Then I remembered my mother, my origin and history and that of the Jewish people, and I thought, 'there's no way that I'm going to let that happen again, no matter what happens to me.' That's what helped me go on that mission."[12]

PLACES TO VISIT: MAKHTESH RAMON

The Ramon Crater is not a stop on a typical tour route through Israel. Located in the wilderness of southern Israel, the nature reserve is teeming with wildlife, desert landscapes, and geological formations. At night, stars can be viewed as far as the eye can see. Don't forget to stop by the visitors center to honor the life of Israel's first astronaut, the late Colonel Ilan Ramon.

SHADI KHALLOUL[13]

Aramean Maronite-Christian Shadi Khalloul is from the Upper Galilee region of Israel, which borders Lebanon. As a proud Zionist,

Khalloul doesn't take his Israeli citizenship for granted. He knows Israel
is the only country in the Middle East that grants him the rights and
freedoms to practice the most significant part of his life: his ancient
Christian faith.

The Middle East has experienced a drastic decline in its Christian
population according to a 2019 report out of the United Kingdom. A
century ago, Christians made up 20 percent of the population; today
it's 4 percent, or 15 million people.[14] The vanishing presence of Middle
Eastern Christians didn't happen without a cause—they have experienced relentless persecution. Those who belong to some of the most
ancient Christian sects have been forcibly removed from their homes,
murdered, imprisoned, and discriminated against, causing many to
flee Muslim extremism.

Shadi is keenly aware of the fact that, just beyond the border, Christians are suffering in countries like Egypt, Iraq, Syria, and Saudi Arabia. In stark contrast, Israel is experiencing growth in its Christian
population.

After serving in the Israel Defense Forces, Shadi became a spokes-
person for the Christian Israel Defense Forces and founded the Israeli
Christian Aramaic Association (ICAA), whose work advances the
Aramean culture and national identity in Israel.

Aramean Christians, who speak Aramaic—the language spoken in
the Holy Land during the time of Christ—identify as descendants of
Jesus' earliest followers. There are some 15,000 Israeli Christians who
pray in the ancient Aramaic language; many of them associate with the
Syriac Maronite Church of Antioch.

For decades, the Israeli government incorrectly identified Arame-
ans as "Arab Christian." Shadi led the effort to distinguish his people from the "Arab" label, advocating for their heritage and rights as a
minority within-a-minority to be recognized in Israel.

The effort played out in the realm of education. There were
Aramean families that wished to educate their children in a nearby
Jewish school, but the local municipality refused to pay for transportation to the school. Being assigned the identity of Arab, Aramean children were placed in Arabic-speaking schools. Shadi and the families

argued that the curriculum of the schools didn't align with their values. Parents preferred a Hebrew education over an Arabic one, and wanted a school for their children that promoted Israel Defense Forces service.

The Israeli Supreme Court sided with Khalloul and the Aramean-Christian community in a landmark decision. Shadi said, "We were struggling to fix this identity, and, thanks be to God, we succeeded. It means they recognize the early Christians who inhabited this place with them and spoke the language of Jesus."[15]

Shadi continues to advocate for his people. He's currently seeking permission from the Israeli government to build an Aramean town to preserve the Aramaic culture and language. Khalloul said, "We as a minority want to live as indigenous Aramaic Christians and to be able to have one sole Aramaic town that can preserve our Christian faith, Aramaic language, ethnic identity, and our heritage and explain more about our common roots with the Jews."[16]

I hope you leave this chapter with a broader grasp of the Israeli people. There's no monolithic citizenry in Israel. Since its birth, the country has been a patchwork of peoples, languages, religions, and cultures. In Israel's Declaration of Independence, the founders of the Jewish state promised—irrespective of race, religion, or sex—it will guarantee freedom of religion, conscience, language, education, and culture for all citizens, ensuring freedom, justice, and peace as envisaged by the prophets of Israel.

These lofty ideals are etched in the foundational documents that guide the modern State of Israel. And while they are tantamount to Israeli law, history will show that the practice of these ideals has not always been executed perfectly. Minority communities, like Shadi Khalloul's, still need to fight to have their voices heard. Among all of Israel's people, there are significant social, political, and economic disagreements on how Israel should function as a Jewish state.

But that's ok!

Israel is a vibrant democracy. In fact, it's the only democracy in the Middle East, giving minority communities a voice.

CHAPTER 13

THE MIRACLE
OF ISRAEL

*"Moses dragged us for 40 years through
the desert to bring us to the one place in the
Middle East where there was no oil."*[1]

GOLDA MEIR

American billionaire Warren Buffett declared, "If you're going to the Middle East to look for oil, you can skip Israel. If you're looking for brains, look no further."[2]

Buffett should know; he's invested millions in the country that holds the nickname "Start-up Nation." Israel's citizens have looked beyond the typical way of building wealth in the Middle East and have invested their time, money, and energy in what would be considered uncommon ventures during their time in Israel's neck of the woods: science and technology.

DID YOU KNOW?

Israel boasts one of the highest numbers of start-ups per capita in the world.

The risk has reaped a great reward. Israel's tech-savvy communities have become a resource to several Fortune 500 companies who are looking for the next big discovery. Israeli ingenuity makes the little country seem much bigger than it looks.

To understand what I'm talking about, just look at the NASDAQ stock exchange in New York City. A 2012 *Bloomberg* article revealed, "China has more companies traded on the Nasdaq than any country outside of the U.S., while Israel ranks second, according to Wayne Lee, a spokesman for the New York-based bourse."[3]

Let's put that into perspective: With only eight million citizens at that time, Israel managed to take more companies public on the NAS-DAQ than all of the countries in Europe, Korea, India, and Singapore. Many of those publicly traded companies today have been acquired by larger tech giants like Facebook, Apple, Intel, and Google.

"We have enormous admiration for Israel, not just as an important ally for the US, but as a place to do business."[4]

Tim Cook, CEO of Apple

Even savvy investors want a piece of what Israel has to offer. At the end of the first half of 2021, Israel's financial tech firms raised a record $2.3 billion in venture capital.[5]

In this chapter, we will feature a few of Israel's technological advancements that have impacted nations all around the globe.

AGRICULTURE

After the War of Independence, Israel's borders started to take shape. The final armistice agreement of that war, coming in July 1949, produced the first view of the new Jewish state. A quick glance at a map from that time would reveal that more than 60 percent of the land they acquired was barren desert. Even today, more than 70 years later,

Israel's Negev desert makes up 50 percent of the country's land. A country with little usable land is unsustainable, especially for a new state.

Most would consider this predicament a setback for the Israelis, who were anxious to settle and work the country they had been fighting so desperately to defend. However, as commentator Dr. Tal Ben-Shahar of the documentary *Israel Inside* said this was an opportunity for the Israelis to turn "adversity into advantage."[6]

Israel, like most Middle Eastern countries, is starved for water, a natural resource vital to the sustainability and growth of a nation. A modern example of Israeli innovation around water use is in desalination. The Sea of Galilee was the only reliable source of clean drinking water until 2005, when the first desalination plant came online in Ashkelon—a city on the coast, next to the Mediterranean Sea.

Desalination is the process of transforming seawater into drinking water, and Israel has become a global leader in this technology. Experts believe that by 2050, 40 percent of the water Israel uses will be desalinated, 28.5 percent will be drawn from natural sources, 26 percent will be reused effluent, 3.5 percent will be brackish water, and 2 percent will be brackish desalinated water.[7]

Also, in 2015, Israel recycled 86 percent of its wastewater for use in agriculture, with the goal of reaching 95 percent recycled by 2025, much more than any other country in the world.[8]

Water management is on the mind of every Israeli and has been a perpetual topic of discussion dating back prior to Israel's independence. The idea of wasting such a precious commodity is unthinkable.

Simcha Blass, a Polish-born Jew, who immigrated to Israel in the 1930s, led Israel's national water company, Mekorot. Blass planned and managed the pipeline that pumped water from the Sea of Galilee to the Negev desert. One day, when out on an inspection he encountered something abnormal. A tree was thriving in the middle of the desert, as if it were planted by a stream. Struck by this oddity, he investigated this miracle in the desert. Blass would come to find that a slow but steady leak from an underground pipe was feeding the healthy tree a manageable amount of water daily, causing it to grow.

A lightbulb switched on for Blass. Instead of using an irrigation system that showers plants and trees from above with inconsistently effective and wasteful sprinklers, Blass envisioned a more targeted approach. In the 1960s, he took the rudimentary components of the leaky pipe that fed the flourishing tree and invented the first drip irrigation system.

DID YOU KNOW?

Israel is one of the few countries in the world that ended the twentieth century with more trees rather than fewer.

Blass then established the world's first drip irrigation system company, Netafim, on the northern edge of the Negev desert. He partnered with Kibbutz Hatzerim, a small town next to Beersheba, to manufacture the world's first commercial dripper. Drip irrigation revolutionized the way Israelis managed the desert land, fulfilling David Ben-Gurion's dream "to make the deserts bloom."[9]

Drip irrigation systems have been used since then, helping Israel become an exporter of fruits, vegetables, and flowers to the European market.[10]

Netafim is the number one provider of drip irrigation systems in the world. With 17 global manufacturing plants, the company conducts business in 110 countries spanning five continents.[11] Netafim's irrigation techniques help to produce 50 percent more crop while using 50 percent less water;[12] a benefit to countries like India, Vietnam, and the Philippines, whose agricultural output is global. Lately, the Israeli irrigation pioneer has been contracted to build automated water systems in countries like Ethiopia and Rwanda. In India, this Israeli technology will improve irrigation standards for 35,000 farmers, in 66 villages, covering more than 120,000 acres of land.[13]

PLACES TO VISIT: **THE SALAD TRAIL**

Nestled in the Negev, the Salad Trail is a guided tour into the world of Israel's high-tech agriculture industry. A professional agronomist guides you through an experience that involves picking and eating your own food.

TECHNOLOGICAL INNOVATION

Even if you've never traveled to Israel, there may be a piece of Israel with you right now. Every day, phone calls, voice mails, and text messages that are used to connect friends and family through mobile devices have become a staple in life. This essential technology had milestones in innovation that started in the Holy Land.

The Motorola cell phone made its first appearance on April 3, 1973, and in less than half a century, more than half of the world's population were carrying mobile devices in their hands.[14] In real numbers, that is 4 billion people. Mobile telecommunications is considered the fastest-growing man-made technology in history.

In 1964, Motorola was the first company from the United States to open a research and development center in Israel. It was a bold move for the pioneer in telecommunications—a gamble that proved to be very profitable. Since then, several Israeli corporations have become vital assets to the economies of China, India, and Latin America due to their early push to prioritize telecommunications.[15]

Israel's fingerprints can be seen in almost every component of your modern mobile experience. From your basic phone call, voice mail, and text message all the way to the microprocessor, Global Positioning System (GPS), camera, and facial recognition used to secure your device. It is the reason that Israel's coastal plain has been dubbed the "Silicon Wadi" of hi-tech innovation.

Intel established its first Israeli development and manufacturing center in 1974. And since then, the world's largest semiconductor chip manufacturer has been a mainstay of Israel's economy as the largest private-sector employer with 14,000 workers spanning five centers in Haifa, Petah Tiqwa, Jerusalem, Kiryat Gat, and Yakum.[16]

Intel Israel's first breakthrough came in the 1980s, when personal computers were on the cusp of becoming desktop fixtures. IBM selected Intel's Haifa-designed 8088 processor to operate its first PC—the first computer to use Microsoft software as an operating system.

Since then, Intel Israel has developed and manufactured processors that are found in most desktop, laptop, and even, mobile devices.

"We think of ourselves as an Israeli company as much as a US company."[17]

Brian Krzanich, former CEO of Intel

Israel's relationship with Intel began when Holocaust survivor and electrical engineer Dov Frohman was working for the company in California after receiving his PhD from the University of California, Berkeley in 1963.

Frohman invented EPROM, the first erasable computer memory chip. When asked how he developed the concept of erasable memory, he responded, "Daydreaming."[18] EPROM was a necessary piece of the puzzle to advance the home computing revolution, a technology that we still use in our modern devices. Gordon Moore, cofounder of Intel, once said EPROM was "as important in the development of the microcomputer industry as the microprocessor itself."[19]

Dov was three years old when his Jewish parents entrusted the care of their boy to a devout Christian family connected to the Dutch Resistance in Holland. That would be the last time young Dov ever saw his parents. The Christian family treated him like he was their own son, risking their lives to hide him from the Nazis, who had invaded the Netherlands. After the war, Dov was adopted by his uncle, who lived in Tel Aviv.

PLACES TO VISIT: MADATECH MUSEUM

The Madatech Museum in Haifa is the largest science museum in Israel. Located in the historic Technion Building, Madatech employs interactive exhibits on mechanics, robotics, aeronautics, communications, and more to create a hands-on learning experience. Don't forget to visit the palm tree planted on site by Albert Einstein back in 1923.

As a graduate of Israel's prestigious Technion, Frohman's dream was to make Israel a center of technological research. His desire fell on deaf ears for several years, but he remained persistent—a quality most Israelis possess. His vision became a reality when Intel agreed to establish a small design center in 1974. But, under the leadership of Frohman, it wouldn't remain small for very long. Intel Israel would grow to become the bedrock of Israel's hi-tech economy.

In 2014, just 40 years after Frohman opened the doors of the small design center, it was reported that Intel Israel had manufactured more than one billion microprocessors and processor components. Today, chip manufacturing companies are pouring billions of dollars into Israel. Thirty-seven multinational firms are operating in the Silicon Wadi, producing the chips needed for powering devices used all around the world.

HEALTH AND SCIENCES

When you see Dr. Amit Goffer moving about around Yokneam Illit, a town on the foothills of the Carmel Mountains, he will be standing tall and proud. Goffer is the founder of ReWalk and UPnRIDE Robotics, unique Israeli start-up companies inventing wearable mobility technology for the disabled.

Goffer, an electrical and computer engineer, founded ReWalk in 2001. He developed a robotic exoskeleton that could be fitted around the legs of those who were paralyzed from the waist down. The robotic exoskeleton gave mobility and hope back to those who were told they would never walk again.

DID YOU KNOW?

Israel has the highest percentage of engineers and scientists per capita in the world.

Just ask Claire Lomas, whose legs wouldn't move after she was thrown from her horse during an equestrian competition in the United Kingdom in 2007. The accident broke her back, damaging her spinal cord, and doctors told her she would never walk again.

Lomas heard the prognosis, but became focused on walking again. She stumbled across ReWalk while scouring the internet. Her friends and family helped raise the funds needed to purchase one of Goffer's exoskeletons. The professional equestrian diligently trained to ride a new type of "horse," one that would give her a new freedom of movement. After four months of ReWalk training, Lomas set her eyes on completing the London Marathon. In 2012, Claire Lomas crossed the finish line with her husband and child by her side, walking nearly two miles a day, for 17 days, to finish the race route.

Goffer's ingenuity has helped so many people who had lost hope in ever feeling the freedom of movement again. Yet one person the ReWalk technology couldn't help was Goffer himself. Before the company's founding, the entrepreneur was riding ATVs with his children through the ancient town of Sepphoris when his ATV careened into a tree due to a brake failure. Laying on the ground, he told his kids not to touch him, and he knew in that moment he was a quadriplegic. Goffer said, "After the injury, it took me a couple of years to get used to being in a wheelchair, and I couldn't understand why the wheelchair was the only solution for the paralyzed."[20] It was his own personal tragedy that led him to establish ReWalk.

Later, Goffer's ultimate vision—to create a device that would help everyone confined to a wheelchair—was achieved when he founded

UPnRIDE. The Israeli entrepreneur's next company invented a wheeled robotic chair that gives the user the option to be seated or upright when mobile.

Despite the tragedy of a debilitating ATV accident, Goffer never lost the dream of having the freedom to move again. He is another great example of taking a challenge presented to him and overcoming that challenge, while benefiting others in the process. And Goffer's ingenuity is just one example that represents the more than 1,500 Israeli companies creating and manufacturing in the health-care and life-sciences industries.

How does Israel do it? What's the secret to the nation's success? Well, there are two elements that are fused into the Israeli culture that I believe helps explain how they thrive.

First, Israelis hold a high view of education.

The precedence of education is embedded in the Jewish culture and can be traced back millennia, even to the origins of the synagogue. In fact, before Israel was an official state, the Jewish people living in Palestine established prominent universities such as the Technion in Haifa, the Weizmann Institute of Science in Rehovot, and the Hebrew University in Jerusalem. Graduates of these schools have gone on to become the innovators in Israel's tech industry.

PLACES TO VISIT:
WEIZMANN INSTITUTE OF SCIENCE

When in Rehovot, spending time in the Levinson Visitors Center will enlighten you about the significant contributions that the Weizmann Institute has made to the fields of science and technology that have impacted the world.

Another aspect of Israel's success is their mandatory military service for most citizens. Their obligatory service in the Israel Defense

Forces offers Israeli young adults a perfect combination of education and life experience. Years back, when I was leading a tour, we planned a visit to an Israel Defense Forces training base. While we were there, I met a 19-year-old girl who was completing her first year of service in the IDF. I asked the young woman, "What are you doing in the military?" She answered, "I'm preparing to be a ballistics engineer." I was stunned. I had never heard a 19 year-old utter the words "ballistics engineer," but mandatory military service in Israel demands many teenagers to become adults after high school. As most high school students in the West prepare for college, Israelis are taking tests on where they would best fit in their country's armed services. Soon after finishing their service, many young veterans transfer and apply what they've learned and practiced in the IDF to their education in universities and to their employment.

Israel's unwavering commitment to education and experience, coupled with its investment in technology and innovation, will continue to reward the Israelis long after the last drop of oil is pumped from the Middle East.

CHAPTER 14

POLITICS IN
ISRAEL TODAY

"The test of democracy is freedom of criticism."[1]

DAVID BEN-GURION

British-Jewish sculptor Benno Elkan designed the four-ton, 14-foot-high menorah sculpture that faces Israel's parliament building, the Knesset. The bronze candelabra was a gift from the British Labor Party to honor the creation of the State of Israel. Elkan started the project in 1950 and it was finally gifted to Israel in 1956. Elkan intended his menorah to be placed within the Knesset halls, but the powers-that-be at the time decided to move the sculpture outdoors so more people could enjoy the artwork.

Each of the menorah's branches contain reliefs depicting Israel's spiritual struggles from the Hebrew Bible. Elkan chose the center branch to convey Israel's rebirth as a nation.

The menorah is more than a candelabra; it's an enduring symbol of the continuity of the Jewish people stretching from ancient Israel in the Bible to the State of Israel that exists today. What first appeared in the book of Exodus as a light source to illuminate the Tabernacle and Temple for worship later became the symbol of Jewish freedom and liberation from tyranny during the Hasmonean period, and today, the menorah stands as the national emblem of the modern State of Israel.

Elkan engraved on the Knesset menorah, "'Not by might nor by power, but by my Spirit,' says the LORD Almighty" (Zechariah 4:6), connecting all the accounts comprised in the reliefs together. This is a biblical reminder of God's providential hand, which has provided for and protected the Jewish people through the ages.

Knesset Menorah in 1956, at the "Menorah garden."

The Knesset building is a modern square-shaped structure skirted by concrete columns. It is perched upon a hilltop in Givat Ram, on land leased from the Greek Orthodox Patriarchate, two miles from the Old City of Jerusalem.

Jerusalem has been the capital of the Jewish state since the beginning years of modern statehood. The Knesset met briefly in Tel Aviv, but transitioned temporarily to the Froumine House in Jerusalem in the spring of 1950, awaiting a more permanent home.

When the Knesset approved a plan to construct a parliamentary building, David Ben-Gurion was informed that James de Rothschild would finance its construction. James was continuing the philanthropic endeavors of his father, Baron Edmond de Rothschild, in supporting the Zionist vision. In 1966, political leaders, public servants, and heads-of-state, along with citizens from all around Israel—nearly 6,000 in total—crowded into the new plaza to dedicate the Knesset building.

PLACES TO VISIT: KNESSET

The Knesset offers free guided tours through Israel's parliament building. Learn about the history of the Israeli government and how the Knesset represents the citizens of Israel. During the tour, you'll be introduced to symbolic artwork and sculptures that tell the story of the Jewish people. And, if you get there at the right time, you may get to see a lively Plenum session taking place in person.

THE KNESSET

The Hebrew word *knesset* means to "gather" or "assemble," a term that has deep historical significance for the modern Jewish state. "Knesset" is the same word used to identify the Great Assembly: the governing body of 120 men who enforced Jewish law after Israel's return from exile. The Great Assembly was led by Ezra, the post-exilic biblical figure. Among other notable leaders were men like Nehemiah, Haggai, Zechariah, and Malachi.

Inspired by their ancestors, the modern founders of Israel emulated the number of leaders in the ancient assembly, which is the reason that today's Knesset has 120 members representing the Israeli people.

Plenum Hall, at the heart of the Knesset building, is the place where members of the Knesset gather to legislate. Tel Aviv-born artist Dani Karavan designed the back wall of Plenum Hall, behind the Speaker's podium, to use Galilee stone to depict one of Judaism's most sacred spaces, the Western Wall. Karavan called his piece "Pray for the Peace of Jerusalem" (Psalm 122:6). The stones are arranged to portray the tension and harmony between the spiritual and the earthly Jerusalem.

As mentioned before, a portrait of Theodor Herzl hangs in the hall as an homage to the visionary who said, "It is no dream" when envisioning a future Jewish state. Herzl's portrait is positioned in such a way that it seems to stare at those who legislate. His presence is felt by those who have an active role in the application of Zionism and its future.

Knesset members are seated in accordance with the party factions that they belong to, in the shape of a menorah on the Plenum Hall floor. The governing coalition that holds the most seats sits to the left, while the opposition government is arranged on the right. The prime minister and cabinet members are also Knesset members and they occupy the center of the hall. The Israeli government blends the roles of executive and legislative duties, while in other countries, the executive and legislative branches of government hold strictly separate duties.

When the Knesset meets, there are a litany of issues they might discuss: voting on bills may be brought to the floor, domestic and international issues may be debated, and motions of no confidence may be raised. As a unicameral legislative body, the Knesset requires a majority vote when passing bills and resolutions.

DID YOU KNOW?

The Chagall State Hall, in the Knesset, serves as a venue for official state events. The three tapestries that drape the back wall were designed by Jewish artist Marc Chagall. The tapestries tell the biblical story of the Jewish people and their unique link to the land of Israel.

POLITICAL PARTIES AND ELECTIONS

Israel functions as one large voting block, due to its small size. This is different from other electoral systems, like in the United States, where proportional representation to divide voters into districts is implemented. Proportional representation, in Israel's case, is best expressed by the sheer number of political parties that make up the Knesset—there are many.

When the state was founded, the Zionist movement was comprised of liberals, socialists, the right, the religious, and even communists. All these Zionists had the same desire to build a Jewish state, but they possessed very different ideas on how to actually accomplish it. To give a voice to each idea in the vast political spectrum, the founders of Israel set the party voting threshold at a measly 1 percent.

This means that if a group of like-minded politicians formed a party and established a winning platform, they only need 1 percent of the public vote to acquire seats in the Knesset. The voting threshold has increased over the years, but not by much. In 1988, it increased to 1.5 percent, it changed to 2 percent in 2003, and today it's 3.25 percent. The vast number of political parties that rise and fall is the best way to see representative government at work in Israel. Major parties focus on big-ticket issues like employment, security, taxes, and the economy (examples are Labor, Likud, and Yesh Atid), while smaller parties can garner votes with a more specific agenda—for example, the pensioner's party (Dor), the Orthodox Jewish factions (Shas and United Torah Judaism), or the Arab parties (Joint List and United Arab List [known as Ra'am]).

DID YOU KNOW?

The members of the Israeli Knesset represent the citizens of the Jewish state; they are comprised of men and women who are Jewish, Christian, Druze, and Muslim.

Parties can merge their lists of politicians to expand their power and reach. A popular merger happened in 1968 when three socialist-labor parties—Mapai, Ahdut HaAvoda, and Rafi—merged to form what is Israel's Labor Party today.

For three decades, the Labor party enjoyed wielding political power in the Knesset. Every prime minister serving up until 1977 was associated with the Zionist socialist-democratic party labor movement.

Labor's agenda fit that of the majority of the early founders, but at the turn of the twentieth century, with the failure of the Israeli-Palestinian peace process that was promoted by Labor leader Yitzhak Rabin in the early 90s, the party's influence waned. At its zenith, the Labor movement held 56 seats, or 46 percent of the vote; but today it can barely scrounge together seven seats, or 6 percent of the vote. However, the failure of the Palestinian-Israeli peace process wasn't the only issue that upended the Labor party. It was also an economic shift that occurred in Israel, almost simultaneously, thanks in part to former prime minister Benjamin Netanyahu.

Between 2003–2005, Netanyahu served as Israel's finance minister. As a graduate of MIT's Sloan School of Management, Netanyahu altered Israel's socialist course and placed it on a path looking to capitalism. He promoted privatization reforms and simplified the tax system, which increased the promoted growth and helped facilitate the creation of the start-up economy. The economic foundation he laid as finance minister was built upon through his leadership as Israel's prime minister (1996–1999, 2009–2021).

Israel's GDP increased 60 percent per capita during Netanyahu's premiership, ranking Israel as one of the top 20 nations in the world.[2]

Netanyahu is often praised for his strong stance on security combined with spearheading economic growth. But he receives heavy criticism for his abandonment of the democratic-socialist Zionism principles that David Ben-Gurion and the founders had promoted. Netanyahu is a formidable leader in Israeli politics. He is the longest-serving prime minister in Israel's history, and when he has held the premiership, many have attempted to unseat him.

By law, Israeli national elections are held every four years in the Jewish month of Cheshvan (October/November). However, elections can be instigated at any point in the four-year term if a Knesset majority votes to move to early elections. The Knesset can also dissolve the ruling government and move to early elections if they fail to approve an annual budget, or three months after the start of the fiscal year on March 31.

Whether an election is held early or at the four-year mark, after the citizens' votes are tabulated, the party with the most votes is permitted by the president to form a coalition government. Just when it seems like the politicking should be over, in some ways, it starts all over again. Typically, the leader of the winning party cobbles together enough seats from each party to exceed the 61-seat threshold to form a government.

Politicians from various parties that have political agreement typically gravitate to each other. However, to win favor with those politicians who are on the fence, some parties may require an incentive to join the coalition that forms a government. You could say that to gain power you have to give a little power. The winning party and potential prime minister will dole out coveted cabinet positions like Minister of Foreign Affairs, or Economy and Industry, or Education, or Defense, etc., to encourage other parties to join their coalition.

PLACES TO VISIT: **SUPREME COURT**

Israel's Supreme Court building, located on the same campus as the Knesset building, provides free guided tours through the halls of Israel's highest judicial authority.

There's no better example of seeing Israeli politics at work than to examine the events of the spring election of 2021. On June 13, 2021, after a total of 15 years serving as Israel's prime minister, Benjamin Netanyahu was unseated by his protégé, Naftali Bennett. For years, Netanyahu withstood a barrage of politicians vying to replace him in the premiership. From 2019–2021, he remained prime minister on three occasions, taking Israel to elections an unprecedented four times in three years. Only through the results from the fourth election of that series was Netanyahu no longer the leader of Israel.

The winning strategy that finally ousted Netanyahu was due to more than Bennett's political prowess. It was actually the willingness of unlikely alliances to partner with each other over the one political issue they all agreed on—dethroning "king" Netanyahu. Netanyahu and his Likud party were successful in winning the most votes during the election, but they couldn't muster the 61 seats needed to form a coalition government.

According to Israeli law, the president can turn to the party with the second-highest number of votes to see if they can form a coalition. After this election, that task was given to Yair Lapid, the head of the liberal party, Yesh Atid. Lapid had the same dilemma as Netanyahu; he didn't have enough allies in the Knesset to form a government. But what Lapid did next shows how you give power to gain power in the Knesset.

Lapid crossed the aisle and offered right-leaning politician Naftali Bennett the coveted prime minister position for the first half of the four-year term, provided that Bennett's Yamina party would join the change-bloc coalition. Negotiations came down to the wire, but in the end, Bennett agreed to the terms.

Lapid also partnered with Mansour Abbas, an Islamist leader of the United Arab List party. Abbas's agreement to join Lapid's coalition government marked a historical moment in the Knesset's history, marking the first time that the United Arab List party joined a coalition government. For 25 years, the United Arab List proudly sat in the opposition government, no matter who was in office.

Israeli journalist Eylon Levy described the unlikely scenario perfectly on Twitter when he wrote, "The Islamist leader just signed a deal with the liberal secular son of a Holocaust survivor to establish a government headed by a religious-nationalist and former settler leader (in a hotel named after the Maccabees). That's where we're at."[3]

PLACES TO VISIT: WOHL ROSE GARDEN

Take a leisurely stroll through the award-winning Wohl Rose Garden that separates the Knesset building from the Supreme Court building. The 19-acre park was formerly used for government purposes only, but it was later opened to the public.

BASIC LAW

Israel's Declaration of Independence vowed that a constitution would be adopted by an "Elected Constituent Assembly" no later than October 1, 1948. On December 10, 1948, two months after the deadline, a proposed constitution was prepared for ratification by a newly elected government that would become seated after the upcoming

January elections occurring a month later. Two years elapsed, and still no constitution was agreed upon. Israel's elected officials couldn't compromise on an official text that would embody the rules of their state.

DID YOU KNOW?

Israel's Declaration of Independence concludes with a line beginning with, "Placing our trust in the 'Rock of Israel'..." The phrase became a source of contention. Aharon Zisling, a left-wing leader, refused to sign the declaration if a God he didn't believe in was printed on it. Rabbi Fishman-Maimon, another signatory, who helped Ben-Gurion draft the declaration, wanted the phrase, "Placing our trust in the Rock of Israel and its Redeemer." Ben-Gurion settled on "Rock of Israel" because "rock" has various interpretations. As it turned out, Maimon had the final word. After Ben-Gurion declared independence, the rabbi stood and recited the *shehecheyanu* blessing—invoking the name of God over the ceremony.[4]

The religious parties didn't help. They refused to adopt any constitution other than the Torah. Even prime minister David Ben-Gurion shelved the topic of a constitution. He argued that time wasn't on their side; other issues like security and immigration were more pressing than a constitution.

The debate was vigorous. Ben-Gurion had a strong argument: his newly formed state was under a lot of pressure. However, the people required a system of laws that would enshrine their values. The Harari Resolution was put forth by Knesset member Yizhar Harari. He proposed a constitution that would be developed over time; it would comprise of a series of basic laws established by a committee and then approved by the Knesset instead of a document written all at once. The Harari Resolution was adopted on June 13, 1950.

The First Basic Law, approved by the Third Knesset in 1958, solidified the rules behind the function of the Knesset, the electoral system, voting rights, and defined that a two-thirds vote would be needed to change Basic Law. Other Basic Laws include the role of Israel's president (1964), the legal standing and place of the Israel Defense Forces military (1976), the establishment of Jerusalem as the unified capital of Israel (1980), the role and authority of the judiciary (1984), the protection of human dignity and liberty (1992), and the law defining Israel as the nation-state of the Jewish people (2018).

"Truth will spring up from the earth and justice
will be reflected from the heavens."

Psalm 85:12

*This psalm inspired the architecture of the Courtyard of
the Arches located in the Israeli Supreme Court.*

The custodian of the state's Basic Laws and other laws created by the Knesset is Israel's judiciary. Because the state has no written constitution to demarcate a total separation from prestate rule, certain regulations that were present at the time of the British Mandate have carried over into the way government is organized in modern statehood.

The judiciary is divided into three courts: the local magistrate courts, six district courts, and the supreme court. The local magistrate courts handle minor offenses like traffic tickets, family disputes, small claims, and issues that carry penalties of less than seven years' imprisonment if convicted. The six district courts take on the trials of cases with more than seven years' imprisonment and more than one million shekels (~$300,000) as penalty. While Israel's supreme court, located in Jerusalem, hears appeals from district court rulings and handles matters related to the government, like Knesset elections.

Israel remains the only democracy operating in the Middle East. The country is comprised of a tapestry made up of diverse individuals: men, women, secular, religious, liberal, conservative, Jewish, Muslim,

Christian, and many more. The domestic and international concerns that distress the electorate are manifest in lively Knesset debate and parties that represent both majorities and minorities. If you're a citizen of the State of Israel, by law, you have a right to stand up and make a difference. It's a right that most people living in the Middle East will never experience.

CHAPTER 15

UNDERSTANDING THE MIDDLE EAST CONFLICT

*"With cunning they conspire against your people; they plot
against those you cherish. 'Come,' they say, 'let us destroy them
as a nation, so that Israel's name is remembered no more.'"*

PSALM 83:3-4

The iconic golden rotunda, noticeable from most vantage points in the Old City of Jerusalem, is called the Dome of the Rock. It's the oldest standing Islamic shrine and it houses the sacred Foundation Stone—the exposed top of Mount Moriah. The Foundation Stone is holy to the Jewish people. It's said to be the spot where the world was formed, it's where Abraham bound Isaac, and it was the exact location of the Holy of Holies in the Jewish Temples.

Built in the late-seventh century AD, the golden-domed, octagonal-shaped monument commemorates the place Muhammad was caught up into heaven to receive divine instruction from Allah. The revered Islamic Prophet arrived atop the Temple Mount after a night journey on a winged horse that transported him from Mecca to Jerusalem.

On the southwestern end of the Temple Mount, Muslims worship at the Al-Aqsa Mosque, the second-oldest mosque in the world. Technically, the Qur'an doesn't mention Jerusalem as Muhammad's destination in the Night Vision, but instead, it says he traveled to "Al-Aqsa

Mosque," the farthest mosque from the Great Mosque of Mecca in Saudi Arabia. The Al-Aqsa Mosque is the third-holiest site in Islam.

The Temple Mount is, without a doubt, one of the holiest places in the minds of Jews, Muslims, and Christians—making it one of the most incendiary pieces of real estate in the world. A single event there can create a Middle Eastern maelstrom. For instance, in 2000, Palestinian terrorists unleashed a nearly five-year-long uprising against Israel, known as the Second Intifada, after Knesset opposition leader Ariel Sharon visited the Temple Mount. Everyone knew that his visit would

Aerial photograph of the Temple Mount: with the Western Wall, the Dome of the Rock, and the Al-Aqsa Mosque.

become a sensitive subject, but at the end of the day, he did nothing more than visit the place considered the holiest site in Judaism.

Muslims worship daily on the Temple Mount, and the numbers of worshippers swells during their holy days. On the final Friday of Ramadan, nearly half a million Muslims can be seen worshipping between the Al-Aqsa Mosque and the Dome of the Rock.

On the western side of the Temple Mount, the Jewish community comes to worship at the Western Wall. The Kotel, as it is also known, is made of retaining wall stones that bolster the platform where the Dome of the Rock stands. According to the rabbis, God's presence remains in all the stones of the Temple Mount, but the Western Wall complex is unique due to its proximity to the Foundation Stone.

In 2021, as Jews were mourning the destruction of the Temples on their most solemn day Tisha B'Av, some Orthodox Jews journeyed to the top of the Temple Mount. A clash erupted between Muslims and Israeli police over the presence of Jewish people on the Temple Mount.

Reuters news published a headline about the event that could be read as a microcosm of the Middle East conflict; it read, "Jewish visits, opposed by Palestinians, spark clashes at Jerusalem holy site."[1] Just the presence of the Jewish people visiting their sacred location was enough to incite violence.

There's no doubt the Middle East conflict is full of religious and political complexity that has unfolded in events over the past century, but the root cause of the conflict is actually pretty simple to explain.

ISLAM

Islam is more than a religion honored in the mosques of the Middle East and worldwide; the tenets of the faith permeate the culture, law, and even the politics of the Middle East. Sadly, Jew-hatred is ingrained in Muslim society; just ask Egyptian Haisam Hassanein, who graduated valedictorian from Tel Aviv University. Hassanein spoke to the crowd of international master's students at their graduation. Instead of giving a typical graduation speech about the bright future set before the graduates, he shared about questioning the assumptions of one's upbringing. Hassanein admitted to growing up in a culture that promoted anti-Israel and antisemitic values:

> My first exposure to Israel was through music and television. On the radio, there were anthems about the destruction Israel had caused. In the movies, Israelis were depicted as spies and thieves. In spite of the fact that the two countries struck a famous peace accord in 1979, the Israelis, I was told, were our eternal enemies.[2]

Antisemitism in Islam begins in their most holy writ, the Qur'an. The text denigrates and vilifies Jewish people, comparing them to "apes and swine" (Qur'an 5:60). In a historical encounter with a Jewish tribe, Banu Qurayza, Muhammad claims divine permission to steal their lands, their belongings, and to slaughter them (Qur'an 33:26-27).[3]

The hadith is an Islamic book that records the actions and words attributed to Muhammad. Inside it's written that in the last days: "The last hour would not come unless the Muslims will fight against the Jews and the Muslims would kill them until the Jews would hide themselves behind a stone or a tree and a stone or a tree would say: Muslim, or the servant of Allah, there is a Jew behind me; come and kill him; but the tree Gharqad would not say, for it is the tree of the Jews" (Sahih Muslim 2922).

The hadith's prophecy trickles down throughout Islamic society. And, when taken to an extreme, Middle Eastern leaders and heads-of-state feel justified by these texts to spout hate-filled speeches against the Jews and Israel.

The Hamas Charter of 1988 quoted the hadith verse mentioned above. Hamas is a modern terrorist organization that governs the Gaza Strip; their charter is a guiding covenant for their resistance against Israel.

At a welcoming ceremony for Pope John Paul II in Damascus, Syrian president Bashar al-Assad chose to use this unique opportunity to promulgate hate toward Israel and the Jewish people. He spoke lies about Israel's relationship with the Palestinians and then publicly stated, "They [Jews] try to kill the principle of religions with the same mentality they betrayed Jesus Christ and the same way they tried to betray and kill the Prophet Mohammad."[4] Such verbiage is similar to the centuries-old antisemitic tropes and blood libels calling all Jews "Christ-killers."

In the mosque, religious clerics regularly preach hate against the Jew and Israel. In 2015, a Jordanian cleric permitted "mandatory jihad" against the Jews, deeming them "among the brothers of apes and pigs."[5] On the other side of the Jordan River, a Palestinian cleric considered it an Islamic religious duty to hate the Jews, and any Muslim who does otherwise is considered a heretic.

"Israel is a malignant cancerous tumor in the West Asian region that has to be removed and eradicated: it is possible and it will happen."[6]

Iranian Supreme Leader Ayatollah Ali Khamenei

Muslim youth, like Hassanein, are raised watching TV, listening to music, and learning in school that Israel could never be an ally for peace. Philippe Lazzarini, the head of the United Nations Relief and Works Agency for Palestine Refugees (UNRWA), has admitted the textbooks used to educate Palestinian youth in Gaza contained "inappropriate" material glorifying terrorism.[7]

The first step to understanding the modern Middle East conflict is not to dive into the foreign policy of the past century, but to examine the Jew-hatred that's woven throughout Muslim society.

However, before we continue, I want to make an important disclaimer. I'm casting a broad net when I assign an antisemitic slant to the entire Muslim world. For decades, Israel has been an outcast in the Middle East because it is a Jewish state in a Muslim world. But it should be made known that there are scores of Muslims who wish to have peace with their Jewish neighbors, and yet those voices are often silenced.

The ethos of the Middle East is bent toward anti-Israel and anti-Jewish sentiment; as seen above, it's heard coming from heads of state, religious clerics, TV, music, film, and even school curriculum. However, when painting with such a broad brush, we can't neglect the lone, scattered voices of those who support Israel's right to exist as the only democratic Jewish state.

THE THREE NO'S

At the end of 2017, Turkish president Recep Tayyip Erdogan summoned the 57-member Organization of Islamic Cooperation (OIC) to Istanbul, Turkey, to discuss the "repercussions" of the United States' recognition of Jerusalem as the capital of Israel. Past US presidents had promised to move the US embassy from Tel Aviv to Jerusalem, but in the end, the US embassy remained in the Israeli city on the coast. President Donald Trump, however, wasn't a politician that was like his predecessors. In 2017, he announced that the United States was moving its embassy to Jerusalem.

At the OIC meeting, Palestinian president Mahmoud Abbas stood and promised that until Jerusalem is recognized as the capital of a future Palestinian state, there will be "no peace or stability" with Israel.[8]

Abbas's statement before the OIC falls in line with the history of the Muslim world saying no to Israel. The UN Partition Plan of 1947 promised the Palestinians a state; it was the original two-state solution. However, the Palestinians said, "No!"

In the aftermath of the Six-Day War of 1967, Israeli leaders thought the defeat of Egypt, Jordan, and Syria could lead to negotiating a strategy for peace, but they were wrong. A delegation of eight Arab heads-of-state drew a line in the sand with the Khartoum Resolution, which established the famous "Three No's": *no* to peace with Israel, *no* recognition of Israel, and *no* negotiations with Israel.

DID YOU KNOW?

The original Palestinian National Charter (1968) deemed Zionism an imperial, fascist, colonial movement. The Palestine Liberation

Organization considered Israel the instrument of Zionism, which they allege threatens peace in the Middle East and around the world.

In 2000, US president Bill Clinton brokered a deal between Israeli prime minister Ehud Barak and Palestine Liberation Organization (PLO) leader Yasser Arafat. Barak offered Arafat 96 percent of the West Bank, along with all of the Gaza Strip. The deal looked promising, but in the end, Arafat said, "No!"

Clinton told Arafat, "I'm a colossal failure, and you made me one."[9] Sixteen years later—while speaking at a 2016 US presidential election campaign fundraising event for then-presidential candidate Hillary Clinton—the former president remarked, "I killed myself to give the Palestinians a state. I had a deal they turned down that would have given them all of Gaza... between 96 and 97 percent of the West Bank, compensating land in Israel, you name it."[10] But, in the end, his hard work was rejected and he's never forgotten it.

In 2008, Israel had a bit of déjà vu when Israel's prime minister Ehud Olmert promised Palestinian president Abbas 93 percent of the West Bank, plus land around Gaza that would have given the Palestinians the equivalent of 100 percent of the total landmass of the West Bank. Abbas said, "No!"

Imagine how different the Middle East would look if the Arabs ever did say yes. If they had accepted the partition plan in 1947, the Arab-Israeli conflict as we know it today might not exist. If they had recognized Israel and negotiated with the Israelis, who were seeking peace with them after the Six-Day War in 1967, reconciliation could have been realized decades ago. On a smaller scale, Israel has already proven with Egypt and Jordan that establishing peace is possible.

If the Palestinians had agreed to either one of Israel's offers, in 2000 or 2008, they could have established a Palestinian state in the West Bank.

Unfortunately, the Palestinian leaders have proven time and again that they do not want peace with Israel. As the renowned Israeli diplomat Abba Eban said at the Geneva Conference in December 1973,

"The Arabs never miss an opportunity to miss an opportunity." Why would they say "No!" to everything Israel offered them?

FROM THE RIVER TO SEA, PALESTINE WILL BE FREE!

"From the river to the sea, Palestine will be free!" is a slogan used by many radical pro-Palestinian supporters. As you've read above, Israel has been willing to take positive steps toward establishing a Palestinian state. However, every offer receives the same response. The constant rejection of peace stems from more than not getting what is wanted in the negotiations. The sentiment in the room seems to be that the "No!" will become a "Yes!" only when all of the land falls under Palestinian control.

DID YOU KNOW?

The Palestinians hold fast to a political position called the Right of Return, which guarantees the first-generation Palestinian refugees and their descendants the right to return to the properties their family left behind or were forced to leave, on some occasions, in what is now Israel and the Palestinian territories.

Arafat and Abbas were both keenly aware of their plight on the subject of peace. Any deal that requires negotiations with Israel will be met with swift opposition by their people and the surrounding Muslim nations. Why? Because, at its core, a rejection of peace is a rejection of Israel's right to exist.

Here's a perfect example: Without any negotiation tactics, Israeli prime minister Ariel Sharon unilaterally handed the Gaza Strip over to the Palestinians in 2005 in what looked like the first installment of future Palestinian statehood. To show the seriousness of this decision, the Israeli government elected to evict 9,000 Israeli citizens from the houses they had called home for nearly 40 years. This historic event was dubbed "The Disengagement Plan."

Upon disengagement, the Palestinians would also acquire farm fields and 3,000 Israeli greenhouses on the land, which netted a lucrative income from exporting vegetables and flowers to Europe. As the last Jew left Gaza in August 2005, the Palestinians looted and destroyed the fields and greenhouses that could have provided employment and income for their people. Why would they do this? Because the fields and greenhouses were Jewish.

Years afterward, on *The Daily Show with Jon Stewart*, the comedian and political commentator questioned former-secretary of state Hillary Clinton on the abysmal status of the Gaza Strip. Her response struck at the heart of the Middle East conflict:

> You know, when Israel withdrew from Gaza…they left a lot of their businesses—there was a really very valuable horticultural business that was set up by the Israelis who had lived in Gaza. And the idea was that this would be literally turned over—money was provided, there would be a fund that would train Palestinians in Gaza to do this work. And basically, the leadership said "we don't want anything left from Israel" [and] destroyed it all. That mentality to me is hard to deal with.[11]

Clinton's assessment of their attitude of "we don't want anything from Israel," even if it's for the good of our people, cuts to the heart of the Middle East conflict. Any plan to stabilize the region or bring peace between Israel and the Palestinians will receive a "No!" as long as the Jewish state has anything to do with it.

Hamas' resistance has influenced the Palestinians of the West Bank. A poll from June 2021 found that 53 percent of the Palestinians in the West Bank believe that Hamas is "most deserving of representing and leading the Palestinian people."[12] This statistic is a hard pill to swallow, given that Article 6 of their Hamas Charter states, "The Islamic Resistance Movement is a distinguished Palestinian movement, whose allegiance is to Allah, and whose way of life is Islam. It strives to raise the banner of Allah over every inch of Palestine…"[13]

Currently, the Middle East conflict is at a stalemate. As things stand today, there's very little movement toward peace between the Palestinians and Israel. However, that doesn't mean that peace isn't achievable. In coming chapters, you'll see some of the steps that have been taken to turn those "No!" answers into "Yes!"

CHAPTER 16

ISRAEL AND THE UNITED STATES

"I will bless those who bless you, and whoever curses you I will curse; and all peoples on earth will be blessed through you."

GENESIS 12:3

A 30-foot-tall bronze American flag waving in the shape of a flame that is pointing to the heavens can be found in the center of the Arazim Valley of Ramot in Jerusalem. The impressive sculpture made of bronze, granite, and aluminum is the centerpiece of the 9/11 Living Memorial, a circular plaza dedicated to the memory of the nearly 3,000 Americans who perished on September 11, 2001.

The 9/11 Living Memorial, dedicated in 2009, was purposefully positioned to face Jerusalem's main cemetery, Har HaMenuchot. Metal plaques skirt the plaza, each one listing the names of the victims of terror who died on that fateful day. Presently, the 9/11 Living Memorial located in Israel remains the only memorial outside of the United States that lists each person's name.

As Americans gather annually on September 11—at the Twin Towers site, at the Pentagon, and in Shanksville, Pennsylvania—to remember that fateful day in American history, Israelis too join in solidarity at the 9/11 Living Memorial in Jerusalem to remember. The event has featured ambassadors, heads of state, and first responders from both Israel and the United States.

The 9/11 Living Memorial is just one of many links in a long historical chain that binds together Israel and the United States, a union that predates both Israel's independence and the American Revolution.

FROM THE LIBERTY BELL
TO ISRAEL'S RECOGNITION

The principles of liberty and freedom remain the cornerstone of the experiment called the United States. These foundational principles were extracted from the Jewish Scriptures by America's Founding Fathers. The biblical inscription etched on the Liberty Bell comes from Leviticus 25:10: "Proclaim liberty throughout all the land unto all the inhabitants thereof" (KJV). This defines the American spirit to this very day.

Thomas Jefferson, Benjamin Franklin, and John Adams viewed themselves as Israelites in the midst of an exodus, escaping the oppression of the king of England. The first official seal of the United States, submitted by these three Founding Fathers, depicted the Israelites on their way through the middle of the Red Sea—behind them was Pharaoh and in front of them was Moses, leading the way to freedom.

America's fourth president, James Madison, proposed the structure of three branches for the US government at the Constitutional Convention of 1787. He based the proposal on Scripture from the prophet Isaiah: "The

Service members from the United States and Israel at the 9/11 Living Memorial, honoring those who perished during the attacks that occurred on September 11, 2001.

LORD is our judge [judicial branch], the LORD is our lawgiver [legislative branch], the LORD is our king [executive branch]" (Isaiah 33:22, Madison's branch proposals added).

The earliest US presidents were vocal about the role the Hebrew Scriptures took in establishing the United States and the hope for the reconstitution of an independent Jewish state. John Adams, for instance, said, "I really wish the Jews again in Judea an independent nation, for as I believe…once restored to an independent government and no longer persecuted, they would soon wear away some of the asperities and peculiarities of their character."[1] In the Emancipation Proclamation, Abraham Lincoln shared that he believed that many Americans wished to see the Jewish people receive their own homeland: "It is a noble dream and one shared by many Americans."[2]

Also, Harry Truman's trusted personal adviser and friend, Clark Clifford, said in an interview that Truman was "a real student of the Bible" and "felt that there was an obligation and a commitment made in the Old Testament that one day the Jews would have a homeland and that appealed to him a great deal."[3] The thirty-third president's approach to the Scriptures was more than likely the impetus for recognizing Israel only 11 minutes after Israel declared its independence in 1948, despite then-secretary of state George Marshall strongly advising against the action.

"I had faith in Israel before it was established; I have faith in it now."[4]

Harry Truman

Marshall warned President Truman that taking sides pitted America against the Arab nations, which would only add gasoline to the volatile Middle Eastern fire. Speaking of gasoline, Marshall was also worried that Truman's decision would upset the nations who controlled the world's oil supply. Finally, the former secretary of state believed that Israel didn't stand a chance in battle against the Arab world.

Marshall's assessment of the situation was valid, but not enough to deter President Truman from recognizing the Jewish state. During his meeting with Truman, Marshall became so irritated that he promised he would not vote for Truman when he would run for reelection.

US PRESIDENTS AND ISRAEL

The United States remains Israel's strongest ally and friend in the world. Many presidents since Truman have commented on the moral and strategic partnership shared between the two nations. President John F. Kennedy was drawn to the "prophetic spirit of Zionism" that encourages all free men to look to a better world.[5]

Yet in the years right after the Truman administration, there was radio silence between the United States and Israel over concerns that Israel's socialist leanings would cause them to walk into the arms of the communist Soviets. For that reason, the US State Department and the Pentagon had no interest in selling arms to Israel, fearing to do so would start a regional arms race. Since its rebirth, Israel had valued American support over that of the Soviets.

The arms embargo was lifted in 1962 during the Kennedy administration. He was the first president to enhance the US-Israeli partnership, greenlighting the sale of Hawk ground-to-air missiles after Egyptian president Nasser entertained the USSR with an $83 million arms deal.

PLACES TO VISIT: YAD KENNEDY

Yad Kennedy is a memorial to US president John F. Kennedy and is located near Jerusalem. The memorial stands 60 feet high and is designed in the shape of the stump of a tree, a metaphor for a life that ended early. Fifty-one columns surround the memorial to represent each US state, plus Washington, DC.

After the Six-Day War in 1967, America changed its outlook on Israel. Israel's identity changed from an indefensible state to a powerful nation that could help put a stop to the spread of communism in the Middle East. Kennedy's successor, Lyndon B. Johnson, expanded ties with Israel. Like Truman, supporting Israel was personal to him. During the Johnson administration, the US became Israel's number-one ally and principal arms supplier—a vital relationship after the Six-Day War.

Johnson once told a Jewish audience that his support for Israel is grounded in the Bible stories from his childhood, and for that reason, "the gallant struggle of modern Jews to be free of persecution is also woven into our souls."[6] Those Bible stories were more than words on a page for Johnson; in 1938, then-US Representative Johnson moved hundreds of Jews through Cuba, Mexico, and South America into Texas, creating a refuge for Jewish people escaping eastern Europe, an action that could have barred him from Congress.[7]

Israel's security needs were the reason America became Israel's principal arms supplier, but Ronald Reagan strengthened ties with the Jewish state to an even greater level. Decades before Reagan was president of the United States, he was president of the Screen Actors Guild, where he befriended Jewish people in the film industry. The former actor was a part of Hollywood's elite, but that didn't mean he sacrificed his morals to be accepted by the glitterati. In the late 1940s, Reagan stood up for his Jewish friends by canceling his membership with the prestigious Lakeside Country Club because they refused to admit Jewish people into their membership.

Once president of the United States, thawing the Cold War was a priority on Reagan's foreign agenda. Israel was the only Middle Eastern ally America could trust, and for that reason, he was the first president to call Israel a "strategic asset."[8] "The Gipper" believed that a strong democratic Jewish state in the Middle East could thwart the Soviets' communist influence.

A Memorandum of Understanding (MOU) was signed on November 31, 1981, in Washington, DC. The MOU was the first formal document that considered Israel a strategic ally of the United States. Reagan invited other Middle Eastern countries to participate in resisting the Soviets, but they were more interested in overthrowing Zionism than combating communism.

DID YOU KNOW?

The Israeli Air Force developed a fighter jet called the Lavi. The prototype was controversial and some feared that the Lavi would create serious competition with the United States' F-16 and F/A-18 fighter jets.

Reagan's successor, George H.W. Bush, stated that the friendship between the two countries remained "strong and solid."[9] As vice president, Bush was influential in helping to free refuseniks—Soviet Jews who were denied visas to emigrate to Israel. On the eve of Mikhail Gorbachev's White House meeting with President Reagan, Vice President Bush spoke to the largest gathering of Jews in American history on the National Mall. In the spirit of Reagan's "Tear down this wall" address, Bush vowed he would urge the Soviet leader to free the Jewish people when he said, "Mr. Gorbachev! Let these people go. Let them go."[10]

Interestingly, during Bush's presidency, the administration had some tense moments with Israeli prime minister Yitzhak Shamir and the American Jewry. Bush lost two-thirds of the Jewish vote in his bid for reelection in 1992 to Bill Clinton.

President Clinton reassured Israel that the United States was a firm partner, with values built on a shared heritage. Clinton attempted to bring peace and stability between Israel and Palestinians. The Oslo Accords were signed in 1993, and Israel and Jordan signed a peace treaty in 1994. And yet by the end of his administration, with one last push for peace, an agreement could not be reached—giving rise to the Second Intifada.

President George W. Bush considered the State of Israel "one of our most important friends in the world."[11] In June 2003, he introduced the "Road Map to Peace" to Israelis and Palestinians as a guide to end the violence of the Second Intifada and establish a peaceful Palestinian state. Israeli prime minister Ariel Sharon did perform a withdrawal from Gaza in 2005, but the Road Map became a dead end.

"Our two nations have a lot in common when you think about it. We were both founded by immigrants escaping religious persecution in other lands. We both have built vibrant democracies. Both our countries are founded on certain basic beliefs, that there is an Almighty God who watches over the affairs of men and values every life. These ties have made us natural allies, and these ties will never be broken."[12]

George W. Bush

By 2008, president Barack Obama reiterated the platitudes of his predecessors by saying, "We're going to keep standing with our Israeli friends and allies."[13] Obama was influential in funding Israel's Iron Dome system. In May 2010, Obama requested Congress to provide $205 million for the production and deployment of the antimissile system, which has saved countless Israeli lives. However, in 2015, the controversial Iran Deal (JCPOA) was heavily criticized by Israel and several Sunni Muslim countries. They viewed the deal as a way for Iran to normalize relations with the Western world, while simultaneously continuing uranium enrichment and funding terrorism throughout the Middle East.

Israel and the United States remained close allies, but in Obama's final years as president, his policies created tensions. As the forty-fourth president's second term was coming to a close, he signaled to his UN Ambassador to abstain from a controversial United Nations Security Council resolution calling for Israel to end settlement building in Palestinian territory, which allowed it to pass easily. The relationship between the two countries was strained upon Obama's departure, but it gave way to four years of positive interaction with the Trump administration.

DID YOU KNOW?

During the Obama administration, the United States provided $1.6 billion in funding to Israel for the Iron Dome. The missile intercept

system is used to shoot down rockets fired by Hamas in Gaza and
Hezbollah in Lebanon.

President Trump made many promises concerning Israel during
his campaign, which he fulfilled during his term. He told the Israeli-
American Council National Summit, "The Jewish state has never had a
better friend in the White House than your president, Donald J. Trump."[14]
Trump took a different approach to the Israeli-Palestinian conflict than
the presidents before him; he cut through the decades of failed Middle East
diplomacy by recognizing Jerusalem as the capital of Israel and by moving the United States embassy from Tel Aviv to Jerusalem. A few months
later, Trump recognized the Golan Heights as sovereign Israeli territory
bordering Syria. He also advanced the "Peace to Prosperity" plan, a vision
to establish peace between Israelis and Palestinians, which was approved
by certain Middle Eastern countries, but was rejected by the Palestinians.

America's chief-executive's support for Israel is best seen played out
in the halls of the United Nations, where anti-Israel sentiment runs wild.
In just eight years, between 2012 and 2020, the UN General Assembly
voted on 225 resolutions: 180 resolutions were against Israel, while 45
were related to the rest of the world.[15] America consistently sides with
Israel on the vast majority of those resolutions—so much so, that many
resolutions are withdrawn knowing a United States veto is certain.

The position of US ambassador to the United Nations is an office
that is occupied by a presidential nominee, then confirmed by Congress. This US spokesperson to the world, in many ways, serves at the
pleasure of the president, which reflects that decisions made by the
United States to support Israel in the United Nations are decisions that
originate from discussions that occur in the Oval Office.

BIPARTISAN CONGRESSIONAL SUPPORT AND ISRAEL

United States foreign policy is driven by the president's agenda,
which means Israeli leaders are quick to adjust from one administration

to another. No modern president has outright neglected to work with Israel, but there have been tense moments between the two countries.

The United States Congress, on the other hand, has maintained a bipartisan support for the State of Israel in both chambers ever since the Yom Kippur War in 1973.

In 1996, Israel commemorated Jerusalem's tri-millennium: 3,000 years as the capital of Israel and the center of Jewish life. Leading up to the celebrations, the US Congress passed the Jerusalem Embassy Act on October 23, 1995. The bill was in motion at the height of President Clinton's peace talks between the Israelis and Palestinians.

The president was worried that the Palestinians could bow out of the peace negotiations if Congress approved the bill that would recognize Jerusalem as the undivided capital city of the State of Israel and require that the United States embassy be moved from Tel Aviv to Jerusalem by May 31, 1999. Congress also vowed to remove 50 percent of the upkeep budget for every embassy and state building around the world if an embassy was not opened in Jerusalem by the 1999 deadline, three and a half years later.

Clinton viewed that the Jerusalem Embassy Act could stall the progress toward peace. In July 2000, he shared the perspective he held during his presidency on what moving the embassy could mean: "I have always wanted to move our Embassy to west Jerusalem. We have a designated site there. I have not done so because I didn't want to do anything to undermine our ability to help to broker a secure and fair and lasting peace for Israelis and for Palestinians."[16]

The White House contested the unconstitutional nature of the bill. Clinton argued it removed his authority over foreign affairs. Congress then amended the bill to include a presidential waiver, postponing the embassy's relocation.

In the end, Congress was not hampered by most of Clinton's concerns. The bill advanced through both chambers with no opposition in the Senate (voted, 93-5) and in the House of Representatives (voted, 374-37). Clinton never signed nor vetoed the bill, automatically ratifying it after ten days of sitting on the Resolute Desk.

The embassy relocation waiver was signed every six months by successive administrations: Clinton, then Bush, then Obama, and also Trump. But President Trump ended this cycle on May 14, 2018, when he officially opened the United States embassy in Jerusalem, on Israel's seventieth anniversary.

PLACES TO VISIT:
UNITED STATES EMBASSY IN JERUSALEM

The United States embassy in Israel, originally located in Tel Aviv, was relocated to the Talpiot neighborhood in Jerusalem under the guidance of the Trump administration. The embassy straddles the 1949 armistice line that once divided East and West Jerusalem, a visible sign that the United States recognizes Jerusalem as the undivided capital of Israel.

Presidents may have their own foreign policy agendas that they wish to see fulfilled, but Congress has substantial powers to influence foreign policy through resolutions, financial assistance, and military aid. Congress has advanced their relationship with Israel through the resolutions of support, friendship, peace, condemning adversaries and boycotts, recognizing Jerusalem, and joint ventures. To this day, Israel remains the largest beneficiary of United States funding since World War II.[17] The military support of Israel remains a Congressional priority in order to ensure the tiny Jewish nation is capable of defending itself.

DID YOU KNOW?

Israel is one of the largest cumulative recipients of United States foreign aid. They are also given more freedom to spend the money readily, compared to other countries that receive foreign aid.

There are disagreements between Republicans and Democrats on the future of a two-state solution, but nonetheless, the members of the two parties still throw their support behind the Jewish state—some more loudly than others. The unique relationship that exists between the United States and Israel shouldn't be taken for granted. As of late, the progressives within the Democratic party have become more vocal about their disgust toward Israel and consider the Congressional support immoral.

For the time being, the special relationship between the United States of America and Israel remains firmly intact. And the reason is because Israel is rooted in the hearts of the American people, who vote for their representatives. According to an annual Gallop poll, 75 percent of Americans in 2021 had a favorable outlook on Israel—which in turn, is reflected in their votes.[18] The goal for Israel is to remain a bipartisan subject of conversation in the halls of the US Capitol and the White House, and in the everyday discourse of the American public.

CHAPTER 17

MESSIANIC JUDAISM

"I am not ashamed of the gospel, because it is the
power of God that brings salvation to everyone who
believes: first to the Jew, then to the Gentile."

ROMANS 1:16

Adjacent to Ben Gurion International Airport is a small, inconspicuous village that probably experiences more traffic in their skies than on their roads. Kfar Chabad has all the character of a typical Jewish village. The houses resemble most Israeli homes made of concrete, stucco, and red-tiled roofs. But the whole Mediterranean vibe is thrown off by a large, obtrusive, stand-alone brownstone house.

The one-off, three-story apartment house wasn't the brainchild of some avant-garde Israeli architect with an agenda. The brownstone is a brick-for-brick replica of the international headquarters of the ultra-Orthodox Jewish Chabad movement that is located on 770 Eastern Parkway in Brooklyn, New York. It was also home to the late ultra-Orthodox rabbi Menachem Mendel Schneerson. Many of his followers believed he was Israel's messiah.

Construction on the Kfar Chabad brownstone reproduction started in 1992 and it was slated to become the home for Rabbi Schneerson; yet the elderly rabbi died two years later.

The Russian-born rabbi never promoted himself as messiah, yet through his charismatic leadership and his prophetic accuracy about both the fall of the Soviet Union and Israel's victory in the Six-Day War, the Hasidim (ultra-Orthodox) considered him their messiah.

The "Rebbe," as he was called, elevated the status of the Chabad movement, and he became the figurehead of Orthodox Judaism. In 1978, US president Jimmy Carter, at the behest of Congress, designated Schneerson's birthday as National Education Day. The rabbi corresponded with Presidents Carter and Reagan throughout their terms.

Schneerson's death divided the Hasidim. Some abandoned hope in his rule, while others claimed he will resurrect one day, and a radical minority still believe Schneerson lives in an invisible form in the Brooklyn Chabad headquarters. Even in his absence, posters with Schneerson's face are plastered all throughout Israel and ultra-Orthodox communities around the world say, "He is the King, the Messiah."

At a Chabad conference in 2017, Rabbi Reuven Wolf announced to 5,000 Hasidic men in Brooklyn that he believed, at his "inner core," that the late Rebbe Schneerson would soon return to prepare the world for redemption.[1]

There's another Jewish group who also believes the Messiah has come and is coming again. He fulfilled the messianic prophecies of the Old Testament, died a sinner's death though He was innocent, was buried in a tomb, and unlike Schneerson, He gloriously resurrected three days later. This Messiah wasn't born in Russia. He was born in Bethlehem and His name is Jesus!

Today, Jesus the Messiah is sitting at the right hand of the Father and, according to the New Testament, He promised to return in glory and power to bring redemption to Israel and rescue the world from Satan's grip.

What's interesting about these two groups of Jewish people is that they are both messianic. However, the ultra-Orthodox who believe Schneerson is the messiah are invited to maintain their Jewish identity. While the Messianic Jews who have placed their faith in Jesus are ostracized and considered outcasts of Judaism.

DID YOU KNOW?

Messianic Jews deal with a certain level of nonviolent persecution in the land of Israel. Additionally, new immigrants may experience opposition to making aliyah to Israel for their profession in Jesus.

WHAT DOES MESSIANIC JUDAISM EVEN MEAN?

Messianic Judaism is a confusing title because, as you read above, those who believe Rebbe Schneerson is the messiah and someone who calls Jesus the Messiah are both labeled "messianic." Additionally, there is a difference between Judaism and Jewishness. Judaism is a religious system of mandatory laws, while Jewishness is a culture. For the purposes of this book's usage, when we talk about a Messianic Jew, we are referring to a person who believes Jesus is the Son of God, Messiah of Israel, and the Savior of the world, while maintaining some degree of Jewishness in their life.[2] Every journey of each Jewish believer is different. Some come to faith and join the local church in their town, while others strive to maintain a Torah-observant lifestyle.

For instance, my dear friend and colleague Steve Herzig was raised in an Orthodox Jewish home in Cleveland, Ohio. After he prayed to receive Jesus as his Messiah, Steve wanted to be baptized, and he knew that baptism was not something that was going to be offered at his Orthodox synagogue. In fact, when his parents found out that he had become a Messianic Jew, they barred him from living at home and going to church—so he moved west, to California.

The idea of going to church was still unsettling for Steve, but at the first service he attended, the pastor preached from the prophet Isaiah and, front-and-center in the church, Steve saw a menorah. These were both symbols that brought him comfort as a new Jewish believer.

Other Jewish believers feel more comfortable attending Messianic synagogues. These congregations worship Jesus as the Messiah, but look and sound more like a synagogue than a church. Instead of meeting on Sunday morning, Messianic synagogues gather on Shabbat. They honor Jewish holidays like Passover and Yom Kippur. Hanukkah is celebrated as more prevalent than Christmas or Easter. And life-cycle events like circumcision and bar/bat mitzvah are central in community life. Essentially, Messianic synagogues allow the Jewish followers of Jesus to maintain a high degree of Jewishness.

"To this day, the Jewish liturgy speaks of God as 'the God of Abraham, the God of Isaac, and the God of Jacob,' referring in the last two phrases to the special son and grandson through whom, according to the biblical narrative, the Jewish people came into existence."[3]

Jon Levenson

Jewish identity is at the heart of Messianic Judaism, and that raises these questions: Should Jewish believers be required to put aside their Jewish culture and customs when they place their faith in Jesus? Is it biblical for Jewish believers to incorporate the Jewish practices in their worship?

MESSIANIC JUDAISM THROUGHOUT HISTORY

We will look at questions like the ones above a little later in this chapter, but first we will look at how Messianic Judaism has been practiced through the years. We will review what Messianic Judaism looked like through three different periods of history: during the time of the early church, after the destruction of the Second Temple, and within the last two centuries.

The Early Church

The earliest church was composed entirely of Messianic Jewish believers. In Acts 2, the apostle Peter, a Jewish man himself, preached the good news of Jesus to his fellow "Israelites" (Acts 2:22). "Therefore let all Israel be assured of this: God has made this Jesus, whom you crucified, both Lord and Messiah" (Acts 2:36).

Peter was preaching to Jewish people from all over the known world. They were celebrating Shavuot (Pentecost), one of the three biblical festivals that required Jews to worship in Jerusalem. Nearly 3,000 Jewish people trusted in the Messiah, Jesus, that day. When they left Jerusalem, they found new life in Christ (Messiah) coupled with the indwelling of the Holy Spirit, yet they didn't abandon their Hebraic heritage.

The issue faced in the early church wasn't, How much Judaism do we maintain as Jewish followers of Jesus? Rather, it was, How do we invite Gentiles into this new community?

In Acts 10, Peter was faced with a change from everything he had previously known. He was flabbergasted that the Lord would entice him to eat unkosher foods that would make him ceremonially unclean. Three times he refused the command, but Jesus said to him, "Do not call anything impure that God has made clean" (Acts 10:15).

The vision Peter had served two functions: First, Peter's vision and the circumstances around it revealed God's call to minister to the Gentile world. Second, Jesus was permitting his disciples to eat with Gentiles in order to bring them the gospel. The first-century Jewish community considered Gentiles unclean, but God deemed them worthy of His grace, so they needed to be presented with the gospel—a baton that would be carried later by the apostle Paul.

"Israel has survived every satanic attempt to destroy it and will continue to do so (Isaiah 54:17). God will preserve Israel and cause the nation to flourish in its own land, as He has promised because it plays a primary role in implementing God's theocratic Kingdom on Earth after Christ's Second Coming."[4]

David Levy

James, the half brother of Jesus, led the Jerusalem Council, the body who oversaw the disputes that arose in the early church. One such dispute appears in Acts 15, and the issue dealt with the circumcision of Gentiles who had placed their faith in Christ.

The Jerusalem Council, which was comprised of the 12 apostles, determined that Gentiles were not required to fulfill the law of circumcision in order to be a part of the body of the Messiah. However, there is no indication that the Jerusalem Council insisted Jewish followers of Jesus were obligated to refrain from circumcision.

Toward the end of Acts, the apostle James confronted Paul as the apostle to the Gentiles was gaining a reputation among Jewish believers in Jesus. They were concerned Paul was teaching Jewish people who live in the diaspora "to forsake Moses, telling them not to circumcise their children or walk according to our customs" (Acts 21:21 ESV). Paul dispelled the rumors when he assisted four Jewish believers in Jesus in purification rites at the Temple to show the spirit of sensitivity toward his Jewish brothers.

What must be seen in the book of Acts is that Jewish believers maintained their Judaic identity in the way they worshipped God. In today's Christian culture, it's an anomaly to consider a Jewish person a follower of Jesus, let alone the fact that he or she may still maintain aspects of Judaism as a form of worship to the Lord.

The Quick Fade

As more Gentiles embraced the gospel, coupled with the destruction of the Temple, in AD 70, and the end of the Second Jewish Revolt led by false messiah, Bar Kochba, in AD 135, the Messianic Judaism of the early church faded quickly.

A prime example of Messianic Judaism being present in the lives of believers during the first century, and into the second century, were the Nazarenes. They were a small sect of Jewish Christians that could be traced back to the earliest church in Jerusalem. The apostle Paul was considered to be a leader of the Nazarenes (Acts 24:5).

The Second Jewish Revolt against Rome (AD 132–135) created a major divide between Jewish believers, like the Nazarenes, from the rest of the Jewish community. No Jewish person wished to see the fall of Jerusalem, but when the military leader Simeon bar Kosiba was hailed as the messiah and given the title "Son of the Star," *Bar Kochba*—referring to Numbers 24:17—the Nazarenes parted ways. They fled to Pella, and after the revolt, settled into cities surrounding the Sea of Galilee, in Syria, and as far as Iraq, until the fifth century.

The fourth-century church father from Judea, Epiphanius, defined the Nazarenes perfectly: "Only in this respect they differ from the Jews and Christians: with the Jews they do not agree because of their belief in Christ, with the Christians because they are trained in the Law, in circumcision, the Sabbath and the other things."[5] The Nazarenes were Jewish Christians in every respect, but they worshipped God through obedience to the law—maintaining their Jewish identity.

During the fourth century, Emperor Constantine established Christianity as the state religion of the Roman Empire. As a result, the church quickly abandoned its Jewish roots. For instance, Sunday was codified as the official day of worship, abandoning those Jewish believers that honored Sabbath but gathered on Sunday to worship the risen Messiah. Also, after the fourth century, Jewish people who did come to faith in Jesus were forced to abandon their Jewish identity altogether.

The Resurgence

On May 2, 1922, Victor Buksbazen, an 18-year-old Jewish teenager, placed his faith in Jesus as his Messiah on a cold winter night in Warsaw, Poland. He was surrounded by Jewish believers in a small chapel; sadly, several of those who celebrated Victor's salvation found their demise less than 20 years later at the hands of the Nazis. Even the chapel building couldn't escape Hitler's fury; it too was destroyed during the Holocaust.

Victor's father first embraced the Lord Jesus and he talked to his young son regularly about the Messiah. Yet he still wanted Victor to receive a Jewish education at a *yeshiva* (a Jewish school that teaches rabbinic literature) so he could learn as much as he could about Judaism.

Victor's father died not long after returning from the battlefields of World War I. Just before his death, he told Victor, "You are young and free. If you ever reach the conviction that Jesus is the true Messiah and your Savior, then do not hesitate to make an open confession of Him."[6]

Victor Buksbazen gave his life to Jesus the Messiah.

In 1935, Victor met Lydia Sitenhof in London; she too was a Jewish believer. Lydia moved to Poland to do ministry with her fiancée. She sensed the rising danger coming from Germany and prompted Victor to move them out of Poland. Lydia and Victor moved to London, got married, and eventually made it to the United States, where he became the first executive director of the Friends of Israel Missionary and Relief Society, which would later become the Friends of Israel Gospel Ministry.

The nineteenth and twentieth centuries saw thousands of Jewish people come to faith. Protestant missions societies were financially supporting missionaries to share the gospel around the world and they became increasingly sensitive to cross-cultural ministry. Jewish believers were permitted to be identified as "Hebrew Christians," which for the previous nearly 2,000 years the church would have considered nonsense.

DID YOU KNOW?

A study done by Israel College of the Bible found that in 1948, there were 23 Messianic Jewish believers in Israel. In 2017, there were 300 Messianic congregations and an estimated 30,000 Jewish believers.[7]

Missions agencies to the Jews formed as early as 1809. The London Society for Promoting Christianity Amongst the Jews (1809) and the Hebrew Christian Alliance of Great Britain (1866) equipped believers to share their faith with Jewish people. It should be noted that these early Jewish missions did not promote Messianic Judaism; they encouraged Jewish believers to attend Protestant churches.

A movement arose of Jewish believers who preferred to uphold Judaism; these Jewish believers eventually labeled themselves "Messianic Jews."[8] They refused to assimilate into what they considered a Gentilized church with all its non-Jewish practices.

The first publication of *The Messianic Jew* in 1910 created quite a stir. Its articles encouraged Jewish believers to live a life guided by the Torah. Pushback from other Jewish believers challenged the Messianic Jewish movement, arguing that a Torah-observant Jew hampers their own spiritual growth and confuses Gentiles; some even considered it heretical.

Messianic Judaism was once an outlier, but today it has become more widely accepted by Jewish believers.

MESSIANIC CONGREGATIONS

Jewish believers can decide how their own Jewishness is integrated into their daily lives. This is practiced both in their homes and in their community worship. Many become part of predominately Gentile churches, while others join Messianic congregations. Remember, Messianic congregations are communities of worship where Jewish believers can maintain a unique Jewish identity. Services often take place on Friday evenings or Saturday mornings to welcome in Shabbat. The congregants honor the Feasts of Israel and observe some Jewish life-cycle events. What makes a Messianic congregation different from a typical Jewish synagogue is their belief in Jesus as the Son of God and the value they place on the New Testament.

IS MESSIANIC JUDAISM UNBIBLICAL?

Is Messianic Judaism contrary to the Word of God? To me, the answer all hinges on the question of whether or not a particular Messianic believer or congregation violates the New Testament teaching concerning the liberty both the Jew and Gentile have in Christ. If a Jewish person wishes to maintain degrees of Jewish life like circumcision, keeping kosher, honoring the Sabbath, and observing Jewish festivals as a form of worship to Christ, they certainly have the liberty to do so. As seen earlier, Paul himself had no problem observing certain Jewish rituals. Messianic Judaism creeps into unbiblical territory when Judaism takes precedence over the core doctrine of belief in Jesus as a prerequisite for salvation, therefore isolating Gentile Christians from fellowship.

LIBERTY IN MESSIAH

Opponents of Messianic Judaism fear that the movement is a resurgence of *Judaizers* from the first century AD, a fear that's duly noted. Judaizers taught that true followers of Jesus must conform to the Mosaic Law. They believed Gentiles had to become Jewish proselytes first, and then they could come to the Messiah. And historically, Messianic Judaism has received pushback because the apostles dealt specifically with the issue of Judaizing in the early church.

When the apostle Paul—"a Hebrew of Hebrews"—came to faith in Jesus, he learned his status in and knowledge of Judaism was rubbish compared to knowing Christ; Judaism was incapable of delivering him from the bondage of sin that separated him from God (Philippians 3:4-9). But remember, the apostle Paul and the Jerusalem Council in Acts 15 wrestled with this issue and agreed that Gentiles and Jews are united as one body under the fellowship of faith in Jesus. It's by faith people are saved, not by the ritual practices of the Mosaic Law that affirm one's Judaism. It all depends on where one places their identity.

Let's go back to my friend Steve from earlier. He values his Orthodox Jewish upbringing; during all his years of following Christ, he's never denied his *Jewishness*. When Steve and his wife, Alice, started a family, they taught their four kids to appreciate the culture and customs he was raised with in the synagogue. I personally had a taste of it myself. I can remember, years ago, visiting their house as a teenager during the Christmas season. It was the first time I lit the candles of the Hanukkah menorah while Christmas carols were playing in the background.

Steve's faith in Christ didn't require him to sacrifice his Jewishness. No! Quite the contrary. He was enlightened by the work of the Holy Spirit in his life to what it really meant to be born as one of God's chosen people. As a Jewish believer, he brought a biblical balance between his Jewish heritage and his faith in the Lord Jesus. Steve's spiritual identity no longer rests in the ritual practices of Judaism, but in the Jewish Messiah, Jesus.

CHAPTER 18

CHRISTIANITY AND MODERN ISRAEL

"How I should like to visit Jerusalem sometime."[1]

ABRAHAM LINCOLN

R on Dermer, former Israeli ambassador to the United States, was quoted saying, "People have to understand that the backbone of Israel's support in the United States is the evangelical Christians. It's true because of numbers and also because of their passionate and unequivocal support for Israel."[2]

The "passionate and unequivocal" support that Dermer experienced from evangelical Christians comes from God's promise to Abraham to "bless those who bless you" (Genesis 12:3). Christian support for Israel is not grounded in Israeli politics or policy; instead, it emanates from the Scriptures. The restoration and rebirth of Israel in their ancient homeland, to the Christians, is a bellwether of God's faithfulness in their own lives.

CHRISTIAN ZIONISM

If you are a Christian reading this book and you believe that God's promises to Israel and the Jewish people are "irrevocable" (Romans 11:29), then that not only makes you a Zionist, it makes you a committed Christian Zionist. You are a Christian who believes the Jewish people have a biblical, historical, moral, and legal right to exist in their ancient homeland.

Biblically, when the apostle Paul wrote that the "gifts and his call are irrevocable," he was highlighting the eternal relationship God has with the Jewish people—that link that goes back to Abraham, a connection that cannot be broken. Paul was reminding the church in Rome and us today, in the twenty-first century, of the continuity of God's eternal covenant that cannot be broken.

Historically, the Jewish people have maintained a unique connection to the land that is not only documented in the Bible and other historical texts, but also verified in archaeological records that show their presence in the land a thousand years before Christianity and Islam existed.

Morally, the Jewish people have faced racism, persecution, and even death. When they would strive to assimilate into the cultures they lived in, they would still be met with ferocious antisemitism, leaving them helpless to defend themselves. Now, Israel is the only country in the world where the Jewish people have a right to self-determination and self-defense.

Legally, the late-nineteenth- and early-twentieth-century Jewish Zionists and pioneers were not stealing Palestinian land, as many would have you believe. The Jews rightfully purchased the land from absentee landlords. Zionists worked with political and religious leaders to convince the world of the need for a Jewish homeland. The Balfour Declaration of 1917, the San Remo Conference of 1920, and the UN Partition Plan of 1947 are all binding legal documents that gave international permission for the Jewish people to establish a sovereign state.[3]

DID YOU KNOW?

Horatio Spafford, who authored the famous hymn "It Is Well with My Soul," moved to Jerusalem after a series of devastating events in his life. He started the American Colony, a Christian utopian society that became of great benefit during World War I. The American Colony ceased being a Christian community by the 1940s. Today, it's a luxury hotel that's known for hosting politicians, journalists, and celebrities. Also, the very first talks between Israelis and Palestinians, which developed into the Oslo Agreement, occurred at the American Colony.

The "passionate and unequivocal" support of Christian Zionists that Ron Dermer experienced is the same support Theodor Herzl and others felt as they were fighting to establish a Jewish state. Christians lend their support to Israel in a way that transcends politics; theirs is a biblical mission.

Reverend William Hechler

For all the talk of Theodor Herzl and his work advocating for Zionism and the establishment of a Jewish state, rarely was the Bible mentioned. That's because Herzl wasn't a religious man. Herzl's basis for Jewish sovereignty was based on Jewish persecution in Europe and a desire for his people to control their own destiny.

The father of modern Zionism was certainly aware of his ancestry and the Jews' biblical and historical connection to the land of Israel, but Herzl's Zionist endeavors were not driven by the prophecies of Israel's restoration. God, however, always has a way of revealing how His hand is the one moving the pieces into place to accomplish His will, like in the book of Esther.

Reverend William Hechler served as the chaplain for the British Embassy in Vienna between 1885 and 1910, the same city Herzl was living in. Hechler voraciously studied the prophecies of Daniel and Revelation, and as a Bible-believing Christian, he was convinced God would one day restore His chosen people to the Promised Land.

Hechler reached out to Herzl after reading his booklet *Der Judenstaat*, "The Jewish State," in March 1896. Herzl detailed his first interaction with Hechler in his dairy as follows: "The Rev. William H. Hechler, chaplain to the British Embassy in Vienna, called on me. A likeable, sensitive man with the long grey beard of a prophet. He waxed enthusiastic over my solution…Hechler declares my movement to be a 'Biblical' one, even though I proceed rationally in all points."[4]

The two became friends with a shared mission. Hechler was the voice of faith in Herzl's ear, connecting him to what the Scriptures taught about God's plan to restore Israel to the land. The Christian chaplain did more than preach to the agnostic Jew, he opened the political floodgates for Herzl to share his Zionist message with world leaders. Hechler connected Herzl to the Grand Duke of Baden, Frederick I, a state leader in the German Empire. The duke was enthralled with Hechler's prophetic message and Herzl's practical approach to establishing a Jewish state in Palestine to solve the problem of antisemitism.

Herzl's connection with Hechler eventually led to his high-profile meeting with Kaiser Wilhelm II. Before knowing Hechler, Herzl's name had no international recognition—and now, he was being introduced to the emperor of Germany as the leader of world Zionism.

In 1889, Wilhelm II carried Herzl's message of Zionism to the Ottoman sultan Abdul Hamid II. Herzl asked the kaiser to implore the sultan if he would be willing to lease Palestine to the Jews, with the backing of the Germans. The sultan turned down his request and the kaiser lost enthusiasm for Herzl and Zionism, but the international press grabbed the story and turned it into a positive meeting. Jewish restoration became a topic of international concern.

When Herzl convened the First Zionist Congress in Basel, Switzerland, he invited Hechler as a nonvoting delegate and called him the "first Christ Zionist."

Hechler visited his dear Jewish friend the day before Herzl died. The chaplain attempted to brighten Herzl's spirits with stories of getting back on his feet and traveling to the Holy Land again, but Herzl knew his fate. He said to the Anglican minister and friend, "Greet Palestine for me. I gave my heart's blood for my people."[5]

God used Hechler to instill in Herzl that he was on a biblical mission, a work that was grounded in the Scriptures.

"The day when Zionism is so secure that it can take a look back to its rise and ponder on its origins and its history, your efforts for it will have the recognition they deserve for their astonishing foresight and for their true Christian generosity."[6]

Max Nordau, co-founder of Zionist organization
with Theodor Herzl, in a letter to Henry Dunant

William E. Blackstone

William E. Blackstone was the most legendary American evangelical Christian in the nineteenth century who promoted the ideals of a restored Jewish state. Even before Herzl branded the political Zionist movement, Blackstone, a wealthy real estate investor and evangelist, saw the need for a Jewish homeland after traveling to the Holy Land in 1888. When Blackstone returned, he invited leaders from both the Jewish and Christian communities to participate in his conference on the past, present, and future of Israel, held at the First Methodist Episcopal Church in Chicago.

At the meeting, a resolution of sympathy was passed on the treatment of the Jewish people in modern nations, specifically those in Russia suffering during the pogroms. World leaders were called upon to consider opening the door for the Jews' restoration to the Holy Land.

Blackstone was dissatisfied with the outcome of his conference; he wanted action, not just words of sympathy. He was confident that the only way for Jewish people to escape the throes of antisemitism was by establishing a Jewish state in Palestine. The entrepreneurial evangelist took matters into his own hands; he wanted to see the American government apply pressure on Russia and other countries who were mistreating the Jews.

He arranged a petition to be presented to secretary of state James G. Blaine, titled "Palestine for the Jews," which later came to be known as the "Blackstone Memorial." To add credibility to the petition, Blackstone acquired 413 signatures from some of the most influential politicians, clergy, businessmen, journalists, and newspapers in America at the time. The list of signatures in support of Blackstone's agenda is, by far, the most stirring part of the petition:

> Among the signatories were John D. Rockefeller and J. Pierpont Morgan; Melville W. Fuller, Chief Justice of the United States Supreme Court; T.B. Reed, Speaker of the House of Representatives; James Cardinal Gibbons, Archbishop of Baltimore; Hugh J. Grant, Mayor of New York City; Edwin H. Fitler, Mayor of Philadelphia; William McKinley, congressman from Ohio and future President of the United States; Robert R. Hitt, chairman of the House Committee on Foreign Affairs; and editors and publishers of ninety-three newspaper and periodicals.[7]

Blackstone instigated a Zionist American movement by involving American leadership from every aspect of life. The Blackstone Memorial remained an influence for many years. Paul Merkley observes:

> While it would be reckless to claim that we can trace a clear line of cause and effect from Blackstone's Memorial of 1891 to the Creation of the State of Israel in 1948, it is not at all far-fetched to say that the Memorial is the place to go to find the clearest expression of the motivation that won President Woodrow Wilson, and which would continue to be the surest, the most constant source of American Christian Zionism.[8]

Orde Wingate

Orde Charles Wingate was a captain in the British Army when he arrived in British Palestine in 1936. He was a devout Christian man, raised Plymouth Brethren, and his mother spoonfed him the Bible in his youth. He knew that God would return the Jewish people to Israel because of what the Scriptures prophesied.

Arab rioters had been attacking both the Jewish community and the British. Wingate received permission to train Haganah fighters to defend communities and train the Jewish community to protect themselves from their Arab attackers. He trained the Haganah to defend themselves using elements of surprise, especially at night. Special night squads were put in place throughout the Yishuv, implementing Wingate's strategies.

Wingate's military tactics were a success—so much so, the British gave in to Arab pressure and eventually banned Wingate from serving in Palestine. The Christian Zionist and British captain left behind the passion and military training to help defend the Jewish people, many of whom would become leaders in the Israel Defense Forces.

CHRISTIAN ZIONISM TODAY

Hechler, Blackstone, and Wingate were all devout Christian Zionists, dedicated to seeing a Jewish state established because of their love for God and His Word. But how does Christian Zionism fare today?

Evangelical Christian Zionism has remained a steady source of support for modern Israel. However, as of late, a new survey found that support among young evangelical Christians dropped 75 percent in just three years. In 2018, 69 percent of young evangelicals said they supported Israel, only 5.6 percent allied themselves with the Palestinians, and 25.7 percent didn't take sides. In 2021, 33.6 percent supported Israel, 24.3 percent sided with the Palestinians, and 42.2 percent reported they sided with neither.[9]

The numbers have Israelis concerned about the future of evangelical Christian support. One poll does not establish a trend, but it would be a mistake to ignore the results. Other surveys in recent years have also demonstrated weaker support for Israel by younger evangelicals.

It's time to ask some tough questions. What is happening? Why has support for Israel declined, especially among young evangelicals?

In the poll, the young adults were asked if their religious beliefs affected their decisions. Nearly 44 percent said that their view on the Israeli-Palestinian issue was not affected by their religious or theological belief. Thirty-eight percent said their faith did influence their support of Israel, while 17 percent said that their religious beliefs encouraged them to support the Palestinians.

The poll also revealed that 65 percent of young evangelicals say they seldom or never hear about the importance of Israel. Hechler, Blackstone, and Wingate all had one thing in common: They read their Bible. These early Christian Zionists studied the Scriptures and saw that Israel was at the center of God's plan of redemption. For the majority of young adults in the church today, their view of modern Israel is strictly political or based on gut feelings.

PLACES TO VISIT:
THE FRIENDS OF ZION MUSEUM

In Jerusalem, the Friends of Zion Museum is a state-of-the-art experience that opened in 2015. The museum tells the stories of those Jewish and non-Jewish dreamers who helped Israel become a reality. The museum highlights those early Christian Zionists who stood alongside the Jewish people as they forged a new nation.

The stats can seem justifiably negative, but there's always a silver lining with God, particularly with the 42.2 percent of young evangelicals who responded that they support neither side over the other. A large percentage of young evangelical Christians are waiting to hear what Hechler, Blackstone, and Wingate read. They are waiting to be reached with the biblical truth that God is not finished with Israel.

Those young Christians in the "neither" category may be apathetic or uninformed on the issues or unsure of what the Bible teaches about Israel, but they are probably more willing to hear about what the Scriptures teach about Israel and the Jewish people than those who have already staked their claim.

The church has a great opportunity here that we shouldn't overlook. After all, if we don't teach our young people biblical truth, they'll continue to be led by politics and gut feelings, instead of by God. Believers can display, to each other and to the world, their trust in God's plan for Israel with prayer, reading Scripture, their words, and their deeds.

CHAPTER 19

MAKING YOUR
PERSONAL PILGRIMAGE
TO ISRAEL

*"Five gospels record the life of Jesus. Four you will find in books
and the one you will find in the land they call Holy. Read the
fifth gospel and the world of the four will open to you."*

SAINT JEROME

Before the days of commercial airlines, five-star hotels, luxury coach buses, and endless buffets of delicious Middle Eastern food, a pilgrim from Spain embarked on a treacherous journey that would, without a doubt, change her life.

Egeria, a devout Christian woman, made one of the earliest documented pilgrimages to the Holy Land around AD 380.[1] A pilgrimage is different from any other type of travel or vacation. It's a journey of deep spiritual significance and expectation. Egeria isn't the first pilgrim to visit the sacred places of the Bible; others like Melito, a bishop from Sardis, made a similar journey. But what makes Egeria's journey so special are the diary entries she penned to the ladies in her spiritual community. The remaining fragments we have of her journal paint a picture of the biblical sites she experienced during the fourth century, and more significantly, include her elaborate explanations of the ways the early church worshipped.

Egeria traversed much of the Middle East. She walked the path of Moses on Mount Sinai in Egypt and climbed Mount Nebo, which is now in modern-day Jordan. She saw Haran in what is now modern-day Turkey, where Abraham lived. And for three years, she worshipped with Christians in Jerusalem and walked the shores of the Sea of Galilee, following in the footsteps of Christ.

Pilgrimages to the Holy Land became increasingly more popular. Maps and itineraries were organized during the Byzantine era to help guide pilgrims from one sacred site to another. Eusebius, a fourth-century church historian who lived in Caesarea, created a travel guide for pilgrims called *Onomasticon*. It would later be translated from Greek into Latin for pilgrims coming from Western Europe.[2]

There's no doubt a lot has changed since the fourth century AD. Egeria's journey took several years, while some other pilgrimages during that time lasted several months. But today, the twenty-first-century pilgrim can have the same spiritual experience in just two weeks.

It doesn't matter where you live in the world, flights from all four corners of the globe arrive daily in Tel Aviv, streamlining travel to the Holy Land to mere hours. Israel's small size is also an advantage that helps you maximize your time on the ground. In just one day you can comfortably see several different biblical sites.

PLACES TO VISIT: JAFFA

Jaffa is an ancient port city dating back more than 4,000 years. Both Solomon and Zerubbabel used the port to transport cedars from Lebanon to build the Temple in their respective times. Jonah boarded a boat in Jaffa in objection to God's call for him. And, the apostle Peter was in this city when he received a vision to take the gospel to the Gentiles. In 1950, the city of Jaffa was incorporated into Tel Aviv; today it's called Tel Aviv-Yafo. Jaffa is a favorite stop on any tour to Israel. The old, narrow streets take you back in time and the views of the Mediterranean Sea and of Tel Aviv stick in your memory.

I know from personal experience that traveling to the Holy Land never gets old. Whenever I lead a group, I'm often asked, "Don't you get bored visiting the same places all the time?"

My response is always the same: "Never!"

For starters, I'm always learning something new, and there's always a new archaeological find or some fresh discovery that adds more depth to the history of the places I visit. With every trip I take to Jerusalem, I feel like I'm visiting a different city, as researchers are constantly uncovering new archaeological finds.

But beyond just the knowledge, what makes each trip new for me is seeing the spiritual emotions and feelings, the look on each face, as sacred places people have read about all their lives in the Bible are seen with their own eyes for the first time.

When people see the Sea of Galilee or the city of Jerusalem from a distance for the first time, they know they are looking at the very same places Jesus saw. They know with certainty this is where Jesus healed the lame, this is where Jesus walked on water, this is where He climbed the steps to enter the Temple, and this is where He died on the cross for our sins. When someone is overwhelmed while sitting in the garden of Gethsemane or staring at Golgotha, I know they are having a moment with God. And it's these moments that make each time in Holy Land a fresh experience. Every aspect of a Christian pilgrimage gives a new dimension to one's relationship with the Lord.

Below are some tips to make your trip to Israel a special journey you'll never forget. I've been leading Holy Land tours since 2007 with the Friends of Israel Gospel Ministry, a Christian organization that's been going to the Holy Land since 1977. Much of what I've learned about organizing and structuring a tour comes from their years of experience and expertise.

DID YOU KNOW?

In 2019, the year prior to the pandemic, Israel's tourism boomed with a record 4.5 million visitors that brought in $6.3 billion to the economy.[3]

KNOW WHO YOU'RE GOING WITH

Before you put down your deposit to secure your seat on the first trip you see, there are a few items you need to investigate.

More often than not, you're joining a tour that's being offered by your church, or maybe you had heard about going to Israel on the radio, or saw on social media that a Christian group is organizing a trip. There's no better way to experience Israel than with a pastor, friend, or group you trust. However, you also want to be able to trust the travel agency that is organizing all of the details of your international travel.

First, if your church or group is organizing a trip without the guidance of a travel agent, do yourself a favor and find another trip that does. There are so many moving parts to a successful tour that one hiccup could have a domino effect for the rest of your trip.

Once I was standing on a dock with a group, waiting to board a boat that would take us out onto the Sea of Galilee. Next to me were 20 young adults grinning from ear to ear; they just couldn't believe they were going to set sail where Jesus had walked on water. When the captain arrived, I handed him my boarding slip with all of the details from our travel agency. He looked at me with a strange face and handed the paper back to me. "Wrong day!" he said.

"What! Wrong day?" I replied.

I frantically looked down. He was right, the paperwork had my boat departing on the same day the next month. I immediately got on the phone with my travel agent in Israel. She calmed me down, and within minutes the issue was fixed. We boarded the next boat and my group never knew the difference.

The clerical error on the boarding slip was a minor problem, but if I hadn't had a knowledgeable team waiting in the wings to help me, we would have probably had to forfeit a very memorable moment during the tour. Now imagine, if your flight was canceled or your hotel room wasn't booked properly, and you traveled to Israel without a reliable agency, that could really ruin a once-in-a-lifetime pilgrimage.

Your best tours are managed when agencies work together to structure and execute your travel. The first agency is stateside; they work with your church or organization to structure the trip. They book your flights, organize the itinerary on the ground, secure all of your international travel information, choose the best hotels that fit the tour budget, and arrange the travel insurance.

The stateside travel agency typically partners with an Israeli-based travel team that does the groundwork where you are traveling to. They handle the actual hotel arrangements and ensure the tour itinerary is fulfilled. The Israeli travel agency also secures ground transportation and, most importantly, hires a licensed tour guide. It was my Israeli travel agent who promptly fixed my boarding slip issue; she spoke both Hebrew and English, which means she understood my problem in English and fixed it by speaking in Hebrew with the captain.

You should be confident in your trust of who is taking you halfway around the world! Find the name of the travel agency on your trip brochure, or ask the person or group leading the tour. Research how long they've been in the business and who they partner with on the ground to ensure you are taken care of.

At Friends of Israel Gospel Ministry, we trust GTI Tours. They handle all the details from soup-to-nuts stateside, from your initial registration to your final return. We love GTI Tours for several reasons, but one of them is their partnership with Diesenhaus, the oldest travel agency in Israel, established in 1926. Diesenhaus has multiple offices and oversees nearly a half-million tourists per year. Their years of expertise provide a sense of comfort and security that someone is looking out for you when you are traveling in a foreign country.

DID YOU KNOW?

Direct flights between China and Israel have opened the door for the growth of Chinese tourism to the Holy Land. The Israeli tourism industry is adjusting accommodations for their visitors from the East. The growing number of Chinese Christians is also adding to the increase in Chinese tourism to Israel.

A BARGAIN ISN'T ALWAYS THE BEST

We're all bargain shoppers; I know I'm always looking for the best deal online. But when you are traveling halfway around the world, a bargain isn't always the best. At first glance, the cost of a tour to Israel can take one into a state of sticker shock. I'll be honest, it's not cheap. If you're embarking on a 12-day tour to Israel from the United States, you have to factor in the price of flights, 10 nights at a hotel, ground transportation, site fees, meals, tips, and travel insurance. It adds up.

So you begin to hunt around for the best price. There are plenty of options online, but you need to read the fine print to find out what's included in the price.

Some tours offer a "land only" price, which means you're required to find your own flights. In some cases, this could work to your advantage, especially if you're a frequent flyer with enough miles with an airline that can get you to Tel Aviv for free. The onus is on you, however, to arrive with enough time to meet your group and guide before they embark on the tour. If your flight is delayed and you get there late, you could miss out on some great biblical sites.

PLACES TO VISIT: BEERSHEBA

Abraham secured a well at Beersheba with the price of seven ewe lambs. It is the southernmost city of Israel in the Old Testament and the location where Abraham worshipped the Lord after planting a tamarisk tree. Beersheba today is considered the "capital of the Negev" and has developed into a center for Israel's high-tech industry.

A very nice lady once registered to go on one of our tours many years ago. She called Friends of Israel requesting her flight information, and to our surprise, her name appeared nowhere on the flight list, but she was registered for the tour. Come to find out, she chose the "land only" option because it was cheaper, but didn't realize that she needed to book her own flights. Our professional staff helped her and she made it to Israel with no problem. Crisis averted.

Beware, cheaper tours are also known to leave out site admission fees, tips, and other small costs that will add up for you once you are there, distracting you from the trip of a lifetime.

The Friends of Israel designs each Holy Land pilgrimage to enhance your experience on the ground. Every detail is included in our trips— from your flights to your lodging, meals, transportation, and even your travel insurance. We want you to have peace of mind on your pilgrimage so it's an experience you'll never forget.

Research the trip brochure before you commit. Below is a checklist of items that should be included with a trip:

1. Flights
2. Ground transportation
3. Accommodations
4. Sightseeing
5. Meal plan
6. Tour guide

Yet even with all the planning and researching to determine the best tour that fits your budget, while ensuring the best experience, life can still throw us curve balls. That's why you need to make sure you purchase the best travel insurance.

The tour you're considering may or may not include travel insurance in the advertised price. And even if it does, you'll want to find out what their protection includes. The travel insurance industry has been upended since the COVID-19 pandemic wreaked havoc on the world. Do not overlook this vital element and cost for your trip.

I say that because I've seen and heard it all. Once, a husband and wife flew into Newark, New Jersey, a day before their departure to Israel. The wife slipped and badly injured herself at the hotel; her injury forced them both to cancel their trip. Had they not had travel insurance, they would have forfeited the cost of the trip.

Once, I was with a group in Jerusalem when one of the tour participants complained of having a debilitating toothache. We located an
Israeli dentist who took care of him, and fortunately, his travel insurance reimbursed him for the treatment.

But the worst I've ever seen was the result of the 2020 pandemic; it
canceled trips all over the world. At Friends of Israel, we were mere days
from boarding a plane bound for Tel Aviv when COVID-19 grounded
all travel. Thankfully, our travel insurance reimbursed every tour par-
ticipant, but that wasn't the case for everyone. I heard other travelers
touring with different groups were told their insurance didn't include
"pandemic" in their protection and they were left to fight to get their
money back.

Once again, don't neglect travel insurance. Do your research
to find out what provisions are buried in the fine print. Because of
COVID-19, it's common now to find pandemic-proof travel insurance. Don't overlook this vital part of your trip, one I hope you never
have to use!

DID YOU KNOW?

The COVID-19 pandemic obliterated the Israeli tourism industry.
Following the record-breaking 4.5 million visitors in 2019, the end
of 2021 saw that only 400,000 tourists traveled to the Holy Land.[4]

MAKING THE MOST
OF YOUR EXPERIENCE

The popular saying "less is more" is a good phrase to keep in mind
when you're traveling to the Holy Land. I know it sounds counter-
intuitive when you want to absorb everything you can while you're
there. But, having too much sightseeing packed into one itinerary
will cause you to never have time to stop and appreciate the special
moments that make each tour unique and special.

PLACES TO VISIT: **GARDEN OF GETHSEMANE**

A garden at the foot of the Mount of Olives that's maintained by the Franciscans and commemorates the location where Jesus cried out to God, "Not my will, but yours be done" (Luke 22:42). The trees in the garden today are probably an outgrowth of the trees from Jesus' day. The Church of All Nations, which is next to the garden, is named after the 16 countries that helped build it.

Tour participants lament that there's never enough time to linger at each biblical location. It's true, there is never enough time. Each sacred location deserves, at minimum, a day, and for some locations, like Jerusalem and the Sea of Galilee, at least a week. But alas, time is not on our side. That's why it's important to evaluate how much traveling you will actually be doing.

If you're gearing up for your first pilgrimage, I highly recommend joining a ten-day tour at minimum. Ten days provides the flexibility to cover all of the regions and climates of the Holy Land like the Mediterranean coast, the Carmel mountain range, the Jezreel Valley, the region of Galilee, the Golan Heights, the Jordan Valley, the Judean Mountains, and the Negev.

Whether you've been to Israel once, twice, or twenty times, you fall in line with a heritage of people, a lineage, a tradition, who want to experience and know Jesus more by visiting where He walked. A pilgrimage is life-changing.

PART 3:

TOMORROW

CHAPTER 20

IS PEACE POSSIBLE IN THE MIDDLE EAST?

"Many nations will come and say, 'Come, let us go up to the
mountain of the LORD, to the temple of the God of Jacob.'"

MICAH 4:2

Naharayim, an inconspicuous plot of land between Israel and Jordan, became the center of international attention in 1994 after Israel relinquished it to Jordanian control. Jordan, in turn, leased it back to the Jewish state so Israeli farmers could continue to work the land. These were big steps for the two countries that were at one time ardent enemies, all of this done in the name of peace.

After the War of Independence, a dispute over the armistice agreement border gave Israel control of Naharayim, "two rivers," where the Jordan and Yarmuk rivers converge. The border dispute only deepened the animosity the two countries had for one another. Israel's willingness to give Jordan sovereignty of the disputed land and Jordan's willingness to lease the land back to Israel was a sign that the two countries were willing to move forward in peace.

In 1997, the image of Naharayim was marred when a Jordanian soldier of Palestinian descent opened fire on a group of Israeli schoolgirls visiting the Island of Peace—a park created in honor of the peace between Israelis and Jordanians. The young girls were there to learn about peace, but on that day, a Jordanian terrorist killed seven innocent children. Afterward, even King Hussein of Jordan crossed the border to personally apologize to the families of the Israeli victims, building a deeper relationship between Israel and Jordan.

The Jordanian lease agreement on Naharayim was set on a 25-year automatic renewal lease according to the 1994 peace plan, but over the years, tensions between the two countries have also escalated.

Jordan's King Abdullah II announced an end to the lease agreements in 2019, banning Israeli farmers from working and tourists from visiting Naharayim and the Island of Peace. In a televised speech, Abdullah received a standing ovation when he announced the end of the peace treaty annexations. The king went to social media and wrote, "Jordan's sovereignty over its land is above all else."[1]

Despite the stress, both countries vowed to maintain the tenets of the 1994 peace treaty. The small plot of land dubbed the Island of Peace, however, is a perfect picture of the uncertain foundations these peace deals are built upon.

UNCERTAIN PEACE

Is peace possible in the Middle East?

Sure.

Israel and the Jewish people have enjoyed moments of peaceful coexistence with their neighbors throughout their history, but there have always been times that, within moments, peace can suddenly disintegrate. The same can be said for the modern Middle Eastern peace agreements and the uncertainty of their strength for withholding changes like the succession of a leader or unpopular sentiments among the people.

DID YOU KNOW?

The United Nations neglects to help assist in establishing peace or communicating the truth about Israel to the world. According to UN Watch, between 2015 and 2021 the UN General Assembly passed 121 resolutions condemning Israel, while the rest of the world only received 45. The United Nations ignores the human rights atrocities of countries like China, North Korea, and Syria, while criticizing the only democracy present in the Middle East.

Israel and Egypt

After the Six-Day War and the Yom Kippur War, Israel maintained control of the Sinai Peninsula. Egyptian president Sadat lost interest in keeping alliances with the Soviet Union and turned his gaze to the United States. Sadat knew peace with Israel would secure a warm relationship with Washington, DC.

On November 20, 1977, President Sadat did the unthinkable: He flew to Tel Aviv to meet an excited Israeli prime minister Menachem Begin and his delegation on the tarmac. Sadat spoke to the Israeli Knesset in Jerusalem, saying, "I come to you today on solid ground, to shape a new life, to establish peace."[2]

Begin and Sadat signed a peace treaty at the White House on March 26, 1979. The treaty called for an end to the state of war that dated back to 1948, mutual recognition and the exchange of ambassadors, normalized relations, and a total withdrawal of Israeli forces and civilians from the Sinai Peninsula. On April 26, 1982, Israel upheld its end of the bargain and Egypt maintained its diplomatic relations, while allowing free Israeli passage through the Suez Canal and the Gulf of Eilat.

The majority of the Arab world scowled at Sadat's decision. The Arab League moved its headquarters out of Cairo and had Egypt suspended for establishing peace with Israel.

To this day, Israel and Egypt maintain peace in accordance with their old agreement, but many consider it a "cold peace." A deep animosity toward Israel still exists among Egyptians and many have called for the end of the peace agreement with Israel. In a 2019–2020 Arab Opinion Index, only 13 percent of Egyptians support diplomatic recognition of Israel, while 85 percent oppose it.[3]

Israel and Palestinians

The Palestine Liberation Organization was founded in 1964 with the purpose of unifying the Arab world under the banner of the liberation of Palestine. From the beginning, the PLO pledged an armed struggle toward the Israelis to accomplish their mission. These armed uprisings are better known as *intifada*. The First Intifada started in 1987: Palestinians would barricade roads, then throw stones and Molotov cocktails in order to taunt and harm Israeli civilians and the Israel Defense Forces.

Palestinian protests, civil unrest, suicide bombings and other acts of violence were commonplace for almost five years. The PLO would even murder their own people, anyone they considered an Israeli co-conspirator or sympathizer.

Yitzhak Rabin told officers at the Israel Defense Forces Staff College that the intifada was "the will of small groups to discover their national identity and demand its realization."[4] Israelis and Palestinians suffered; deaths on both sides mounted, and bitterness grew deeper.

Israel and the PLO met secretly in Oslo, Norway, in 1993, in what became the origins of the Oslo Accords. Their meeting was done covertly, so as not to cause a stir among their people. The Palestinians would be furious to hear that their leadership would even sit in the same room with an Israeli. And Israelis would wonder how any decent Israeli could discuss peace with the PLO—a terrorist organization.

Norwegian deputy foreign minister Jan Egeland played the role of mediator, facilitating the negotiations. One of the biggest obstacles to peace between the Israelis and Palestinians was their mutual recognition of one another. On September 9, 1993, Yasser Arafat officially recognized the State of Israel and its right to exist in peace and security. Mutually, Prime Minister Yitzhak Rabin recognized the PLO as the legitimate representative of the Palestinian people.

By September 13, Rabin and Arafat were in Washington, DC signing the Declaration of Principles at the same desk where Begin and Sadat signed their peace treaty between Israel and Egypt. Israel officially recognized the PLO and the PLO recognized Israel in front of the whole world. The Declaration of Principles permitted Palestinian self-governance and set in place a gradual withdrawal of the Israeli military from Gaza.

Two years later, Oslo II was signed, granting the Palestinian Authority control over areas of Gaza and the West Bank. Rabin, Arafat, and Israeli president Shimon Peres were awarded a joint Nobel Peace Prize for their efforts toward establishing peace.

DID YOU KNOW?

Shimon Peres was the last surviving leader of Israel's founding era; he died on September 28, 2016. Ben-Gurion commissioned Peres as the head of naval services after independence. He served as Israel's prime minister two times and once as president.

On November 4, 1995, Yitzhak Rabin attended a peace rally in Tel Aviv held in support of the Oslo Accords. A religious Israeli student, Yigal Amir, who protested the peace agreement, lunged at Rabin and shot him twice. The prime minister died later that day. His death sent shockwaves throughout Israel and the world.

The Oslo Agreement crumbled with both parties pointing at each other as the cause for the failure of peace. Yasser Arafat and leaders of the Palestinian Authority were known to talk out of both sides of their mouth. In English, they recognized Israel's right to exist, but in Arabic, they would preach a Palestine "from the river to the sea." They also continued to stockpile weapons in abrogation of the peace accord.

Talks between Israel and the Palestinians resumed at Camp David in 2000, just prior to both President Bill Clinton's and Prime Minister Ehud Barak's exits from office. The time to complete the Oslo Agreement from 1993 was now or never.

Barak offered his counterpart 97 percent of the West Bank and 100 percent of the Gaza Strip. The Israeli premier also pledged to give Arab neighborhoods in eastern Jerusalem as a Palestinian capital, maintaining control over their religious sites. In addition, the new Palestinian state would receive $30 billion from an international fund to aid them.

Camp David provided the framework and structure to establish a Palestinian state. Yasser Arafat's response to this offer for a future Palestinian state for his people was "No!"

The failure of the meetings at Camp David are what led to the Second Intifada. Terror in the Holy Land continued while thousands of Israelis and Palestinians lost their lives until a cease-fire was signed in 2005 between the new Palestinian president, Mahmoud Abbas, and Israel's prime minister Ariel Sharon.

DID YOU KNOW?

The Israeli security barriers that can be seen in Jerusalem and around the West Bank perimeter, were built during the Second Intifada, after a rise in Palestinian suicide bombings and terrorist attacks. The security barriers are controversial, but proved successful in lowering terrorist attacks by 90 percent.

The tenants of the Oslo Accords still govern the relationship between the Israelis and the Palestinians, but the two parties are far from peace. Today, 7 percent of Palestinians support diplomatic recognition of Israel, while 91 percent oppose it.[5]

Israel and Jordan

The advancement of the Oslo Accords encouraged Jordan to jump on the peace train. Unlike Egypt and their land-for-peace exchange, King Hussein surrendered Jordan's claim to the West Bank, with the vision of seeing a future Palestinian state formed alongside Israel. Hussein was enticed by President Clinton to engage in peace talks with Israel with the proviso that Jordanian debt would be forgiven—Clinton's negotiation tactics were successful.

On October 26, 1994, Hussein, Rabin, and Clinton signed what's known as the Wadi Araba Treaty. The peace agreement, signed in the

Araba Valley, brought to a conclusion the years of war and bloodshed between Jordan and Israel.

The two countries share diplomatic, security, energy, water resource, and economic ties, but the relationship has grown cold over the years. Many Jordanians have never accepted Israel's legitimacy as a Jewish state. They see the 1994 agreement as just another broken promise. Jordan has remained the custodian of the Temple Mount, and many Jordanians are wary of Israel's influence over their sacred space.

Additionally, as I noted above, Jordan withholding the lease renewal of Naharayim and the Island of Peace is a telltale sign that the relationship may be functional, but it certainly isn't warm. Today, 6 percent of Jordanians support diplomatic recognition of Israel, while 93 percent oppose it.[6]

The Abraham Accords

When I started writing this book, Israel's only signed peace agreements with the Arab countries around them were with Egypt and Jordan. By September 2020, all of that changed. Seemingly overnight, President Trump and his administration brokered the Abraham Accords—peace agreements between Israel and the United Arab Emirates (UAE) and Bahrain.

Soon after the UAE and Bahrain publicly normalized their relationship with Israel, Oman, Morocco, and Sudan moved to do the same.

Sudan hosted the Arab League Summit back in 1967, which resulted in the Khartoum Resolution containing the "three no's" we discussed earlier: no peace with Israel, no recognition of Israel, no negotiations with Israel. In 2021, Sudan repealed a law from 1958 that prohibited diplomatic and business relations with Israel in order to enter the Abraham Accords.

Even Saudi Arabia was hinting at potential public peace with its longtime enemy. All this happened as the United States moved its embassy from Tel Aviv to Jerusalem, signaling to the world that Jerusalem is the capital of Israel.

> "If the Arabs put down their weapons today,
> there would be no more violence. If the Jews put down
> their weapons today, there would be no more Israel."[7]
>
> *Benjamin Netanyahu*

The Abraham Accords signaled cooperation between Israel and the broader Middle East. These relationships, however, had been brewing below the surface for a few years, outside of the public eye. Israel and its Muslim neighbors have a new common foe, and it isn't the Jewish state anymore, it's Iran. Former Israeli national security adviser Major General Uzi Dayan said, "The Israeli-Palestinian conflict is not on the agenda and Iran is."[8]

President Barack Obama's Iran deal, designed to prevent Iran from building a nuclear weapon, was highly praised in the Western world, but it was severely criticized by Israel and Sunni Muslim countries in the Middle East. Obama's insistence to ram through the Joint Comprehensive Plan of Action (JCPOA) built stronger ties of security cooperation between the Arab world and Israel.

The Middle East of today looks vastly different from the past. Peace between Israel and several of its neighbors does exist. But the peace in the Middle East today could look very different in just 25 years—which always keeps it in an uncertain status.

PERMANENT PEACE

Psalm 122 is a song of ascent, a prayer that was offered as Jewish pilgrims climbed the mountains of Judea to ascend to Israel's capital, Jerusalem. This psalm of David says, "Pray for the peace of Jerusalem: 'May those who love you be secure'" (Psalm 122:6). The pilgrimage trail to peace in the Middle East—and dare I say, the world—does not go through Washington, DC or Oslo—it goes through Jerusalem.

Jerusalem: The Peace of God's Presence (Psalm 122:1-2)

King David begins Psalm 122 with a feeling of ecstatic joy at the very thought of entering Jerusalem. The king was excited that he and other worshippers would experience the joy of God's physical presence in the City of Peace. David knew that the creator of heaven and earth dwelled there and in His presence was peace. "For the LORD has chosen Zion, he has desired it for his dwelling, saying, 'This is my resting place for ever and ever; here I will sit enthroned, for I have desired it. I will bless her with abundant provisions; her poor I will satisfy with food'" (Psalm 132:13-15).

There was a sense of peace in David's life. He knew that as long as God was physically dwelling with Israel in Jerusalem, no enemy could overtake the city and God would be their refuge, strength, and provision. Jerusalem becomes the focal point of *shalom* because it is from there that God will administer peace. *Shalom* is Hebrew for "peace," "wellness," and "completeness."

PLACES TO VISIT: **TEMPLE MOUNT**

It's never easy to visit the top of the Temple Mount. There are restrictions, such as it only being open to visitors during certain hours of the day and that only Muslims are permitted to enter the Dome of the Rock. Relying on the experience and wisdom of a good tour guide will assist you in avoiding any pitfalls that could occur during a visit. But the long lines and the wait are worth it, since the site is the holiest location to the Jewish people because it is where the Temples once stood.

Jerusalem: The City of Peace for Everyone (Psalm 122:3-5)

For the Jews, Jerusalem is not only the center of worship, it's also the focal point for the administration and practice of God's law. "Jerusalem is built like a city…there stand the thrones for judgment, the thrones of the house of David" (Psalm 122:3, 5).

The City of Peace is the hub of God's righteous justice. The "thrones for judgment" was the place where Israel's leaders sat to make legal decisions according to the law of God. The justice and righteousness of God were executed from Jerusalem, a biblical justice and righteousness from where peace arose.

The "thrones for judgment" would not only be administered to the people of Israel, but would one day spread throughout the world, bringing peace and stability to every kingdom and to every nation. Both the prophets Isaiah and Micah prophesied Jerusalem being the center of where this would take place in the future. Micah proclaimed,

> In the last days the mountain of the LORD's temple will be established as the highest of the mountains; it will be exalted above the hills, and peoples will stream to it. Many nations will come and say, "Come, let us go up to the mountain of the LORD, to the temple of the God of Jacob. He will teach us his ways, so that we may walk in his paths." The law will go out from Zion, the word of the LORD from Jerusalem (Micah 4:1-2).

Both Isaiah's and Micah's visions not only had Israel's tribes coming to Jerusalem to find justice, righteousness, and peace, but also had all of the nations pouring in to the City of Peace to find divine instruction. This prophetic imagery has Jerusalem standing as the place where peace could be found and given to the rest of the earth, in the midst of a world that is longing for it.

Jerusalem: The Wellspring of Peace (Psalm 122:6-9)

Now that we know and understand the significance of this little city both locally and globally, we can now see why David would say, "Pray for the peace of Jerusalem" (verse 6). To pray for Jerusalem's peace is to pray for a permanent peace, both in the Middle East and globally.

But, this can only happen when the "Prince of Peace"—the Messiah of Israel, Jesus Christ—sits on His throne in Jerusalem (Isaiah 9:6). When you pray for the peace of Jerusalem, you are asking the

Lord Jesus to return to establish His righteous reign on earth (Isaiah 9:7). And Daniel foresaw that after He returns, "He was given authority, glory and sovereign power; all nations and peoples of every language worshiped him. His dominion is an everlasting dominion that will not pass away, and his kingdom is one that will never be destroyed" (Daniel 7:14).

Is peace possible in the Middle East? Yes! But, only when Jesus Christ rules and reigns from His throne in Jerusalem!

CHAPTER 21

THE PLACE OF ISRAEL IN BIBLE PROPHECY

*"And so after waiting patiently, Abraham
received what was promised."*

HEBREWS 6:15

The best place to stand in Israel to get a panoramic view of Bible prophecy is atop the Mount of Olives. In one glance, all of Jerusalem can be seen, from the City of David to the Old City and the Temple Mount. On a side note, a highlight of the experience is taking a photo-op riding on a camel with Jerusalem in the background—it's great social media fodder.

There are numerous biblical events that occurred between the Temple Mount and the Mount of Olives. Jesus prophesied of Jerusalem's fate and His glorious return (Matthew 24–25). He entered Jerusalem on a donkey after riding down the Mount of Olives into the Kidron Valley in fulfillment of Zechariah 9:9 (Matthew 21:1-11). Later, He would journey from the upper room in Jerusalem to the garden of Gethsemane, on the eastern slope of the Mount of Olives, where He would cry out to His Father in agony, "Not my will, but yours be done" (Luke 22:42).

The book of Acts begins with the resurrected Jesus with His disciples, standing on the Mount of Olives. Jesus spent the last 40 days

The Mount of Olives.

teaching them about the kingdom of God. As the disciples were listening to Jesus, they asked Him, "Lord, are you at this time going to restore the kingdom to Israel?" (Acts 1:6).

The question was apropos to where their feet were planted. The disciples—probably going through their index of biblical prophecy—recalled Zechariah's vision of the Messiah's feet touching down on the Mount of Olives in the last days (Zechariah 14:4). In their minds, all the pieces of the prophetic puzzle fit together. Of all the times to "restore the kingdom to Israel," then would have been the best, with the Messiah standing on the Mount of Olives.

But the Father had other plans; kingdom restoration would happen, but not then. The disciples were given a task to be witnesses for Christ throughout the world with the Holy Spirit's assistance (Acts 1:8).

As Jesus ascended from the Mount of Olives to sit at the right hand of the Father, angels appeared to the bewildered disciples, promising them, "This same Jesus, who has been taken from you into heaven, will come back in the same way you have seen him go into heaven" (Acts 1:11). The angels communicated a divine promise that Jesus would return to the Mount of Olives, just as Zechariah had promised.

Israel remains at the center of God's prophetic plan. But is there a place for modern Israel in biblical prophecy?

ISRAEL'S RECONSTITUTION

After two millennia of being scattered throughout the world, May 14, 1948, became a date of biblical proportions for the Jewish people. There is no other group of people who were exiled from their homes, dispersed, maintained their unique identity, resurrected their original language, and then returned to their ancient homeland. The very thought of Israel's rebirth is a modern miracle, but some Christians think otherwise.

As David Levy writes concerning Israel's rebirth:

> Some Christians say it is totally unrelated to prophecy and that modern Israel's reestablishment is a historical event that has no relevance to biblical fulfillment. Others teach there will be a literal, national restoration as prophesied in the Bible, but not until Jesus Christ comes back. They believe today's return in unbelief does not follow the proper sequence of repentance, then restoration. Both views are flawed. The first denies that this or any future return of the Jewish people to their homeland is a fulfillment of biblical prophecy. The second denies any biblical fulfillment until Israel repents of sin and unbelief—a view not taught in Scripture.[1]

Is the modern state of Israel a mere happenstance, a coincidence of history? Does Israel's return to the land have no meaning until Christ's return? Or are we living in one of the most extraordinary of times as we experience Israel's reconstitution according to the promises of God? The prophet Ezekiel gives us clarity on the best answer to the place of modern Israel in Bible prophecy.

DID YOU KNOW?

Jewish and Christian tradition both place the Mount of Olives as the epicenter of Messiah's future return. Jesus promised to return

to it and Jewish people have been burying their dead on its slopes
for thousands of years. According to the sages, the resurrection
will begin on the Mount of Olives when Messiah appears.

GOD'S ABOUT TO "ACT"

In the first chapter of this book, I showed you the unconditional
covenant God made to Abraham concerning a land, descendants, and
a blessing. God's vow is the anchor that is linked to Israel—past, present, and future. His holy reputation is hitched to Israel. God has to
fulfill His promise to Abraham or else He's a liar—and God is no liar!
(Hebrews 6:18).

> Therefore say to the house of Israel, Thus says the Lord
> GOD: It is not for your sake, O house of Israel, that I am
> about to act, but for the sake of my holy name, which you
> have profaned among the nations to which you came. And
> I will vindicate the holiness of my great name, which has
> been profaned among the nations, and which you have
> profaned among them. And the nations will know that I
> am the LORD, declares the Lord GOD, when through you I
> vindicate my holiness before their eyes. I will take you from
> the nations and gather you from all the countries and bring
> you into your own land (Ezekiel 36:22-24 ESV).

If you notice from Ezekiel's prophetic passage, God's faithfulness to
restore Israel isn't predicated on the people's own righteousness. As long
as Israel is covenantally out of sync and resided outside of the Promised
Land, they profane His name among the nations. It's for this reason
God will "vindicate" His holy reputation through the act of regathering the Jewish people "into [their] own land" (Ezekiel 36:24).

God's "act" to restore Israel serves as a double-edged sword to mag-
nify His glory. First, restoring Israel to the land validates His faithfulness to the promise He swore to the patriarchs Abraham, Isaac, and

Jacob. Second, their rebirth is a sign to the nations that the God of the Jewish people is the living God who plans to fulfill His mission through Israel.

DRY BONES RISE

There are several prophets who envisioned Israel's restoration to the land, but none so detailed and graphic as Ezekiel's vision of the valley of dry bones. Two-thousand six-hundred years prior to Israel's independence in 1948, Ezekiel was led by the Spirit of God into a valley full of human bones. The bones were "very dry," a literary descriptor for the reader to grasp that these individuals are beyond dead. Each body has been lying unburied for quite some time, the muscles and flesh have long been stripped off the bones, and the sun has bleached them dry.

Ezekiel climbed over piles of bones, maybe in the Kidron Valley between the Mount of Olives and the Temple Mount.[2]

PLACES TO VISIT: KIDRON VALLEY

The Kidron Valley originates in Jerusalem and spans nearly 20 miles to the Dead Sea. The valley divides the Mount of Olives and the Temple Mount. During times of reform, Israel's kings would dump pagan idols used for worship in the valley. It was also called the Valley of Judgment (Joel 3:2, 12).

The God of Abraham, Isaac, and Jacob asks what many would consider an outlandish question to the prophet standing among the dead. He asked, "Son of man, can these bones live?" (Ezekiel 37:3). Ezekiel's response to God could be seen as "sitting on the fence"—after being dragged through a valley of death, living seems far off. Yet Ezekiel is also talking to the One who spoke life into existence. Ezekiel responded, "Sovereign LORD, you alone know" (verse 3).

The God of the living orders the prophet to speak life over the bones, commanding them to rise:

> This is what the Sovereign LORD says to these bones: I will make breath enter you, and you will come to life. I will attach tendons to you and make flesh come upon you and cover you with skin; I will put breath in you, and you will come to life. Then you will know that I am the LORD (verses 5-6).

As the prophet preached the Word of God, the dry bones "rattled" and shook! Ezekiel saw death defeated by God's Word. Muscles and skin covered those dry bones until they took on human likeness.

Ezekiel was both amazed and confused. The bones resurrected into bodies, but they were lying before him, lifeless: "there was no breath in them" (verse 8).

In the prophetic vision, God doesn't seem concerned like Ezekiel; it's as though this is all part of His sovereign plan. He commanded Ezekiel to call for the breath of life to awaken the bodies, an image reminiscent of God's breath entering Adam after he was formed in the garden (Genesis 2:7). Suddenly, the multitude stood on their feet, "a vast army" (Ezekiel 37:10).

Then God gave a clear and concise explanation to Ezekiel's vision: "Son of man, these bones are the people of Israel. They say, 'Our bones are dried up and our hope is gone; we are cut off'" (verse 11). But because God vowed to act according to His loyal love and faithfulness to the covenant He made with Abraham, He said,

> My people, I am going to open your graves and bring you up from them; I will bring you back to the land of Israel. Then you, my people, will know that I am the LORD, when I open your graves and bring you up from them. I will put my Spirit in you and you will live, and I will settle you in your own land. Then you will know that I the LORD have spoken, and I have done it, declares the LORD (verses 12-14).

In the midst of one of Israel's darkest moments in their history, God gave Ezekiel a glimmer of hope. Exile, diaspora, or even Holocaust does not spell the end for God's chosen people. The nation that's been scattered; beaten; subject to the whims of pharaohs, kings, and emperors; religiously oppressed; mocked; and even victims of genocide would rise again into a vast army.

Fast-forward to today, a large stone edifice stands over the threshold of the Yad Vashem Holocaust memorial. As you come into and go from the memorial, you will observe that Ezekiel 37:14 is permanently etched in the stone for all to see: "I will put my breath into you and you shall live again, and I will set you upon your own soil..."

THE PROPHETIC PAUSE

The modern State of Israel is a secular country; a large number of Israeli Jews would consider themselves secular, or nonreligious at best. A WIN/Gallup International poll found that out of 65 countries, Israel is one of the least religious nations in the world.[3]

Is the modern State of Israel that we see today what God intended when He commanded Ezekiel to speak life to the dry bones that surrounded him? Is modern Israel the resurrection of the dry bones?

If you return to Ezekiel 37, you will note that God's original command to the prophet to speak life over the dry bones included both the resurrection of the body and the life-giving breath. In fact, if you look closely, breath was the first and most significant component of God's prophecy: "This is what the Sovereign LORD says to these bones: I will make breath enter you, and you will come to life" (verse 5).

The prophecy and the process play out in Ezekiel 37—the dry bones took on human form, but there was no breath. In the previous chapter, Ezekiel 36, God promises to return Israel to the land and give them His Spirit (breath): "I will put my Spirit in you and move you to follow my decrees and be careful to keep my laws. Then you will live in the land I gave your ancestors; you will be my people, and I will be your God" (verses 27-28).

God seems to intentionally postpone conferring His Spirit to Israel, indicating there is a process to the prophecy. First, the dry bones reconstitute taking on the shape and likeness of human form. The first stage could be the rebirth of the State of Israel, Jewish people from the four corners of the world returning to their ancient homeland. The bones that have dried out for two millennia are resurrecting. The prophetic pause seems to indicate that Israel will return to its own land in unbelief—that there is evidence, in the Scriptures, that the modern phenomenon of Jewish regathering and Israeli sovereignty is a stage in the process of God's prophetic plan. The fulfillment of the dry bones prophecy is still waiting for its completion, when God's breath will give spiritual life to Israel.

That can only happen when Israel repents and turns to "the one they have pierced" (Zechariah 12:10). The apostle Peter was preaching to the nation of Israel just a little while after Jesus ascended to heaven, and said, "Repent, then, and turn to God, so that your sins may be wiped out, that times of refreshing may come from the Lord, and that he may send the Messiah, who has been appointed for you— even Jesus. Heaven must receive him until the time comes for God to restore everything, as he promised long ago through his holy prophets" (Acts 3:19-21). The breath of life that Ezekiel watched rush over the dry bones will become a reality when Israel repents and turns to their Savior and Messiah, Jesus Christ.

The apostle Paul also highlights Israel's prophetic future when he writes this concerning Israel's hardened hearts as being allowed by God due to His purpose for saving the Gentiles: "in this way all Israel will be saved. As it is written: 'The deliverer will come from Zion; he will turn godlessness away from Jacob. And this is my covenant with them when I take away their sins'" (Romans 11:26-27). Here the apostle Paul gives hope that God's not through with Israel. He has a bright future for them: Jesus the Messiah of Israel will return to Zion, forgive Israel's sins, and usher in a messianic kingdom, where He will rule and reign from Jerusalem.

PLACES TO VISIT: **MOUNT OF OLIVES**

The Mount of Olives, at 2,641 feet above sea level, is the mountain to the east of the Temple Mount. Its name is derived from the olive groves that once covered the area. The Chapel of the Ascension sits at the northern summit and a Jewish cemetery covers the slope that is opposite the Temple Mount. Prophetically, the Mount of Olives is the exact location of Jesus' return (Zechariah 14:4; Acts 1:11).

DON'T IGNORE THE SIGNS

In the 2,000 years of church history, we live during a most exciting and unique time. Israel has returned to the land and it's no coincidence or historical happenstance—it's God's providence. The dry bones are gaining their tendons and flesh. Marvel at God's goodness that He would be gracious to invite us to experience such a momentous moment in history, because Israel's prophetic hope is linked to our prophetic hope.

"Blessed is the one who reads aloud the words of this prophecy, and blessed are those who hear it and take to heart what is written in it, because the time is near."

Revelation 1:3

The apostle Paul writes, "If their rejection brought reconciliation to the world, what will their acceptance be but life from the dead?" (Romans 11:15). Paul is commenting on Israel's rejection of Jesus. It was purposed by God to bring the gospel to the world. Their refusal "brought reconciliation to the world"—that means that now also Gentiles are turning to Christ, and through Christ, mankind is being reconciled to God. That's good news. But the good news isn't done; Paul writes that there's more. The "more" for the Christian comes when Israel also turns to the Savior. When Jesus returns we will *all* experience "life from the dead"—the hope of resurrection.

> The perishable must clothe itself with the imperishable, and the mortal with immortality. When the perishable has been clothed with the imperishable, and the mortal with immortality, then the saying that is written will come true: "Death has been swallowed up in victory" (1 Corinthians 15:53-54).

Don't ignore the signs. How does a country the size of New Jersey become the center of the world's attention and land in the news headlines the world over? How could they rise from the ashes of the Holocaust to become one of the world's most powerful countries—a beacon of hope and freedom as the only functioning democracy in the Middle East? How could they go from swamp-infested farmland and desert to becoming a global leader in economics, agriculture, the sciences, technology, health, the arts, and security? Could it be, that God is drawing attention to Himself through His chosen people? He did promise to do that:

> This is what the Sovereign LORD says: On the day I cleanse you from all your sins, I will resettle your towns, and the ruins will be rebuilt. The desolate land will be cultivated instead of lying desolate in the sight of all who pass through it. They will say, "This land that was laid waste has become like the garden of Eden; the cities that were lying in ruins, desolate and destroyed, are now fortified and inhabited." Then the nations around you that remain will know that I the LORD have rebuilt what was destroyed and have replanted what was desolate. I the LORD have spoken, and I will do it (Ezekiel 36:33-36).

A SIGN OF GOD'S FAITHFULNESS

Let God's faithfulness to Israel be a spiritual lesson for you today! God's mercy, grace, and faithfulness is evident in every moment and aspect of Israel's existence—yesterday, today, and tomorrow. Throughout the Bible, the Jewish people are called a "stiff-necked," stubborn people (Nehemiah 9:16; Acts 7:51), and yet God pledged to remain faithful to them till the bitter end.

I always like to remind people that "Israel's story is my story," meaning that I have moments of great spiritual clarity and growth in Christ, and then I also can feel myself wandering, *prone to leave the God I love.* The roller-coaster ride of a Christian's spiritual walk with God can often mimic Israel's spiritual ups and downs. And despite Israel's sin and shame, God promised to fulfill what He started through them. He said to Israel, "Be strong and courageous. Do not be afraid or terrified because of them, for the LORD your God goes with you; he will never leave you nor forsake you" (Deuteronomy 31:6).

God promised the same to us in Christ Jesus: "Never will I leave you; never will I forsake you" (Hebrews 13:5). When I see Israel today, it's far from perfect; it hasn't arrived. But through Israel, on this side of heaven, my faith recieves a glimmer of sight when I tangibly see God's faithfulness at work.

NOTES

CHAPTER 1—THE BIBLICAL STORY OF THE JEWS

1. Jennifer Polland, "10 Most Read Books in the World," *Business Insider* (December 27, 2012), at https://www.businessinsider.com/the-top-10-most-read-books-in-the-world-infographic-2012-12.

2. Victor P. Hamilton, *The Book of Genesis, Chapters 1–17*, in *The New International Commentary on the Old Testament*. Accordance electronic ed. (Grand Rapids, MI: Eerdmans, 1990), 430.

CHAPTER 2—THE PROMISED LAND AND THE TEMPLE

1. Yehuda Amichai, et al. *The Selected Poetry of Yehuda Amichai* (University of California Press, 2013), 54.

2. David A. Dorsey, *The Roads and Highways of Ancient Israel* (Eugene, OR: Wipf and Stock Publishers, 2018), 37.

3. Michael Hesemann, *Jesus of Nazareth: Archaeologists Retracing the Footsteps of Christ* (United States: Ignatius Press, 2021), 86.

4. Josephus (*Antiquities* 15.380).

CHAPTER 3—THE EXILE AND THE RETURN

1. Thomas V. Brisco, *Holman Bible Atlas: A Complete Guide to the Expansive Geography of Biblical History* (Nashville, TN: Broadman & Holman, 2014), 131.

2. Eugene H. Merrill, *Kingdom of Priests*, 2nd ed. (Grand Rapids: Baker Academic, 2008), 492.

3. Neil MacGregor, "The Whole World in Our Hands," *The Guardian* (July 23, 2004), at www.theguardian.com/artanddesign/2004/jul/24/heritage.art.

CHAPTER 5—ISRAEL IN THE TIME OF JESUS

1. Josephus (*Antiquities* 18.1.2§11).

CHAPTER 6—THE DIASPORA JEWS:
SCATTERED TO ALL THE NATIONS

1. Chris Katulka, "The Reason Why," *Israel My Glory* (January/February 2020), at https://israelmy glory.org/article/the-reason-why/.

2. Museum of the Bible Books, Lawrence H. Schiffman and Jerry Pattengale eds., et al., *The World's Greatest Book: the Story of How the Bible Came to Be* (Franklin, TN: Worthy Publishing, 2017).

3. Tom Simcox, "Important Events in Diaspora History," *Israel My Glory* (January/February 2020), at https://israelmyglory.org/article/important-events-in-diaspora-history/.

4. Peter Colón, "From Rome to the Turks," *Israel My Glory* (September/October 2013), at https://israel myglory.org/article/from-rome-to-the-turks/.

5. The Editors of Encyclopaedia Britannica, "Ashkenazi," *Encyclopedia Britannica* (August 28, 2020), at https://www.britannica.com/topic/Ashkenazi.

6. American Technion Society, "Nearly Half Of Ashkenazi Jews Descended From Four 'Founding Mothers,'" *ScienceDaily* (January 17, 2006), at https://www.sciencedaily.com/releases/2006/01/060117083446.htm.

7. Andrew Tobin, "Ashkenazi Jews Descend from 350 People, Study Finds," *The Times of Israel* (September 10, 2014), at https://www.timesofisrael.com/ashkenazi-jews-descend-from-350-people-study -finds/.

8. Bernard Rosensweig, "The Origins of Ashkenazic Jewry in Germany," *Tradition: A Journal of Orthodox Jewish Thought*, vol. 15, no. 1/2 (Spring-Summer 1975), 130–36, at http://www.jstor .org/stable/23258494.

9. David Shyovitz, "Yiddish: History & Development of Yiddish," *Jewish Virtual Library*, at https:// www.jewishvirtuallibrary.org/history-and-development-of-yiddish.

10. AFP in Madrid, "Spain Passes Law Awarding Citizenship to Descendants of Expelled Jews," *The Guardian* (June 11, 2015), at https://www.theguardian.com/world/2015/jun/11/spain-law -citizenship-jews.

11. Rebecca Weiner, "Judaism: Sephardim," *Jewish Virtual Library*, at https://www.jewishvirtual library.org/sephardim.

12. Andrea Mifano, "The Expulsion of Jews from Arab Countries and Iran—An Untold History," *World Jewish Congress* (February 2, 2021), at https://www.worldjewishcongress.org/en/news/ the-expulsion-of-jews-from-arab-countries-and-iran--an-untold-history.

CHAPTER 7—THE MODERN FOUNDERS OF ISRAEL

1. Joseph L. Baron ed., *A Treasury of Jewish Quotations* (Lanham, MD: Rowman & Littlefield, 1985), 34.

2. Martin Gilbert, *Israel: A History* (New York: HarperCollins, 1998), 4.

3. Benjamin Glatt, "The Prophetic Revival of the Hebrew Language," *The Jerusalem Post* (January 3, 2016), at https://www.jpost.com/christian-news/the-prophetic-revival-of-the-hebrew-language -439241.

4. Francine Klagsbrun, *Lioness: Golda Meir and the Nation of Israel* (New York: Schocken Books, 2019), 308.

5. Gilbert, *Israel*, 9–15.

6. Shlomo Avineri, "Theodore Herzl's Diaries as Bildungsroman," *Jewish Social Studies*, vol. 5, no. 3 (1999), 1–46.

7. Theodor Herzl, *The Jewish State: The Historic Essay that Led to the Creation of the State of Israel* (New York: Skyhorse, 2019), conclusion.

8. Tom Segev, *A State at Any Cost: The Life of David Ben-Gurion*, trans. Haim Watzman (New York: Farrar, Straus and Giroux, 2019).

9. Gilbert, *Israel*, 46–47.

10. "Chaim Weizmann Joins British Admiralty," *Center for Israel Education*, at https://israeled.org/chaim-weizmann-joins-british-admiralty/.

11. "History," *Weizmann Institute of Science*, at https://www.weizmann.ac.il/pages/about-institute/history.

CHAPTER 8—THE HOLOCAUST

1. Elie Wiesel, *Night*, trans. Marion Wiesel (New York: Hill and Wang, 2006), xv.

2. Justin Martyr, *Justin Martyr: The Dialogue with Trypho*, trans. A.L. Williams (London: S.P.C.K, 1930), Dialogue 135.

3. Martin Luther, "On the Jews and Their Lies, 1543," *The Christian in Society IV*, trans. Martin H. Bertram, eds. Jaroslav Pelikan, Helmut Lehmann, et al., in *Luther's Works*, vol. 47 (Philadelphia: Fortress Press, 1955–1986), 137.

4. Richard Steigmann-Gall, "Old Wine in New Bottles? Religion and Race in Nazi Antisemitism," in *Antisemitism, Christian Ambivalence, and the Holocaust*, ed. Kevin P. Spicer (Bloomington, IN: Indiana University Press, 2007), 290–291.

5. As cited in Richard Steigmann-Gall, *The Holy Reich: Nazi Conceptions of Christianity, 1919–1945* (New York: Cambridge University Press, 2003), 30.

6. Adolf Hitler, *Mein Kampf*, trans. Ralph Mannheim (Boston: Houghton Mifflin, 1962), 65.

7. Andrew Grant, "The Scientific Exodus from Nazi Germany," *Physics Today* (September 26, 2018), at https://physicstoday.scitation.org/do/10.1063/PT.6.4.20180926a/full/.

8. Walter Isaacson, *Einstein: His Life and Universe* (London: Simon & Schuster UK, 2008).

9. "'Remembering the Holocaust, Fighting Antisemitism' The Fifth World Holocaust Forum Makes History at Yad Vashem," *Yad Vashem* (January 24, 2020), at https://www.yadvashem.org/events/24-january-2020.html.

10. "Remembering the Holocaust," *Yad Vashem*.

11. Lorraine Boissoneault, "The First Moments of Hitler's Final Solution," *Smithsonian Magazine* (December 12, 2016), at https://www.smithsonianmag.com/history/first-moments-hitlers-final-solution-180961387/.

12. Abraham Joshua Heschel, *Israel: an Echo of Eternity* (New York: Farrar, Straus and Giroux, 1969), 115.

CHAPTER 9—THE REBIRTH OF ISRAEL

1. Martin Gilbert, *Israel: A History* (New York: HarperCollins, 1998), 80.

2. Gilbert, *Israel*, 82.

3. Gilbert, *Israel*, n.p.

4. Shlomo Avineri, "Theodore Herzl's Diaries as Bildungsroman," *Jewish Social Studies*, vol. 5, no. 3 (1999), 1–46.

5. Benjamin Netanyahu, speech given to a joint meeting of the US Congress, May 24, 2011.

6. Provisional Government of Israel, "Declaration of Independence," *Official Gazette*, no. 1 (Tel Aviv: 5 Iyar 5708, May 14, 1948), 1, at https://m.knesset.gov.il/en/about/pages/declaration.aspx.

7. Israel, "Declaration of Independence," 1.

CHAPTER 10—HANGING ON BY A THREAD: THE EARLY YEARS OF THE STATE OF ISRAEL

1. John F. Kennedy, *John F. Kennedy in Quotations: A Topical Dictionary, with Sources*, comp. David B. Frost (Jefferson, NC: McFarland, 2013), 94.

2. Martin Gilbert, *Israel: A History* (New York: HarperCollins, 1998), 262.

3. Provisional Government of Israel, "Declaration of Independence," *Official Gazette*, no. 1 (Tel Aviv: 5 Iyar 5708, May 14, 1948), 1, at https://m.knesset.gov.il/en/about/pages/declaration.aspx.

4. Ronn Torossian, "Menachem Begin To Joe Biden: I Am Not A Jew With Trembling Knees," *The Jewish Press* (April 3, 2015), at www.jewishpress.com/indepth/opinions/menachem-begin-to-joe-biden-i-am-not-a-jew-with-trembling-knees/2015/04/03/.

5. Charles Abrams, "Israel Grapples with Its Housing Crisis: The New State's Number One Problem," *Commentary* (April 1951), at https://www.commentarymagazine.com/articles/charles-abrams/israel-grapples-with-its-housing-crisisthe-new-states-number-one-problem/.

6. Francine Klagsbrun, *Lioness: Golda Meir and the Nation of Israel* (New York: Schocken Books, 2019), 367.

7. Jonathan Kaplan, "The Mass Migration of the 1950s," *The Jewish Agency for Israel* (April 27, 2015), at archive.jewishagency.org/society-and-politics/content/36566.

8. *The Observer* (December 29, 1974).

9. Kaplan, "The Mass Migration."

10. Guy I. Seidman, "Unexceptional for Once: Austerity and Food Rationing in Israel, 1939–1959," (February 26, 2009), *Southern California Interdisciplinary Law Journal*, vol. 18, no. 1, 2008.

11. Tom Segev, *The Seventh Million: The Israelis and the Holocaust*, trans. Haim Watzman (New York: Farrar, Straus and Giroux, 2019), 348.

CHAPTER 11—OUTNUMBERED: FROM THE WAR OF INDEPENDENCE TO THE YOM KIPPUR WAR

1. "We Won Our Wars—We Don't Need Victories," *Time* (October 3, 1969), 32.

2. "A Window Into a Top-Secret Bullet Factory—and the Israeli Spirit of Determination," *Jewish National Fund* (July 19, 2015), at https://www.jnf.org/blog/historical-preservation/a-window-into-a-top-secret-bullet-factory-and-the-israeli-spirit-of-determination.

3. "Old City of Jerusalem Falls to Arabs; Jews Gain in Battle for Tel Aviv Highway," *Jewish Telegraphic Agency* (May 30, 1948), at https://www.jta.org/archive/old-city-of-jerusalem-falls-to-arabs-jews-gain-in-battle-for-tel-aviv-highway.

4. Netanel Lorch, "The Arab-Israeli Wars," *Israel Ministry of Foreign Affairs* (November 23, 2017), at https://www.gov.il/en/departments/general/the-arab-israeli-wars.

5. Martin Gilbert, *Israel: A History* (Rosetta Books, 2014), electronic edition.

6. Benny Morris, *1948: A History of the First Arab-Israeli War* (New Haven, CT: Yale University Press, 2008), 398.

7. Andrew Tobin, "Israeli Paratroopers Re-Create Iconic Photo Of Six-Day War," *The Forward* (May 10, 2017), at https://forward.com/news/371474/israeli-paratroopers-re-create-iconic-photo-on-50th-anniversary-of-the-six/.

8. Martin Gilbert, *The Routledge Atlas of the Arab-Israeli Conflict*, 7th ed. Routledge Historical Atlases (London, Routledge, 2002), 66.

9. Gilbert, *The Routledge Atlas*, 65.

10. Michael Bar-Zohar, "The War Nobody Wanted," *The Jerusalem Post* (June 9, 2013), at https://www.jpost.com/opinion/op-ed-contributors/the-war-nobody-wanted-315965.

11. Lahav Harkov, "Israel's Secret Weapon: We Have Nowhere Else To Go—Comment," *The Jerusalem Post* (May 23, 2021), at https://www.jpost.com/israel-news/israels-secret-weapon-it-has-nowhere-else-to-go-comment-668916.

12. Morris, *1948*, 399.

CHAPTER 12—THE LAND AND THE PEOPLE

1. Theodor Herzl, *The Jewish State: The Historic Essay that Led to the Creation of the State of Israel* (New York: Skyhorse, 2019), conclusion.

2. JPost.com Staff, "I Know What Apartheid Was, and Israel Is Not Apartheid, Says S. African Parliament Member," *The Jerusalem Post* (August 25, 2015), at https://www.jpost.com/israel-news/politics-and-diplomacy/i-know-what-apartheid-was-and-israel-is-not-apartheid-says-s-african-parliament-member-413101.

3. TOI Staff, "Israel's Population up to 9.25 Million, Though Growth Rate, Immigration Down," *The Times of Israel* (September 16, 2020), at www.timesofisrael.com/israels-population-up-to-9-25-million-but-growth-rate-immigration-down/.

4. Hezki Baruch, "12th Child Born to President's Chief of Staff," *Arutz Sheva* (September 16, 2019), at https://www.israelnationalnews.com/news/268968.

5. Baruch, "12th Child Born."

6. Lin Arison and Diana C. Stoll/The Desert and Cities Sing, et al., "A GPS System for the Brain," *ISRAEL21c* (September 27, 2017), at www.israel21c.org/a-gps-system-for-the-brain/.

7. Provisional Government of Israel, "Declaration of Independence," *Official Gazette*, no. 1 (Tel Aviv: 5 Iyar 5708, May 14, 1948), 1, at https://m.knesset.gov.il/en/about/pages/declaration.aspx.

8. TOI Staff, "Arab Muslim Twins Go from Violent Delinquents to Proud Golani Soldiers," *The Times of Israel* (May 9, 2020), at www.timesofisrael.com/arab-muslim-twins-from-east-jerusalem-go-from-delinquents-to-israeli-soldiers/.

9. TOI Staff, "Arab Muslim Twins."

10. Irene Brown, "Israeli Astronaut Busy up in Space," *Jewish Telegraphic Agency* (January 27, 2003), at https://www.jta.org/2003/01/27/lifestyle/israeli-astronaut-busy-up-in-space.

11. Lisa J. Huriash, "Keeping Kosher to Be an Out-of-This-World Experience," *Sun Sentinel* (April 8, 2001), at https://www.sun-sentinel.com/news/fl-xpm-2001-04-09-0104090196-story.html.

12. Sharon Wrobel, "In Rare Footage, Israeli Astronaut and War Hero Ilan Ramon Shares Motivation as Son of Auschwitz Survivor," *The Algemeiner* (June 22, 2021), at www.algemeiner.com /2021/06/22/in-rare-footage-israeli-astronaut-and-war-hero-ilan-ramon-shares-motivation-as -son-of-auschwitz-survivor/.

13. Nicole Jansezian, "One Israeli Christian Is on a Mission to Reclaim the Identity of His People," *All Israel News* (April 13, 2022), at https://www.allisrael.com/one-israeli-christian-is-on-a-mission-to -reclaim-the-christian-identity-of-his-people.

14. Rt. Rev. Philip Mounstephen, "Bishop of Truro's Independent Review for the Foreign Secretary of FCO Support for Persecuted Christians," *Christian Persecution Review* (Easter 2019), at https:// christianpersecutionreview.org.uk/interim-report/.

15. Will Maule, "Israel Supreme Court Rules in Favor of Aramean Christians, Granting Them More Rights," *CBN News* (October 28, 2019), at https://www1.cbn.com/cbnnews/israel/2019/october/ israel-supreme-court-rules-in-favor-aramean-christians-granting-them-more-rights.

16. Kassy Dillon, "Meet The Christian Israeli Who Is On A Mission To Create The First Aramaean Christian Town In Israel," *The Daily Wire* (August 28, 2018), at www.dailywire.com/news/ meet-christian-israeli-who-mission-create-first-kassy-dillon.

CHAPTER 13—THE MIRACLE OF ISRAEL

1. "Mrs. Meir Says Moses Made Israel Oil-Poor," *The New York Times* (June 11, 1973), 3.

2. Ron Friedman, "Buffett: 'Israel Has a Disproportionate Amount of Brains,'" *The Jerusalem Post* (October 13, 2010).

3. Leon Lazaroff, "China to Capitalize on Nasdaq Jump With Tech IPOs, BNY Says," *Bloomberg* (May 7, 2012), at www.bloomberg.com/news/articles/2012-05-07/china-to-take-advantage-of-nasdaq -jump-with-tech-ipos-bny-says.

4. Viva Sarah Press, et al., "Apple CEO Tim Cook: We Have an Enormous Admiration for Israel," *ISRAEL21c* (February 26, 2015), at www.israel21c.org/apple-ceo-tim-cook-we-have-an-enormous -admiration-for-israel/.

5. Luke Tress, "Israeli Fintech Firms Raised Record $2.3 Billion in First Half of 2021," *The Times of Israel* (July 27, 2021), at https://www.timesofisrael.com/israeli-fintech-firms-raised-record-2-3 -billion-in-first-half-of-2021/.

6. Tal Ben-Shahar, "Israel Inside: How a Small Nation Makes a Big Difference," JerusalemOnlineU .com (2011), CD-ROM.

7. Alan Rosenbaum, "Is Israel's Scarcity of Water a Blessing in Disguise?," *The Jerusalem Post* (January 7, 2021), at https://www.jpost.com/jpost-tech/is-israels-scarcity-of-water-a-blessing-in-disguise -654578.

8. Max Kaplan-Zantopp, "How Israel Used Innovation to Beat Its Water Crisis," *ISRAEL21c* (April 28, 2022), at https://www.israel21c.org/how-israel-used-innovation-to-beat-its-water-crisis/.

9. David Ben-Gurion, "Why I Retired to the Desert," *The New York Times Magazine* (March 28, 1954).

10. Jon Fedler, "Focus on Israel: Israel's Agriculture in the 21st Century," *Israel Ministry of Foreign Affairs* (December 24, 2002), at https://www.gov.il/en/departments/general/focus-on-israel-israels -agriculture-in-the-21st-century.

11. "About Us—Everything about Netafim," *Netafim*, at https://www.netafim.com/en/Netafim -irrigation-company_about-us/.

12. Sharon Udasin, "'A Drip Revolution' Around the World," *The Jerusalem Post* (April 23, 2015), at https://www.jpost.com/israel-news/a-drip-revolution-around-the-world-398660.

13. ILH Staff, "Netafim Announces $85M Deal to Supply Hi-Tech Irrigation to India," *Israel Hayom* (August 17, 2020), at https://www.israelhayom.com/2020/08/17/netafim-announces-85m-deal -to-supply-hi-tech-irrigation-to-india/.

14. "Strategy Analytics: Half the World Owns a Smartphone," *Business Wire* (June 24, 2021), at https://www.businesswire.com/news/home/20210624005926/en/Strategy-Analytics-Half-the -World-Owns-a-Smartphone.

15. Dan Senor and Saul Singer, *Start-Up Nation: The Story of Israel's Economic Miracle* (New York: Twelve, 2009), 16.

16. "Israel Science & Technology: Intel & Israel," *Jewish Virtual Library*, at https://www.jewishvirtual library.org/intel-and-israel.

17. Sharon Udasin, "Intel CEO: We Think of Ourselves as an Israeli Company as Much as a US Company," *The Jerusalem Post* (March 15, 2017), at www.jpost.com/israel-news/ intel-ceo-we-think-of-ourselves-as-an-israeli-company-as-much-as-a-us-company-484209.

18. "Intel at 50: Q&A with Intel's Dov Frohman, Inventor of EPROM," *Intel Newsroom* (July 5, 2018), at https://newsroom.intel.com/news/intel-50-qa-intels-dov-frohman-inventor-eprom/.

19. "Intel at 50: Dov Frohman," *Intel Newsroom*.

20. Joanne Pransky, "The Essential Interview: Exoskeleton Inventor, UPnRIDE Founder Amit Goffer," *Robotics Business Review* (April 30, 2018), at https://www.roboticsbusinessreview.com/ interview/essential-interview-exoskeleton-inventor-upnride-founder-amit-goffer/.

CHAPTER 14—POLITICS IN ISRAEL TODAY

1. James G. McDonald, *My Mission in Israel: 1948–1951* (London: Gollancz, 1951), 247.

2. Zev Stub, "What Economic Legacy Does Netanyahu Leave Behind?—Analysis," *The Jerusalem Post* (June 13, 2021), at https://www.jpost.com/israel-news/what-economic-legacy-does-netanyahu -leave-behind-670895.

3. Chris Katulka, "Like William Henry Hechler," *Israel My Glory* (September/October 2021), at https://israelmyglory.org/article/like-william-henry-hechler/.

4. Golda Meir, *My Life* (New York: Putnam, 1975), 223–34.

CHAPTER 15—UNDERSTANDING THE MIDDLE EAST CONFLICT

1. Jeffrey Heller, Hugh Lawson ed., "Jewish Visits, Opposed by Palestinians, Spark Clashes at Jerusalem Holy Site," *Reuters* (July 18, 2021), at https://www.reuters.com/world/middle-east/ jewish-visits-opposed-by-palestinians-spark-clashes-jerusalem-holy-site-2021-07-18/.

2. Yair Rosenberg, "Tel Aviv University's Egyptian Valedictorian: 'We Must Always Question Our Assumptions,'" *Tablet Magazine* (August 17, 2015), at https://www.tabletmag.com/sections/news/ articles/tel-aviv-universitys-egyptian-valedictorian-we-must-always-question-our-assumptions.

3. For this book, the version of the Qur'an used was Farida Khanam, ed., *The Quran*, trans. Mau-lana Wahiduddin Khan (Delhi, India: Goodword Books, 2012).

4. Associated Press "U.S. Criticizes Assad Comments," *AP News* (May 7, 2001), at https://apnews.com/article/73d72e5260fb2f39eb8e9ccd580c34d6.

5. TOI Staff, "WATCH: Jordanian Cleric Now Says Jews Must be Killed, Just Not Yet," *The Times of Israel* (November 4, 2015), at https://www.timesofisrael.com/watch-jordanian-cleric-now-says-jews-must-be-killed-just-not-yet/.

6. Tamar Pileggi, "Khamenei: Israel a 'Cancerous Tumor' That 'Must Be Eradicated,'" *The Times of Israel* (June 4, 2018), at www.timesofisrael.com/khamenei-israel-a-cancerous-tumor-that-must-be-eradicated/.

7. Melissa Weiss, "U.N. Agency Head Admits Printing 'Inappropriate' Content in Palestinian Classroom Materials," *Jewish Insider* (January 14, 2021), at https://jewishinsider.com/2021/01/unrwa-textbooks-gaza-west-bank/.

8. Dov Lieber, "Abbas Says No Future US Role in Peace Process, Threatens to Void Past Agreements," *The Times of Israel* (December 13, 2017), at https://www.timesofisrael.com/no-more-us-role-in-peace-process-abbas-declares/.

9. Michael Hirsh, et al., "Clinton To Arafat: It's All Your Fault," *Newsweek* (June 26, 2001), at https://www.newsweek.com/clinton-arafat-its-all-your-fault-153779.

10. Brianna Gurciullo, "Bill Clinton: 'I Killed Myself to Give the Palestinians a State,'" *Politico* (May 13, 2016), at https://www.politico.com/story/2016/05/bill-clinton-palestinians-israel-223176.

11. Yair Rosenberg, "Watch Hillary Clinton vs. Jon Stewart on Gaza," *Tablet Magazine* (July 17, 2014), at https://www.tabletmag.com/sections/news/articles/watch-hillary-clinton-vs-jon-stewart-on-gaza.

12. Joseph Krauss, "Poll Finds Dramatic Rise in Palestinian Support for Hamas," *AP News* (June 15, 2021), at https://apnews.com/article/hamas-middle-east-science-32095d8e1323fc1cad819c34da08fd87.

13. "The Hamas Covenant: Selected Excerpts," *Israel Ministry of Foreign Affairs* (November 19, 2012), updated August 31, 2021, at https://www.gov.il/en/Departments/General/hamas_covenant-excerpts.

CHAPTER 16—ISRAEL AND THE UNITED STATES

1. Benjamin Netanyahu, *A Durable Peace: Israel and Its Place Among the Nations* (New York: Grand Central Publishing, 2009).

2. Michael B. Oren, *Power, Faith, and Fantasy: America in the Middle East, 1776 to the Present* (London: W.W. Norton & Company, 2007), 221.

3. Michael T. Benson, *Harry S. Truman and the Founding of Israel* (Westport, CT: Praeger, 1997), 54.

4. Mitchell Bard and Moshe Schwartz, *1001 Facts Everyone Should Know about Israel* (Lanham, MD: Rowman & Littlefield, 2005), 156.

5. "Z.O.A. Convention Opens; Kennedy Lauds 'Experience of Zionism,'" *Jewish Telegraphic Agency* (June 29, 1962), at https://www.jta.org/archive/z-o-a-convention-opens-kennedy-lauds-experience-of-zionism.

6. Bernard Reich, *Securing the Covenant: United States-Israel Relations After the Cold War* (London: Greenwood Press, 1995), 10.

7. Lenny Ben-David, "A Friend in Deed," *The Jerusalem Post* (September 9, 2008), at https://www.jpost.com/features/a-friend-in-deed.

8. David Tal, *The Making of an Alliance: The Origins and Development of the US-Israel Relationship* (Cambridge: Cambridge University Press, 2022), 268.

9. "U.S. Presidents & Israel: Quotes About Jewish Homeland & Israel," *Jewish Virtual Library*, at https://www.jewishvirtuallibrary.org/u-s-presidential-quotes-about-jewish-homeland-and-israel-jewish-virtual-library#hwbush.

10. David Friedman, "More Than 200,000 Rally on Behalf of Soviet Jewry in Massive D.C. Gathering," *Jewish Telegraphic Agency* (December 7, 1987), at https://www.jta.org/archive/more-than-200000-rally-on-behalf-of-soviet-jewry-in-massive-d-c-gathering.

11. "U.S.-Israel Relations: Roots of the US-Israel Relationship," *Jewish Virtual Library*, at https://www.jewishvirtuallibrary.org/roots-of-the-u-s-israel-relationship.

12. George W. Bush, speech given at National Dinner Celebrating Jewish Life in America (September 14, 2005) National Archives and Records Administration, at georgewbush-whitehouse.archives.gov/news/releases/2005/09/20050914-24.html.

13. "Roots of the US-Israel Relationship," *Jewish Virtual Library*.

14. Meridith McGraw, "'Never Had a Better Friend': Trump Touts Israel Record at Jewish Gathering," *Politico* (December 7, 2019), updated December 8, 2019, at https://www.politico.com/news/2019/12/07/trump-iac-speech-jewish-americans-077798.

15. Mitchell Bard, "The UN Relationship with Israel," *Jewish Virtual Library* (2021), at https://www.jewishvirtuallibrary.org/the-u-n-israel-relationship.

16. "Public Papers of the Presidents of the United States: William J. Clinton, 2000-2001" (N.p., Best Books on, 2000), 1497.

17. Jeremy M. Sharp, Carla E. Humud, and Sarah R. Collins, "US Foreign Assistance to the Middle East: Historical Background, Recent Trends, and the FY2021 Request," *CRS Reports* (May 5, 2020), at https://crsreports.congress.gov/product/pdf/R/R46344/3.

18. Lydia Saad, "Americans Still Favor Israel While Warming to Palestinians," *Gallup News* (March 19, 2021), at https://news.gallup.com/poll/340331/americans-favor-israel-warming-palestinians.aspx.

CHAPTER 17—MESSIANIC JUDAISM

1. Ari Feldman, "Is Rebbe Schneerson the Jewish Messiah? Faith Survives In Chabad," *The Forward*, (December 10, 2017), at https://forward.com/news/388439/is-rebbe-schneerson-the-jewish-messiah-faith-survives-in-chabad/.

2. David Rudolph and Joel Willitts eds., *Introduction to Messianic Judaism: Its Ecclesial Context and Biblical Foundations* (Grand Rapids, MI: Zondervan, 2013).

3. Jon D. Levenson, *Inheriting Abraham: the Legacy of the Patriarch in Judaism, Christianity, and Islam* (Princeton, NJ: Princeton University Press, 2012), 3.

4. David M. Levy, "Israel's Primacy in God's Program," *Israel My Glory* (March/April 2010), at https://israelmyglory.org/article/israels-primacy-in-gods-program/.

5. Rudolph, *Introduction to Messianic Judaism*.

6. Victor Buksbazen, "After a Half Century," *Israel My Glory* (April/May 1992), at https://israelmyglory.org/article/after-a-half-century/.

7. "Findings of New Research on the Messianic Movement in Israel," *ONE FOR ISRAEL Ministry* (April 11, 2018), at https://www.oneforisrael.org/bible-based-teaching-from-israel/findings-of-new-research-on-the-messianic-movement-in-israel/.

8. Rudolph, *Introduction to Messianic Judaism*.

CHAPTER 18—CHRISTIANITY AND MODERN ISRAEL

1. Michael B. Oren, *Power, Faith, and Fantasy: America in the Middle East, 1776 to the Present* (London: W.W. Norton & Company, 2007), 188.

2. Jacob Magid, "Dermer Suggests Israel Should Prioritize Support of Evangelicals Over US Jews," *The Times of Israel* (May 10, 2021), at https://www.timesofisrael.com/dermer-suggests-israel-should-prioritize-support-of-evangelicals-over-us-jews/.

3. "Christian Zionism—The Real Story," *Israel My Glory* (May/June 2012), at https://israelmyglory.org/article/christian-zionism-the-real-story/.

4. Theodor Herzl, et al., *The Complete Diaries of Theodor Herzl* (Herzl Press Thomas Yoseloff Ltd, 1960), 312.

5. "Theodor Herzl Dies," *Center for Israel Education*, at https://israeled.org/theodor-herzl-dies/.

6. Philip Earl Steele, "Henry Dunant: Christian Activist, Humanitarian Visionary, and Zionist," *Israel Journal of Foreign Affairs*, vol. 12, no. 1 (2018), 81–96.

7. Jonathan Moorhead, "The Father of Zionism: William E. Blackstone?" *Journal of the Evangelical Theological Society*, JETS 53/4 (December 2010), 787–800.

8. Paul Charles Merkley, *The Politics of Christian Zionism, 1891-1948* (Frank Cass, 1998), 92.

9. Jacob Magid, "Support for Israel Among Young US Evangelical Christians Drops Sharply—Survey," *The Times of Israel* (May 25, 2021), at https://www.timesofisrael.com/support-for-israel-among-young-us-evangelicals-drops-sharply-survey/.

CHAPTER 19—MAKING YOUR PERSONAL PILGRIMAGE TO ISRAEL

1. "EGERIA—Mediterranean Medieval Places of Pilgrimage," *The Egeria Project*, at http://www.egeria project.net/about_egeria.aspx.

2. William L. Krewson, *Jerome and the Jews: Innovative Supersessionism* (Eugene, OR: Wipf & Stock Publishers, 2017), 102.

3. Jerusalem Post Staff, "Record 4.5 Million Tourists Visited Israel in 2019," *The Jerusalem Post* (January 5, 2020), at https://www.jpost.com/israel-news/record-45-million-tourists-visited-israel-in-2019-613161.

4. "Tourism to Israel in April Far Below 2019 Levels," *Globes English* (May 8, 2022), at https://en.globes.co.il/en/article-tourism-to-israel-in-april-far-below-2019-levels-1001411245.

CHAPTER 20—IS PEACE POSSIBLE IN THE MIDDLE EAST?

1. Adam Rasgon, "Jordan's King Visits Naharayim Enclave After Israelis Clear Out," *The Times of Israel* (November 11, 2019), at https://www.timesofisrael.com/jordans-king-visits-naharayim-enclave-reclaimed-from-israel/.

2. "American Foreign Policy Basic Documents, 1977-1980," *United States, Department of State* (1983), 625.

3. "The 2019-2020 Arab Opinion Index: Main Results in Brief," *Arab Center Washington DC* (November 16, 2020), at https://arabcenterdc.org/resource/the-2019-2020-arab-opinion-index-main-results-in-brief/.

4. Martin Gilbert, *Israel: A History* (Rosetta Books, 2014), electronic edition.

5. "The 2019-2020 Arab Opinion Index," *Arab Center Washington DC.*

6. "The 2019-20 Arab Opinion Index: Main Results in Brief," *Arab Center for Research & Policy Studies,* at https://www.dohainstitute.org/en/Lists/ACRPS-PDFDocumentLibrary/Arab-Opinion-Index-2019-2020-Inbreef-English-Version.pdf.

7. Alan M. Dershowitz, *Defending Israel: The Story of My Relationship with My Most Challenging Client* (New York: St. Martin's Publishing Group, 2019).

8. Charles Bybelezer and Maya Margit, "The Jewish State and Sunni Muslim World Against Shiite Iran," *The Medialine* (February 14, 2019), at https://themedialine.org/news/the-jewish-state-and-sunni-muslim-world-against-shiite-iran/.

CHAPTER 21—THE PLACE OF ISRAEL IN BIBLE PROPHECY

1. David M. Levy, "Modern Israel in Biblical Prophecy," *Israel My Glory* (July/August 2008), at israelmyglory.org/article/modern-israel-in-biblical-prophecy/.

2. Julian Morgenstern, "The King-God Among the Western Semites and the Meaning of Epiphanes," VT 10 (1960), 138–197.

3. Sam Sokol, "WIN/Gallup International: Israel One of Least Religious Countries," *The Jerusalem Post* (April 21, 2015), at www.jpost.com/israel-news/gallup-israel-one-of-least-religious-countries-398823.

PHOTO CREDITS